The Evolution of Atheism

The Evolution of Atheism

The Politics of a Modern Movement

STEPHEN LeDREW

OXFORD
UNIVERSITY PRESS

OXFORD

UNIVERSITY PRESS

Oxford University Press is a department of the University of Oxford.
It furthers the University's objective of excellence in research, scholarship,
and education by publishing worldwide. Oxford is a registered trade mark
of Oxford University Press in the UK and in certain other countries

Published in the United States of America by Oxford University Press
198 Madison Avenue, New York, NY 10016, United States of America

Library of Congress Cataloging-in-Publication Data
LeDrew, Stephen.
The evolution of atheism : the politics of a modern movement / Stephen LeDrew.
p. cm
ISBN 978–0–19–022517–9 (cloth : alk. paper) 1. Atheism. I. Title.
BL2747.3.L4155 2015

211'.8—dc23

2015010010

1 3 5 7 9 8 6 4 2

Typeset in Scala Pro

Printed on 45# Cream stock 400 ppi

Printed by Edwards Brothers, North Carolina

For my son, Erik.
Thanks for waiting.

Contents

Acknowledgments

THIS BOOK IS based on my doctoral dissertation, and thanks are therefore due first and foremost to Ratiba Hadj-Moussa, my supervisor at York University. I am deeply grateful for her guidance, encouragement, support, and friendship. The other two members of my supervisory committee, Philip Walsh and Fuyuki Kurasawa, offered invaluable critical feedback throughout the writing process and were a source of many inspirational ideas. The rest of my examining committee—Lori Beaman, Lesley Wood, and Walid El Khachab—also offered useful and challenging comments and questions. Going back a little further, I also want to thank Stephen Crocker, my supervisor as a Master's student at Memorial University of Newfoundland. This book feels like the culmination of a long journey that began when he introduced me to critical social theory and opened my eyes to the world in exciting ways.

I completed a significant portion of the writing while a Postdoctoral Fellow at Uppsala University, where I benefitted from discussions with my colleagues at the Centre for the Study of Religion and Society, and in the Department of Theology. Thanks to those who attended my presentations at the higher seminars in sociology of religion and philosophy of religion, including Mia Lövheim, Anders Sjöborg, Evelina Lundmark, Jonas Lindberg, Martha Middlemiss Lé Mon, Maria Klingenberg, Erika Willander, Jonna Bornemark, Francis Jonbäck, Mattias Gardell, Johan Eddebo, Lotta Knutsson Bråkenhielm, and Olof Franck. Mikael Stenmark's interest in my work was a major reason I came to Uppsala, and I thank him for the many stimulating conversations over *fika*. I appreciate his efforts in helping with the transition to life in Sweden, and making me feel at home by inviting me to play innebandy—or what we Canadians know as floor hockey.

Parts of this book were presented at various workshops and seminars, where I benefitted from a good deal of constructive criticism. I would like to thank the participants of the workshop *Atheist Identities: Spaces and Social Contexts* at the University of Ottawa: Lori Beaman, William Stahl, Richard Cimino, Amarnath Amarasingam, Peter Beyer, Lorna Mumford, Ryan Cragun, Christopher Cotter, Steven Tomlins, and Spencer Bullivant. Helpful comments were also provided by my friends and colleagues in the Canadian Network for Critical Sociology, including Mike Christensen, Marcia Oliver, Matthew Hayes, Mervyn Horgan, Fuyuki Kurasawa, Saara Liinamaa, Peter Mallory, Liz Rondinelli, Phil Steiner, Steve Tasson, and Cathy Tuey.

At Oxford University Press, I want to thank my editor, Theo Calderara, for his interest and his support for this book, and Marcela Maxfield for her assistance with the details of the publication process. I also want to thank the anonymous reviewers, who get no public credit, but perform an invaluable service in the development of a book. Portions of Chapter 1 were published in History of the Human Sciences and I also thank those reviewers.

I am grateful as well for the support of many friends and family members. I have had countless conversations about the subject of this book with Jesse Kristensen, whose enthusiasm for it was inspiring. Marc Carver was always there to help me escape from the daily grind of writing. Nearing the end of writing my dissertation I spent two months in Little Harbour, Newfoundland, at my grandfather's house up on the hill. My aunt and uncle, Irene and Harry Pardy, kept my energy up by keeping me well fed with fish cakes and moose soup, and my cousins Calvin Pardy and Colin Pardy provided good company. My brother Ryan LeDrew assisted with compiling the index, and I thank him for his diligent work. Most importantly, I am thankful for the love and support of my parents, Paul and Daphne LeDrew. In the final stretch of completing my dissertation, they gave me what no one else could: the comfort of home.

No words can convey what Liz Rondinelli has meant to me while writing this book, but I can say that without her it wouldn't exist. She has been there for me during many dark storms, and in the brightest moments shared my joy. Our greatest joy, Erik, was born five days after I completed the manuscript, and he has been my inspiration ever since.

The Evolution of Atheism

Introduction

IT IS AMAZING that in the many years that sociologists have studied religion, very few have bothered to study, or even think very much about, secular people. Doubtless this is a result of the doctrine of secularization, a cornerstone of the discipline in its earliest years, when the question of why societies become less religious as they modernize was a central concern. This 'question' was in fact a taken-for-granted assumption long at the heart of the Western world's self-understanding—certainly within intellectual circles—but today no one could seriously claim that religion is no longer an important force in the world or, even more obtusely, that studying it is a waste of time because it is disappearing anyway. We now recognize that it is crucial to understand not only religion and religious people, but those who are without religion and how they fit into the complex picture of late modern culture.

This book is about the "New Atheism" and its relationship to a movement for secularism that is well over a hundred years old. The New Atheism is the name given to an antireligious group of writers and thinkers—the most important of whom is the Oxford evolutionary biologist Richard Dawkins—who in the mid- to late 2000s successfully fueled a public debate about science, religion, and their place in the modern world. A great deal has been said about the New Atheism, but much of it is the work of ideologues, either atheistic or religious, eager to dismiss their opponents as the loser in an epic historical struggle between science and religion. One exception is Terry Eagleton's book *Reason, Faith, and Revolution*, which steps around the theological–scientific debate and examines it as a cultural and political phenomenon. I want to engage much more thoroughly with the New Atheism on this level, systematically examining it as ideology, identity, and practice through an analysis of the discourse of the New Atheism and its profound impact on the secular movement (a loose network of organizations dedicated to atheism, rationalism, secularism, and/or humanism). Most importantly, I want to bring a sociological perspective to this topic, which to date has primarily been the province of philosophers and theologians. This perspective is crucial because the New Atheism is not abstract philosophy—it is a thoroughly social phenomenon.

My approach to the New Atheism combines an analysis of the thinkers and writings that constitute its intellectual canon with a study of the dynamics of the secular movement. This dual approach reflects my view that the New Atheism is a *secular fundamentalism*, a modern utopian ideology that is also an active movement for social transformation. Like all fundamentalisms, it is not only a position on metaphysical questions but an essentially political phenomenon. It is only manifestly a critique of religion, while its latent project is the universalization of the ideology of scientism and the establishment of its cultural authority. Its critique is therefore not just about religion but more precisely about cultures, belief systems, and forms of knowledge—most importantly the social sciences and humanities, redundant in the New Atheism's Darwinistic master narrative—that are perceived as challenges to this authority.

While ostensibly a critique of the dangers of irrational superstitions, then, the New Atheism is ultimately about *power*—more specifically, socially legitimate authority. It is a response to challenges to the authority of science and, by extension, those who practice science and regulate its institutions. By a further extension, it is a defense of the position of the white middle-class Western male, and of modernity itself, which is perceived to be under threat by a swirling concoction of religious ignorance, epistemic relativism, identity politics, and cultural pluralism. The New Atheism is a reaction to twenty-first-century challenges to the established modern social hierarchy and structure of cultural authority, seeking to eliminate perceived challenges to scientific authority not only from "premodern" religion but also "postmodern" social science. This is an attempt at placing an ideological manifestation of the natural sciences in a position of uncontested authority in the production of legitimate knowledge and in the cultural sphere of meaning and normativity.

I argue that we need to rethink in various ways the prevailing understandings of the New Atheism and the social movement it is a part of. Most importantly, I will challenge the assumption that the secular movement is liberal and progressive, and argue that there is a deeply conservative dimension to it that compels us to recognize the existence of an "atheist Right" that turns sharply away from the radical nineteenth-century political movements from which both intellectual atheism and the secular movement emerged. The rightward political drift of atheism is an amazing development for a movement with roots in socialism, revolution against established powers, and social justice. It is therefore not surprising that the influence of the New Atheism and the rise of the atheist Right are highly controversial within the secular movement. I will examine these tensions in light of the historical development of this movement and the impact of the New Atheism on its goals and strategies, which reveal more fundamental political and normative tensions that have propelled the movement into a period of internal turmoil, the effects of which are still playing out.

As a result of its popular appeal and staggering publishing successes, the New Atheism became the central focus of the secular movement and its primary mobilizing force. Its effects were felt in many countries, particularly in Western Europe and North America, though this book focuses on the movement in Canada and, primarily, the United States, where an aggressive attack on religion was welcomed by those concerned about the rise of the Christian Right and the new threat of Islamic terrorism. While the New Atheism came to dominate movement discourse for a time, however, it does not represent the movement as a whole. A casual observer might equate secular activists with Richard Dawkins' antagonistic atheism, but I will highlight the fact that the New Atheism's goal of destroying religion and entrenching scientific rationality as the dominant form of cultural authority is challenged by other groups within the movement motivated by very different goals and ideologies. The conflicts and debates that have emerged from these tensions have given shape to the secular movement as it is today and have produced deep divisions that threaten movement fragmentation or even a massive breakdown. The analysis in this book offers a picture of a movement confounded in its attempts to define itself by a complex and sometimes self-contradictory set of discourses, and of groups of people united only by their lack of faith struggling to maintain cohesion in the face of deep divisions in their politics.

I will examine these events in historical perspective, which reveals that the conflicts of the present are only the most recent manifestation of tensions and debates that have persisted throughout the history of the secular movement. Indeed, the New Atheism is "new" only to the extent that it is current, while the ideology it advances is no different from the scientific atheism that arose from a fusion of Enlightenment rationalism and Victorian Darwinism in the nineteenth century. It is only the most recent manifestation of a kind of "secular revolution" that began in that period, which tied religious criticism to a political project to advance the authority of science and scientists, particularly within educational institutions.[1] The tensions within the secular movement today, meanwhile, can largely be understood as an extension of an essential tension between scientism and humanism, and between liberal individualism and socialism or social justice, that has characterized the movement since the early days of the National Secular Society in the mid-nineteenth century.

The title of this book, then, is somewhat ironic. It refers to the centrality of the concept of evolution, and the impact of its social history, in atheist thought—a fact that has not been sufficiently recognized in scholarship on the history of atheism. This concept is used by New Atheist thinkers to explain not only the origins of life as a refutation of religious explanations but also social and intellectual progress. This is itself an irony for a group of self-proclaimed Darwinists, since a proper Darwinian model of evolution has no conception of progress or "improvement," but only adaptation and differentiation, a point Darwin himself made in his use of the metaphor of evolution as a "radiating bush" of increasing complexity. Unlike the New Atheists' ideological vision of social progress toward a climactic scientific civilization, Darwinism is not teleological. The irony of the idea of an "evolution of atheism" in the intellectual sphere, meanwhile, is that the content of the New Atheism's critique of religion is over a hundred years old. If anything, it is a regression to a simplified Enlightenment critique that ignores the reservoirs of knowledge offered by the social sciences, which add complexities to our understanding of religion that the New Atheists prefer to ignore, indulging in the kind of willful ignorance that they disparage religion for promoting. Finally, there is also an irony in the idea of an evolution of atheism as a social movement, since the same essential tensions that shaped the birth of the secular movement also shape its dynamics today. There is, however, some truth to the idea in that these tensions are giving rise to some new forms, most importantly a group of libertarian rationalists who connect scientism to radical individualism and economic freedom, and a group of feminists who embrace a scientific version of atheism while advancing humanistic ethics and a program for social justice. These groups combine ideology, politics, and strategy in novel ways, and thus we can see these aspects of the movement in terms of a radiating bush of expanding forms that evolve from common ideological antecedents. But these new forms are still manifestations of the essential tension within atheism between scientism and humanism, which gives rise to the divergent goals of advancing the authority of science and the autonomy of the individual, and advancing human equality and an ethic of social justice.

Secularism and Fundamentalism

A number of scholars have taken a view of the New Atheism as a kind of fundamentalism, but none offers a substantive definition of the concept or a rigorous analysis of how it applies in this case.[2] I want to argue that the New Atheism is a *secular fundamentalism* that is both a utopian ideology of scientism that defends the Western social order and a social movement aimed at reinforcing the cultural authority of science and the advanced status of Western values. I should first note that there is a vast literature on fundamentalism and much disagreement on the meaning of the concept, but these debates are not my concern here. I draw on a very select set of sources and one particular interpretation of the concept that applies to this case. The concept of secular fundamentalism as outlined here is, in my view, an appropriate means to understand the nature of the New Atheism and the relationship between its two dimensions: belief system (or, more precisely, ideology) and social movement.

Rather than a vestige of premodern beliefs, Eisenstadt argues that fundamentalism is an expression *of* modernity as much as a reaction to it, at once an antimodern utopian ideology and a modern social and political movement, or set of movements.[3] Fundamentalisms are anti-Enlightenment but also distinctly modern in the sense that they react to challenges to traditional patterns of belief and share the totalizing and utopian aspirations of many modern political movements and ideologies (communism is the primary example here). Like these political movements, fundamentalism seeks to remake society in accordance with a vision of some essential truths. Davie adds that these truths are reaffirmed within the context of profound upheavals, including an expanding global economy and modernity's clash with traditional cultures.[4]

An example is the evangelical fundamentalism that drives the Christian Right, which defends established beliefs and traditional values against secular values and scientific understandings of the nature of life. It is totalizing in seeking to bring an entire nation under religious rule and also utopian in promising salvation through the establishment of a Christian nation in God's favor.⁵ The enemy of the Christian Right is secularism, or secularization, a force its members wish to reverse. The Christian Right is antimodern (or, more specifically, anti-Enlightenment) to the extent that it associates science and reason with the process of secularization, understood both as the functional differentiation of religious and political spheres and as the relativization of all belief systems that comes with constitutional pluralism and some important characteristics of late modernity, including globalization and multiculturalism. It thus advances a totalizing ideology and political program that reaffirms the essential truths of a particular tradition and its authority in all spheres of life and takes concrete action, attempting to exert political power by influencing government and electing representatives sympathetic to the cause. As such, it is both ideology and a social movement.

While we might typically associate fundamentalism with religion, Davie argues that this need not be the case and that some secular ideologies also fit the description. She explains that in late modernity faith in the universal emancipatory powers of science and reason begins to wane and the "secular certainties" that provided the ground for religious criticism themselves come under attack:

> precisely those ideologies which have threatened (and to some extent continue to threaten) the traditional certainties of a whole range of religious groups become, at least potentially, the victims rather than the perpetrators of economic and cultural change. No longer are they seen as the confident alternatives, but become instead— like the religious certainties they once sought to undermine—the threatened tradition, themselves requiring justification and, at times, aggressive rehabilitation.⁶

Thus we see the emergence of *secular fundamentalism*, which seeks to reassert the "secular certainties" of science and reason. In this view, then, fundamentalism is an attempt to recreate certainty and authority in response to challenges to established patterns of belief: religious fundamentalism in response to modernity (more precisely its Enlightenment manifestations) and secular fundamentalism in response to late modernity or postmodernity (specifically, relativism and pluralism, which challenge the universality of reason and scientific authority).

Davie argues that the New Atheism may be understood as just such a fundamentalist secular ideology, a view I support. I analyze the New

Atheism as a politicized reaction to two major developments in late modern society: (1) the rise of religious fundamentalism and (2) epistemic relativism (represented in academic postmodernism) and cultural pluralism (represented in policies of multiculturalism). Both of these developments are perceived as challenges to the universal authority of science. With respect to the first, the New Atheism may be understood as a response to anti-Enlightenment fundamentalism, substituting its own reverse form of fundamentalism: an Enlightenment utopia based on faith in the emancipatory powers of science and reason and the progressive nature of social evolution in modern societies, which involves a transition from religious authority to a secular science-based social order (thus they defend a version of the traditional secularization thesis).

The New Atheism, then, is a response to religious fundamentalism (i.e., the Christian Right and Islamicism), which it considers to be "premodern" and thus opposed to modernity. But just as importantly in my view, it also reacts to what it considers the "postmodern" forces of pluralism and relativism, which undermine scientific authority and the universalization of Enlightenment values. The New Atheism advances an ideology that is universalist and absolutist; more than a critique of religion, it is a critique of all epistemological and ethical belief systems that are perceived to conflict with the hegemony of scientific rationality. The *modern* utopia it envisions must be defended against these two antimodern forces, and it does this by offering its belief system in the "marketplace of ideas" and by promoting and defending atheism and scientific rationalism through the structure of a social—or, more specifically, cultural—movement. The New Atheism is much more than just the writings of Richard Dawkins, Sam Harris, Christopher Hitchens, and Daniel Dennett.[7] These four are influential leaders within a broader movement. I understand the New Atheism as a secular fundamentalism that advances a rigid set of beliefs and values—or an ideology—that legitimate a certain conception of modernity and secularization and an associated form of authority. This takes the form of an intellectual and social movement that is essentially political but adopts "cultural" goals and strategies.

This atheist movement and the religious fundamentalism that it is in part a response to are deeply intertwined. Indeed, the atheist movement would not exist without the Christian Right and radical Islamism (or it would at least be very different and much smaller in scale). Cimino and Smith argue that the Christian Right served as a "tonic" for the secularist movement even before the New Atheism came about by presenting an "other" or an enemy to rally against.[8] But it is clear that the movement would never have expanded the way it has without Dawkins and the others to lead this growth by drawing unprecedented public attention to atheism. As noted above, the Christian Right is similarly dependent on secularism for its strength, portraying Christians as "embattled" by encroaching secularism and thus enhancing group solidarity.[9] This interdependence is clear in a billboard advertisement appearing in New York and San Francisco in October 2013 sponsored by Answers in Genesis, a creationist organization founded by Ken Hamm, who is also the founder of the Creation Museum in Petersburg, Kentucky. The billboards carried the message, "To all of our atheist friends: Thank God You're Wrong" along with a link to the organization's website. According to Hamm, the message was necessary because "We're in a battle. We're in a spiritual war and we're to be out there wielding our swords, the word of God."[10]

Hamm is correct that this "spiritual war" is being waged by the New Atheism as well, though this competition might be better understood in terms of the "religious economies" approach developed by Stark and Finke that applies rational choice theory to religion and suggests that in religiously pluralistic societies, actors will choose religious beliefs and organizations based on a cost/benefit calculation, and further, that greater religious supply produces greater demand.[11] The New Atheism actively engages in this "religious marketplace," increasing the supply by offering its own belief system to compete with others that also offer firm answers, essential truths, and a program for the organization of social and political life. Its strategy for advancing its essentially political ideology, then, is a cultural one that involves entering the "marketplace of ideas" and seeking a broad transformation in beliefs—that is, a conversion to its belief system of scientism or "scientific atheism." The New Atheists attempt to do this by proselytizing atheism, which in turn is done primarily by a scathing critique of religion (atheism as an intellectual current) and also by constructing and promoting a positive atheist identity that emphasizes morality (atheism as a social or, more specifically, cultural movement). The New Atheism's reductionist critique of religion presents it as a false set of beliefs regarding nature, a premodern attempt at scientific explanation that relies on the supernatural to fill in gaps in understanding. This is typical of many reductionist, transhistorical and transcultural concepts of religion as different sets of incompatible and nonrational truth claims that inevitably lead to conflict and violence, which Cavanaugh argues is one of the foundational myths of modern Western society and is used to legitimate neocolonial violence against non-Western others (particularly the Muslim world).[12]

This is precisely how the ideology of the New Atheism functions. Its discourse on religion is an ideological legitimation of scientific authority, and more specifically, its discourse on Islam is a legitimation of Western society that constructs a vision of "civilization" through a contrast with its "barbaric" other. The New Atheism might in fact be understood as a renewed defense and promotion of the idea of secularization—which crystallized in the social sciences in the twentieth century but has been present since the Enlightenment—against a perceived *failure* of secularism in practice in late modern society. This failure, which is ultimately considered only temporary, is a result of the "premodern" and "postmodern" threats of religion and relativism. Like religious fundamentalism, the New Atheism is a reaction to the explosion in possibilities of belief that characterize our "secular age."[13] Though they are both totalizing ideologies that seek to eradicate opposing worldviews, both are also themselves manifestations of the expanding possibilities in ways of being—or not being—religious.

PART 1

Atheism as Ideology

I

The Evolution of Atheism

"ATHEISM" IS A complex term with an even more complex history, and it is notoriously difficult to define.[1] A basic distinction is frequently made between "negative atheism," which is a *lack of belief* in God, and "positive atheism," or *disbelief* in the existence of God.[2] Negative atheism, sometimes also called "soft" atheism, is essentially the same as agnosticism, which is the position that the existence of God cannot be proven and skepticism is therefore appropriate. Unlike agnostics, true atheists assert that *God does not exist*, and therefore when we speak about atheism we are really speaking about "positive" atheism. But this is only a starting point, and this definition tells us little about what atheism means to the people who hold this position, and what it has meant in its brief history.

This chapter defines Western atheism by examining its historical development and the various meanings and beliefs that have been attached to it since explicit, "avowed" atheism emerged in the Enlightenment.[3] From this historical point of view, atheism is a modern movement of thought and practice emerging from political turmoil and revolutions in various intellectual fields, and a form of belief—rather than a lack of belief—shaped by its socio-historical context. To understand the New Atheism, then, we need to begin with an historical examination of atheist thought and practice. Such an examination reveals that "atheism" is inextricably bound up with a tradition of Enlightenment principles, including emancipation through reason, liberal democracy, the primacy of the individual, scientific rationality, and the notion of progress, which is closely related to the theory—or as Asad describes it, the "political doctrine"[4]—of secularization (more on this in Chapter 2). This short review is not intended to provide a comprehensive account of the history of something so elusive and contested in its meaning, and there are a number of more extensive works on the topic. Drawing on these existing theories and histories of atheism—most importantly David Berman's *A History of Atheism in Britain* and Michael J. Buckley's twin volumes, *At the Origins of Modern Atheism* and *Denying and Disclosing God: The Ambiguous Progress of Modern Atheism*—I will review several key events and thinkers that characterize a particular conception of modern Western atheism, rooted in the Enlightenment and the rise of reason and empiricism. These thinkers outline a theory of how atheism emerged from a dialectical relationship between religion and science in early modernity, which gradually gave way to a dichotomy in the Enlightenment, and particularly in the nineteenth century as Darwinists used the theory of evolution by natural selection as a case for the emancipation of science from the fetters of institutionalized religion. These Darwinists cultivated a "scientific atheism" that views religion primarily as the antithesis of science and an obstacle to social and scientific progress (progress of the former type being contingent upon the latter in this view). At the same time, another distinct tradition of atheist thought emerged from the social sciences, which I call *humanistic atheism*. It considered religion to be primarily a social phenomenon rather than an attempt at explaining nature.

Both approaches are much more than a critical inquiry into religious faith: they are essentially political projects, and the salient point to be taken from this historical analysis is that the division between the two major forms of atheism is essentially a political one, with each offering a distinct vision of what it means to live in a world free of religion, and how to arrive there. Scientific atheism understands religion as an obstacle to science-driven social progress and seeks to eradicate this relic of the premodern world through science education and "enlightenment." Humanistic atheism rejects the structure of a world that gives rise to religion, which from this perspective is not a challenge to modernity but rather provides ideological support for modernity by rationalizing its inequities. It imagines alternative social formations that would cause religion to vanish. These different positions on religion and understandings of what atheism means—and, crucially, how it should be put into action—are still debated within the atheist movement today. This historical review of the meanings of atheism, then, helps us to understand the dynamics and tensions shaping the contemporary atheist movement's development, most importantly with respect to the impact of the New Atheism, which carries on the scientific tradition while ignoring humanistic approaches. The New Atheism is not "new" but just the most recent incarnation of a particular kind of nonbelief from a particular intellectual tradition. It excludes other kinds of religious criticism that developed diverging lines of critique in the nineteenth and early twentieth centuries because of political and epistemological irreconcilabilities. The New Atheism is much more than a critical inquiry into religious faith. It is an extension and manifestation of the modern project of scientific mastery of the world and the rationalization of society, and its critique is only ostensibly about religion. More implicitly, it is a critique of other perceived challenges to this political project, wherever they may come from—even from other kinds of atheism.

Atheism and Enlightenment

Michael J. Buckley has offered a compelling account of the dialectical origins of modern atheism, with atheism emerging not out of an antagonism between religion and science but rather a relative harmony in early modernity.[5] In the seventeenth century, science was not opposed to Christianity; rather, science was considered work in the service of Christianity. Buckley argues that atheism came not from a contradiction between religion and science but from an internal contradiction within theism itself that led to theology turning to science for its foundations. Gavin Hyman endorses Buckley's theory, suggesting that in early modernity a modern concept of God arose that did away with transcendence as his essential property, instead offering a conception of God as a "thing" in the world of definite substance and location.[6] When theologians determined that God was a material thing that exists within nature, God by definition became an object of scientific inquiry, according to both science and orthodox theology.

Scientists, meanwhile, thought it natural to ground apologetic arguments through empirical evidence, and were encouraged to do so by theologians and clerics alike. The most important figure in the development of this early modern dialectic was perhaps Isaac Newton, a devout Christian who devoted much of his later life to writing about the Bible rather than the natural sciences. He filled in some gaps in his scientific theories with God, claiming that only divine intervention could account for certain irregularities within nature.[7] Newton's discoveries brought about a profound shift and step forward in our understanding of the universe that signaled the possibility that science might be able to find answers to questions that had long been the province of theology, transforming the enchanted universe into a "system of intelligible forces."[8]

With time, even Newton's claim that the universe was created by a supreme being who intervenes in its operations for maintenance work from time to time began to appear dubious to many scientists, simply because it seemed to be an unnecessary addition to a fairly self-sufficient set of theories. By the mid-eighteenth century science had rejected the notion of a static universe with laws generated by God in favor of a view that accepted nature as a product of great revolutionary transformations over an immense period of time, thereby making the addition of God to existing explanations superfluous.[9] This development represented a new phase in the science/religion dialectic as the ideological foundation of atheism, with science making discoveries that did not need the concept of the divine designer. Buckley does point out, however, that not needing a designer to explain things is not the same thing as saying there is no designer. Scientists were not arguing that God does not exist; indeed, most prominent thinkers of the Scientific Revolution were passionate believers and many developed theological positions to accompany their naturalistic theories.[10] Science did, however, begin to claim primary entitlement to what many considered to be the primary function of religion: an explanation of the origin and nature of material reality.

Buckley suggests that this development paved the way for atheism, since theism that was built on scientific knowledge eventually generated its own negation. For modern rationalist critiques to apply to God, there first had to be some change in theology that made God an object that could be critiqued rationally and investigated scientifically. Atheism, then, was not an external challenge to theism but rather the result of a revolution within theology itself, which is to say that the origins of modern atheism are ultimately theological.[11] In this theory atheism is not the result of a *conflict* between science and religion—this false notion of the enduring and intractable conflict between the epistemologies and institutions of religion and science is referred to by some historians simply as the "conflict myth"[12]—but on the contrary, atheism arose from an immanent contradiction within orthodox theology produced by its apologetic strategies.[13]

This theory of the origin of atheism dominates the literature on the topic, finding further support (with slight differences) from Alan Charles Kors and James Turner in their studies of the origins of modern unbelief in France and the United States, respectively.[14] Turner suggests that atheism in America emerged from a dialectical relationship between religion and the rise of modern science and Enlightenment rationalism, and that ultimately it was theology itself that generated its own negation by attempting to adapt religious beliefs to social and cultural changes and to the standards of scientific knowledge. In so doing, "the defenders of God slowly strangled him."[15] Like Buckley, Turner sees atheism arising immanently from within theology as it adapted to the modern world. Kors argues that in France, atheism emerged immanently from within the orthodox tradition in its attempt to defend the existence of God against agents of "natural philosophy" (what would become modern science). Debates between two major theological schools on how best to philosophically demonstrate the existence of God ironically produced better arguments *against* the existence of God, resulting in the negation of both positions. Supporting Buckley's theory, Kors explains atheism as arising out of a contradiction within theology.

Science and natural theology were principal among these apologetic strategies, and in the early days of concurrent revolutions in science and theology there was thus no real conflict. To the contrary, science and religion were bound closely together. The shifting theological understanding of God—that is, the move from transcendence to materiality—resulted in a shift of emphasis from revelation to natural theology, which was predicated upon the idea that the existence of God could be inferred by reason and that science could provide evidence of his presence in nature.[16] This relationship would evolve and give birth to a modern form of atheism that rejected a modern form of theism that was ultimately unsustainable.[17] That is, a theism grounded upon a conception of God as a natural entity amenable to scientific investigation would inevitably fail when the evidence failed to demonstrate his role in nature but rather seemed to demonstrate more and more that the concept of God was not required to explain nature.

It must be noted, however, that these developments generally did not lead directly to atheism, but rather to skepticism of revelation and to a belief in "natural religion" or *deism* (or in other words, a move from revelation to natural theology). Deists rejected the specificities of revealed religion (which was based on hearsay and thus could not be verified rationally or empirically) while embracing the view that religion should be founded upon rational proofs and that evidence of God's design could be found in nature.[18] The prevailing Enlightenment sentiment was that religion that could not be established by reason was nothing but superstition. This transitional phase to true atheism emerged out of the dialectical relationship between religion and science, a product of the Scientific Revolution and a revolution within theology. Many skeptics of this period famous for their critiques of religion were in fact deists, including David Hume, Denis Diderot, and notably Voltaire, whose scathing attacks on religion were not motivated by atheism but rather were directed at corruption within the church. Voltaire was a critic of religious institutions and revealed religion, rather than the idea of God, which he, like Hume, sought to situate within nature and to establish through reason.

The deism trend was not restricted to Europe. In his history of unbelief in the United States, James Turner argues that in eighteenth-century America "unbelief in fact remained unthinkable to all but a tiny handful," but the changes wrought by science and Enlightenment rationalism meant that even here the nature of faith had to change: "if belief were to remain secure, it needed footings solid enough to endure the buffetings of changing times. Thus, by the 1790s its underpinnings had altered drastically, at least for the educated, as believers sought to anchor God firmly in the modern world."[19] Hence, deism became popular among many intellectuals and elites, most notably revolutionary figures such as Thomas Jefferson and Thomas Paine. Rejection of religious authority in favor of liberal democracy, then, was an important element in revolutionary politics in America as it was in France, and the grounds for this rejection were found in deism, which undermined the authority of traditional religious institutions.

The major exception to the rule of deism during the Enlightenment was a watershed event in the history of atheism: the publication in 1770 of Baron d'Holbach's *System of Nature*, which is generally considered the first published work of avowed (explicit and publicly stated) atheism in Europe.[20] D'Holbach considered atheism to be directly connected to the Enlightenment project of emancipation from ignorance, traditional authority, and the tyranny of church and king. His criticism of religion may be distilled to three essential points: it is unscientific and its teachings are contrary to scientific truth; it supports a corrupt social order by diverting attention away from the here-and-now and instead toward the afterlife; and it is not a useful foundation for morality.[21] These points refer to three dimensions of critique—epistemological, political, and moral—corresponding to the dimensions of the Enlightenment critique of religion as outlined by Casanova, which includes the categories "cognitive," "practical-political," and the unwieldy "subjective expressive-aesthetic-moral," which can be more succinctly stated as the "moral-subjective" critique.[22]

The critical engagement with religion among eighteenth-century Enlightenment thinkers, for the most part, was rarely as boldly and proudly atheistic as the work of d'Holbach and never quite escaped the influence of deism and the problem of design. Atheism, however, would find new life in the nineteenth century. It was in this period that atheism evolved from its Enlightenment origins and took shape according to several new points of origin, from which we can derive most contemporary forms. These new strands of atheism grew from the Enlightenment's approach of general skepticism and gave it new grounding in the nascent disciplines of biology, anthropology, sociology, and psychology.

Evolution, Religion, and Society

The impact of the concept of evolution in the history of atheism has been unjustly ignored and undertheorized. In the nineteenth century, Enlightenment notions of progress found expression in the idea of evolution, which was not only a scientific theory but became a dominant narrative in depictions of the history and nature of Western civilization. It also became a cornerstone of atheism, solving (to some minds) the problem of the argument from design and the question of human origins. Before Darwin brought it into the scientific mainstream, evolutionistic thinking was applied in the emerging science of society that August Comte would come to call "sociology." It appeared most infamously in the work of Herbert Spencer, whose influential theories granted legitimacy to the political doctrine of Social Darwinism. The atheism of this period, which connected Enlightenment skepticism to the expanding influence of evolutionary theories of both the natural and social worlds, is what I call *scientific atheism*.

Comte's theory of society was developmental rather than evolutionistic, but it was a precursor to the Darwinistic vision of progress at the heart of scientific atheism, as well as Spencer's later fusion of the fields of sociology and evolutionary biology into what we know today as sociobiology. A theory of religion was integral to his general theory of society. Comte considered religion a slowly disappearing relic of a lower stage of social development. This idea was expressed in his famous "Law of Three Stages," which posited that all societies pass through three historical phases: theological, metaphysical, and positive. In the theological stage, marking all of human history up until the advent of modernity, humans understand themselves and their world in thoroughly religious terms, believing that all phenomena are caused by the action of supernatural beings.[23] Subscribing to the animist theory of the origins of religion,

Comte argues that man has a natural tendency to conceive of "all external bodies as animated by a life analogous to his own."[24] This is essentially a less refined version of the "intentional stance" theory of religious origins derived from contemporary evolutionary psychology—a theory advanced most famously by Richard Dawkins, Daniel Dennett, and Pascal Boyer[25]—which holds that a propensity for religious belief is a byproduct of adaptive mental processes that enhanced our ancestors' prospects for selection. The intentional stance is the tendency to attribute agency to all animate and inanimate objects, as well as natural events and processes (storms and volcanic eruptions, for example). Comte similarly describes "the primary tendency of Man to transfer the sense of his own nature into the radical explanation of all phenomena whatever," referring to primitive humanity's projection of humanlike agency to all phenomena, which is due to the fact that "The only way that he can explain any phenomena is by likening them, as much as possible, to his own acts."[26] Further, in Comte's view early attempts to control the course of the stars through religious rituals constitute "the first symptoms of the awakening of human intelligence and activity" and perhaps, as the New Atheists argue, our earliest attempt at science.[27] Comte seems to have taken this view, explaining primitive religion as a form of knowledge based on "the only theories then possible."[28]

The dominance of theological understandings of self and nature begins to sway in the intermediate metaphysical stage beginning in early modernity, when supernatural beings are replaced by abstract forces as the cause of all phenomena, and philosophy turns to speculating about the nature of these forces. Finally we arrive at the positive stage, where speculation concerning abstract forces is abandoned in favor of empirical investigation into observable natural and social phenomena and the laws that regulate their relationships—in other words, modern science. Comte's positivism assumes that all phenomena can be understood with respect to natural laws and that all natural laws should be reduced to the smallest possible number.[29] Echoes of this sentiment resonate in Dennett's chapter section titled "Who's Afraid of Reductionism?" in *Darwin's Dangerous Idea*, while Dawkins (always in search of "ultimate" explanations) is dismayed by the fact that reductionism has become a "dirty word" in academic circles.[30]

Unlike some New Atheists, however, Comte did not go so far as to suggest that social phenomena are reducible to biological phenomena. He argued instead that the social world required its own science, a "social physics" that recognized society as a distinct field of laws and processes that could not be grasped by the theories and methodologies of the natural sciences. Nonetheless, his thought is compatible with contemporary scientific atheists who consider religion an outdated pseudoscientific theory or explanation of natural phenomena. Comte's ideas could be considered a proto-secularization theory, outlining a teleological path of social development that is characterized by a decline in religious belief, which is replaced by science, the modern form of knowledge. The New Atheism is, in fact, a Comtean ideology of secularization. This is to say that it sees religious decline as a function of intellectual and scientific progress rather than the more recent sociological account of secularization as a process of functional differentiation, with the retreat of religion to the private sphere seen as part of the rationalization of society. This ideology is examined in detail in Chapter 2, but to understand it we first need to understand atheism's historical relationship to the idea of evolution. We must therefore understand the impact of Darwinism.

The publication of *The Origin of Species* in 1859 is not only one of the most significant events in the history of science, but perhaps also the most significant event in the history of atheism. Charles Darwin's theory of evolution by natural selection was one of the most provocative and controversial ideas in human history, chiefly due to its implicit challenge to religious explanations of human origins. This simple but astonishingly successful explanation of life had no need for invocation of the divine. It was self-sufficient and for the first time provided an answer to the riddle of the existence of life that was for thousands of years answered with God, and thus provided atheism with an answer to the lacuna that had plagued it for centuries. Darwin's theory not only challenged the argument from design but nullified it by providing a rational, evidence-based alternative explanation of the appearance of design in life.[31] Darwin himself notes the implications of his theory for the oldest argument for religion in his autobiography: "There seems to be no more design in the variability of organic beings, and in the action of natural selection, than in the course which the wind blows."[32] Though he never called himself an atheist, he expressed an agnosticism that grew out of the implications of his theory of evolution, which provided new scientific grounding for atheism and the critique of religion.[33] Darwin himself pointed to the implications of his theory for the understanding of religion, explaining it, like Comte, in evolutionary terms as an early attempt at explanation of nature:

... the belief in unseen or spiritual agencies ... seems to be almost universal ... nor is it difficult to comprehend how it arose. As soon as the important faculties of the imagination, wonder, and curiosity, together with some power of reasoning, had become partially developed, man would naturally have craved to understand what was passing around him, and have vaguely speculated on his own existence.[34]

Darwin, a shy and chronically ill recluse, rarely spoke publicly and instead left the defense of his highly controversial theory in the public sphere mainly to Thomas Huxley, who would become famous for, among other things, coining the term "agnosticism" and gaining a reputation as "Darwin's bulldog" by arguing vigorously on behalf of Darwin's theory. Huxley and a handful of others took to defending and promoting the theory of evolution in the academy and in the more inclusive public sphere and "effectively collaborated to take over the scientific establishment, with the goal of enthroning naturalism as the ideology of science and science as the mainspring of modern society."[35] Darwin's theory, of course, met with resistance from religious authorities (as well as dissenters from the scientific community), and this coupled with the fact that the Biblical account of the creation and significance of human beings contradicted evolution led some early Darwinists to engage in a public conflict with religious ideas. This conflict still shapes the discourse of the New Atheism today.

It is crucial to note that for these early Darwinists, the theory of evolution was not simply a scientific fact that needed to be defended against irrational forces that would seek to discredit it. The theory of evolution was, from the beginning, tied to a certain political orientation. Darwin was born into a wealthy family of capitalists and scientists.[36] This socialization proved determinative of his character and political views, which in turn were instructive in the development of his scientific theory. Informed by Darwin's liberal-capitalist worldview, natural selection doubled as a metaphor for the right of individuals to pursue their self-interest in a free and competitive society.[37] Soon after its publication, Huxley declared *Origin of Species* to be a gun in the armory of liberalism, the most effective new weapon for attacking superstitious beliefs and thus promoting rational materialism.[38]

Evolution was clearly not politically neutral in the minds of its defenders. Rather, the idea was tied to liberalism and rationalism and used to promote modern goals and values, and thus transcended science to become a cornerstone of the political ideology of the Victorian liberal intelligentsia.[39] Indeed, many scholars agree that Darwin's theory not only validated his political views but itself was a product of Victorian culture, with Darwin early in his scientific career committing himself to a theory of nature that reflected the Malthusian socioeconomic inclinations of British high society. In this view, the theory of natural selection was a contingent result of social history rather than an inevitable conclusion.[40] As atheism became tied to the theory of evolution, it moved from simple negation of religious beliefs to an affirmation of liberalism, scientific rationality, and the legitimacy of the institutions and methodology of modern science—and thus from religious criticism to a complete ideological system.

In addition to linking evolution with liberalism and capitalism, Darwinists found in the theory support for the idea of Western Europe as the world's most advanced (or highly evolved) society. The theory of evolution thus took on enormous significance outside the realm of science, shaping the social and political thought of the day.[41] To this extent, it became as much an instrument of conservative political ideology as it was an instrument of liberalism. This is most clear in the example of Herbert Spencer, who drew on both Darwinian and Lamarckian ideas for his conception of social evolution. In Spencer's social theory, evolution defines the stages that a society passes through.[42] The mechanism that drives this process is natural selection, or competition between the more and less "fit" members of society: "Society advances where its fittest members are allowed to assert their fitness with the least hindrance, and where the least fitted are not artificially prevented from dying out."[43] In this sentence we see Spencer's radical *laissez-faire* individualism and a warning against the danger posed to the advancement of society by welfare state programs and support for the poor, all with the legitimacy provided by a scientific theory.[44] While Spencer did not concentrate on religious criticism and was not directly involved in the development of atheism, he was directly involved in the development of evolutionistic social theories. His view of religion was firmly in line with that of both Comte and Darwin, which is clear in this statement: "Religions that are diametrically opposite in their dogmas agree in tacitly recognizing that the world, with all it contains and all that surrounds it, is a mystery seeking an explanation."[45] Religion, then, is a false explanation of nature, and both Spencer and Comte believed that social evolution and the rise of science would bring it to an end.

It is important to note that this idea of progressive social evolution, with its vision of a "natural unfolding of social complexity," is predicated upon a misreading of Darwin, who viewed evolution as a process with no fixed direction and invoked the metaphor of a "radiating bush" to describe adaptation and differentiation.[46] For Spencer, who inflected biological evolution with his own prejudices and politics, evolution was a journey down a singular line of improvement, and the key to this improvement was creating the conditions whereby the fittest could flourish and would not be hindered by the lesser elements in society. With Spencer, evolution moved from liberal-rationalist ideology to what would become known as Social Darwinism, a political ideology modeled after the conditions of survival in nature—it is, in short, *society* red in tooth and claw. In many circles, scientific and otherwise, atheism became intertwined with this ideology, even though Darwin himself considered atheism to be an untenable position and instead preferred agnosticism.[47]

Despite Darwin's reservations, the theory of evolution meant for some that science was able to complete the break from religion instigated by the Scientific Revolution and a contemporaneous revolution in theology, now having an explanation of the origin of life to supplement the explanation of the cosmos. The atheism of the Victorian Darwinists, constituted by this explanatory model of religion, as well as political liberalism and a defense of the Enlightenment principles of progress, universalism, and scientific-rationalism, is *scientific atheism*. It carries on the cognitive critique, focusing on the irrationality of religious beliefs, with the expectation that the lights of reason would eliminate the darkness of religious ignorance and superstition. It emerged out of the dialectic described by Buckley, which, in the Victorian period following Darwin's theory of the origin of life, culminated in the view that science had replaced religion as the explanation of the material world and that modern scientific society must reject religion.[48] With science claiming the sole right to explanation of nature, critique of religion was in essence a rejection of worldviews that stood in the way of the legitimation and institutionalization of modern scientific methods.

It is crucial again to point out that scientific atheism was not restricted to those in the fields of the natural sciences. Thinkers in the fields of sociology and anthropology also took to positing religion as a lower stage in the evolution of humanity, such as in Comte's Law of Three Stages. E. B. Tylor shared the scientific atheist view of religion as a pseudoscientific hypothesis (what Dawkins calls the "God Hypothesis") and believed that religion's function is the same as that of science: to account for events in the material world.[49] It is equally important to note that not all Darwinists took the Spencerian view of progressive evolution, and that scientific atheists in the Darwinian tradition today—Dawkins is the prime example—are inclined to warp the theory of natural selection to fit their own particular visions of social progress. These facts taken together tell us that scientific atheism is not a necessary consequence of a Darwinian worldview but rather an ideology that uses "evolution" and "natural selection" as metaphors in the advancement of what is in fact a deeply political position.

From Heaven to Earth

The atheist defenders of Darwin, emboldened by the revolutionary theory of evolution by natural selection and the answer it provided to the argument from design, extended and refined the Enlightenment tradition of religious criticism, most importantly the cognitive critique. At the same time, another revolution in thought was taking place, one founded on the notion that the cognitive critique did not account for the nonrational forces that spawn and sustain religious belief. This revolution produced what David Berman calls the "anthropological approach" to criticism of religion, which steers atheism away from ontological questions concerning God's existence.[50] Instead, thinkers in this tradition assumed God's nonexistence, focusing their attention on the question of why people believe in God and how that belief is sustained despite the revelations of science. If the "light" of reason and science failed to illuminate the "darkness" of religion—that is, if people continued to believe even after Newton, Darwin, and the rationalist philosophers—then ignorance alone could not explain religion.

This move might be understood as a departure from scientific atheism, which is a denial of the existence of God and the refutation of religious (as opposed to scientific) explanations of nature, and toward an approach that shifted focus from "nature" to "humanity," as nineteenth-century atheism directed its energy toward ennobling humanity rather than attacking the irrationality of religion.[51] The atheism of the anthropological approach to criticism, and subsequent criticism rooted in this tradition—which understands religion as a social and psychological phenomenon and emerged from the human sciences, including the social sciences and humanities—may therefore be called *humanistic atheism.*

This approach surfaced largely as a response to discontent with the promise of the Enlightenment that modernity would lead to greater prosperity for all, as well as a recognition that the rationalist cognitive critique of religion did nothing to address the nonrational sources of religious belief, which include alienation, suffering, infantile neurosis and insecurity, and fear of death. In its early formulation it understood God as a projection of alienation and suffering, thereby centering humanity and its earthly interests, rather than theological constructions of God and the supernatural realm, as the object of inquiry. Its origin may be traced to Ludwig Feuerbach, while Berman identifies Karl Marx, Friedrich Nietzsche, and Sigmund Freud as the other major pioneers in this tradition.

Of these four, only Marx could be considered a true social scientist, while the others come from the perspectives of philosophy and psychology, but all took account of the social in their theories of religion. It may seem a strange collection, and indeed this is a very diverse group of thinkers. Nonetheless, these four are representatives of a turn in atheist thought toward a conception of religion as a product of the human/social condition, rather than strictly an outdated form of pseudoscientific knowledge or simple ignorance. The chief objection to religion in this approach is not that it is a false explanation of nature and human origins (what Feuerbach terms a "false theological essence" with respect to Christianity) but rather its role in the degradation of humanity and in various forms of oppression. The problem with religion, then, is that it is an obstacle not to knowledge but to human flourishing, and thus the strategy in this approach is not attacking religious beliefs as much as addressing the nonrational social and psychological forces that give them life. As Berman writes, "Although these great German writers were opponents of theism, they were almost entirely uninterested in the substantive question of God's existence: they largely assumed His nonexistence, and offered absorbing accounts of the causes which have brought about, and sustain, belief in God."[52] These diverse thinkers arrived at different conclusions that reflected their own epistemologies and politics, but they all shared the belief that to study religion is really to study the social and psychological condition of humanity (as Feuerbach puts it, "theology is anthropology"), as opposed to the scientific approach that treats religion as a set of hypotheses regarding material reality that can be empirically tested. There are many others from this period who take similar approaches, but Berman identifies four in particular as the most significant, and in terms of influence in the academic world and on the general public, it is difficult to imagine a more significant trio than Marx, Freud, and Nietzsche. Feuerbach, meanwhile, was a precursor to these three and was particularly influential in the development of Marx's views.

Given his role as a principal architect of one of the most important streams of atheist thought of the past two centuries, it is striking that Feuerbach is rarely mentioned today in popular or scholarly religious criticism. Feuerbach's seminal contribution to the development of atheism was his theory of God as a projection of the human onto the divine figure, which is a projection of alienation: "Religion is the disuniting of man from himself; he sets God before him as the antithesis of himself."[53] That is, everything that is great about God is alienated from humanity. Feuerbach understands this act of projection and what it reveals about the human condition as the true, "anthropological essence" of Christianity, while rejecting its theological claims as a "false essence."[54] His project was thus to repair the division with the human by revealing the secret or "true" essence of religion, which is that it is not God that is worshipped, but humanity alienated from itself.

This philosophical project seeks to reclaim the divine properties for humanity; hence, the basis of Feuerbach's atheism is not a scientific-rationalist discrediting of theological claims, but a recognition of the essentially human character of God. With this recognition established, he declares that "By his God thou knowest the man, and by the man his God; the two are identical," an insight that led him to a different kind of approach to religion that involved turning theology into anthropology.[55] Feuerbach believed that to understand (and effectively critique) religion we must understand the conditions of life that give rise to it. Hence, he sought to replace the science of God with the science of Man.[56] This shift in emphasis, from theological claims to the human condition, and from an understanding of religion as a false explanation of nature to one that considers it a social phenomenon, is the essence of humanistic atheism. This approach was adopted by Marx, who reconfigured Feuerbach's theory by defining more precisely the nature of the human experience that resulted in the projection of God—that is, alienation.

Marx sought to expose the distorting ideas about social life within religion and the underlying interests sustaining it and argued that religion could not be analytically separated from the social world it resides in.[57] In his analysis religion could not somehow be siphoned off from social context, in particular the material conditions of social life. For him religion is an ideological manifestation of alienation or an expression of, and protest against, earthly human suffering. Roughly speaking, he echoed Feuer-bach's theory of God as projected alienation: "The basis of irreligious criticism is: man makes religion, religion does not make man. Religion, indeed, is the self-consciousness and the self-esteem of the man who has not yet found himself or who has already lost himself."[58] The alienated self, buried by oppressive conditions, is projected onto the divine figure, which in turn promises relief from this oppression in the next world.

Marx's description of religion as the "opium of the people" and "the heart of a heartless world" elucidates what Feuerbach meant by the "true" anthropological essence of religion as opposed to its "false" theological es-sence.[59] Religion is true not in its theological claims, but in the sense that it is a real expression and manifestation of the human experience of op-pression and suffering; thus, the critique of religion is really the critique of an unjust and oppressive world, and "the critique of heaven turns into the critique of earth."[60] Marx insists that if the world were recreated ac-cording to his socialist vision it would have a heart of its own, and religion would be reduced to a vestigial organ of an oppressive social body, even-tually to be left in the dustbin of history along with capitalism. He agreed with Feuerbach that the elimination of religion is necessary for human beings to be restored to their humanity, and by extension this requires the end of alienation, which is at the heart of religious faith: "The criticism of religion ends in the teaching that *man is the highest being for man*, hence in the *categorical imperative to overthrow all those conditions* in which man is a debased, enslaved, abandoned, contemptible being."[61]

Marx diverges from the Enlightenment tradition in his outline of the method for the abolishment of religion, claiming that when the oppres-sive conditions that necessitate religious belief are transformed, the com-forting illusion of religion will no longer be necessary and it will simply disappear—the ideology vanishes as its material foundation crumbles. While scientific atheism focuses on rational-scientific education and anal-ysis of religion's transcendent ideas, Marx pointed out that this would do nothing to transform the earthly social relations that constitute their foun-dation. He argued that the strategy of rational deliberation was bound to fail because it did not address this true essence of religion. Just as Feuer-bach wanted to turn the science of God into the science of Man by "re-solving the religious world into its secular basis," Marx similarly argued that the critique of heaven necessarily becomes the critique of Earth.[62] He notes that "Feuerbach resolves the religious essence into the *human* essence," while adding that this is not an individual abstraction but rather "the ensemble of the social relations."[63] The point of emphasis is therefore not enlightenment, but social transformation.

This shift in perspective reflects a new understanding of the essence of religion, moving beyond the simple point that Judeo-Christian doctrine is at odds with modern science, and particularly an evolutionary account of the origins of human life. Marx's theory of religion signals a progressive development in atheist thought, moving from rational-scientific refutation of theology to consideration of religion as a social phenomenon, including its sources and its social and political consequences. It also signals a point of divergence among different schools of atheist thought. The Darwinists continued the project of the emancipation of science that originally gave birth to atheism, and they specifically sought to establish scientific hegemony within the academy and employed evolutionary biology as a strategy to this effect while virtually ignoring Marx's more sociological and anthropological brand of criticism.[64]

Like Marx, Freud described religion as an illusion, and though the specifics of this are quite different, these thinkers do share an understanding of the essential value of religion to the believer. Religious illusions, for both thinkers, are in part a mechanism for coping with suffering and the harsh realities of life. Freud located the roots of this illusion not in the material conditions of production but in something much less tangible: the human unconscious. He conceives of the religious believer as a fearful and wondering child—helpless, afraid, and ignorant of the nature of the world, which appears before him as a terrifying and threatening place. He paints a portrait of humans desperate for some measure of control over terrifying forces of nature. This is possible only if nature is controlled by an anthropomorphic figure who might exercise that control on their behalf. The result is the idea of God, who can be persuaded by various means to prevent volcanic eruptions, droughts, hurricanes, and pestilence, to name just a few of his limitless powers.[65]

This helplessness experienced by the adult in relation to nature is much like the helplessness experienced by the child in relation to his parents.[66] Putting these two elements together—the helplessness against nature and infantile helplessness—we get a picture of religion as

the system of doctrines and promises which on the one hand explains to him the riddles of this world with enviable completeness, and, on the other, assures him that a careful Providence will watch over his life and will compensate him in a future existence for any frustrations he suffers here. The common man cannot imagine this Providence otherwise than in the figure of an enormously exalted father.[67]

Here Freud complements the explanatory view of religion with a psychoanalytic account of the adoption of these beliefs. In this respect he diverges from scientific atheism, which is not influenced by humanistic considerations but concentrates entirely on the conflict between the factual claims of science and religion. At the same time, his empiricism and derision of nonscientific explanations of reality, including his attitude regarding religion as a failed ancient explanation of natural processes analogous to Dawkins' God Hypothesis, raises echoes of scientific atheism so clear that it is stunning that the contemporary New Atheists utterly ignore his contribution to atheism.

While the notion of religion as irrational, infantile wish fulfillment dominates discussion of Freud's work on religion, another crucial aspect of his thought on the issue is often overlooked. This is the place of the adult's experience of oppression and suffering in civilization, that state of affairs that guarantees humans a certain degree of security and protection from harm in exchange for a renunciation of our most antisocial instincts and a submission to external authority, which results in a general unhappiness.[68] While civilization in any form is bound to result in repression and psychic discontent, for which religion is a remedy, the problem is exacerbated by the particular configuration of civilization we are presented with, which is characterized by exploitation and oppression. Here a link to Marx emerges, revealing a common understanding of the source of religion's value to the believer. Like Marx, Freud sees in the concepts of God and heaven a means of coping with earthly injustice through the promise of divine justice: "In the end all good is rewarded and all evil punished, if not actually in this form of life then in the later existences that begin after death. In this way all the terrors, the sufferings and the hardships of life are destined to be obliterated."[69] Like Marx, Freud directs criticism away from ontological questions of God's existence and toward the social and psychological conditions of life.

Another pioneer of humanistic atheism is the self-declared antihumanist Friedrich Nietzsche. His philosophy rejects any epistemology of transcendence or universality. His famous declaration that "God is dead" is not, of course, a statement of fact about God's existence.[70] Rather, Nietzsche here refers to the condition of modernity, characterized

foremost posits that minimizing suffering and maximizing well-being and fulfillment in life are the only things likely to make religion vanish. This means that the social order must be questioned and transformed, a position that sets humanistic atheism apart from the more conservative *laissez-faire* liberalism of scientific atheism. In short, the distinction is this: scientific atheism seeks to release modernity from religious shackles, while humanistic atheism questions the foundations of modernity itself and seeks to resolve the inequities that characterize it.

In the twentieth century both forms of atheism became highly politicized and were involved in major social, political, and cultural transformations. Other kinds of atheism emerged and garnered some interest, notably existentialism, which enjoyed a period of popularity, but its influence was not as great or as durable as the others. In this period the most important strands of atheist thought were scientific atheism and Marxism—or at least these were the two that had the greatest impact on society. In terms of the social significance of atheism in the twentieth century, the major example is the Soviet Union, which ostensibly took up Marx's dictum that religion is an ideology of oppression and class society, and thus sought to eradicate it. Interestingly, early Soviet antireligious activity involved a strategy of enlightenment employed primarily through a propaganda campaign that focused on rational and scientific proofs against the existence of God.[80] This was the subject of great debate and created divisions within the highest ranks of the Communist Party, but generally enlightenment was the favored strategy, ironically defying the Marxian idea that social transformation would make enlightenment on the question of religion superfluous. Nonetheless, the purported atheism of the Soviet Union was a manifestation and expression of the politicized atheism of Marxism. The project of rapid secularization in the Soviet Union was largely a failure, and the masses defiantly held to their religious beliefs despite their supposed liberation from oppression, a massive propaganda campaign, and fear of persecution.[81] It is perhaps the connection to the oppression and violence within the Soviet Union and other communist nations (particularly China) that has left the Marxist atheist tradition in ruins, even if in practice these nations generally did not meet the condition of the eradication of oppression upon which Marx's theory was based. In other instances, such as in Latin America, religion itself was an emancipative force that united the masses in revolution, quite the opposite role from that which Marx relegated it to. Religion there was indeed the sigh of the oppressed, but hardly the opium of the people.

Scientific atheism and its relationship with evolution also played an important role in twentieth-century history. This is particularly true in the United States, where scientists and educators have been defending their practices against attack from religious quarters—though the religious would surely also claim to be under siege by science and secularism—since John Scopes was prosecuted and convicted in Dayton, Tennessee, in 1926 for violating a new law prohibiting the teaching of evolution in public schools. This case—popularly known as the Monkey Trial in reference to the notion that humans and apes share common ancestors—famously pitted celebrated defense attorney and avowed atheist Clarence Darrow against prosecutor William Jennings Bryan, political populist and "America's foremost champion of Christian government."[82] In a dramatic twist, Darrow cross-examined Bryan, one of the prosecutors, and the trial became a seminal event in American cultural, scientific, and legal history. Darrow's cool (and often scathing) rationalism represented the Darwinist side of the debate, while Bryan's evangelical defense of revealed religion represented the voice of conservative Christianity.

Scopes was convicted of breaking the law, but in the court of public opinion Darrow was perhaps the victor, with Bryan repeatedly confounded by Darrow's questions requiring him to defend inconsistencies within scripture. By the time they got through the first few verses of Genesis some newspapers had taken to ridiculing Bryan, though his "impassioned objections made anti-evolutionism all but an article of faith among conservative American Christians."[83] Obviously both sides claimed victory, and the trial had the lasting effect of polarizing both sides of the debate and setting the stage for a century of political struggle between religious "creationists" on the one hand and scientific rationalists and secularists on the other. This struggle has largely played out on the issue of public education, and in 2006 a second "Monkey Trial" took place in Dover, Pennsylvania. This time it was secularists who mounted a successful challenge against the teaching of intelligent design theory in public schools, which the presiding judge ruled was equivalent to religious instruction and thus prohibited from state education by the Constitution. Most importantly, it was in this trial that atheism and Darwinism were permanently fused in the American context. Among many conservative American Christians, believing in evolution is tantamount to denying God, hence the rejection of the theory that constitutes the foundation of the science of biology and that, for most people in the Western world and almost all scientists, is simply a scientific fact.

The Scopes trial was one of the most important events in the politicization of atheism (certainly the scientific version). This politicization was, however, largely restricted to the United States, where science frequently came under attack from religious quarters. In Western Europe scientists faced no similar interference from the church or religious activists. Highly politicized atheism returned with renewed vigor in the infancy of the twenty-first century with the emergence of the New Atheism and its celebrated leaders, and an increasingly vocal and radical secular public, particularly in the United Kingdom and North America. This New Atheism was new only in the extent of its impact in the public sphere, where debates regarding religion and its relationship to science suddenly became common features in mass media. Its discourse on science and religion, on the other hand, is quite familiar, reflecting the same debates that shaped scientific atheism in the nineteenth century.

2

The New Atheism

IN AN ESSAY appearing in the first major collection on the New Atheism, Stephen Bullivant asks a simple question with no clear answer: why here and why now? Atheism has a long history, but this history is mostly restricted to developments in the intellectual sphere. In the public sphere more broadly, atheism has been virtually invisible, unless the term was invoked to assert the immorality of the "godless communists" who were the West's principal antagonists in the latter half of the twentieth century. In the early years of the twenty-first century, there was a sudden explosion of public interest in religion and expressions of atheism. Much of this revolved around the staggering success of Richard Dawkins' *The God Delusion*, which sold millions of copies and made the author an international celebrity. What were the conditions that allowed this to happen at this particular time?

Bullivant offers several plausible explanations, though these vary depending on context (he focuses on the United Kingdom and the United States). For Britain, the explanation Bullivant offers is that people there are in fact more interested in religion than is commonly thought based on the results of survey data on belief and church attendance. Turning to the United States, he notes that the question is why strong avowals of atheism have suddenly become popular when the country has been so religious for so long. He cites surveys indicating that atheists are the least-trusted group in America and suggests that these studies have contributed to a "consciousness of being a marginalized and misunderstood minority in American society,"[1] though he also points out that these kinds of studies have been carried out many times over the years with similar results. The major difference today, he argues, may be that whereas America's biggest enemy was once "godless communists," it is now Islamic fundamentalists, so atheism can no longer be equated with a great threat.

Here Bullivant points to the key catalyst for the rise of popular atheism: 9/11 and the subsequent "war on terror." This event brought us into a new world where the locus of conflict revolved around tensions with the Middle East that were framed in terms of what Samuel Huntington famously called a "clash of civilizations."[2] Rather than West versus East, this was more precisely Christendom versus the Islamic world, a cultural conflict as much as a political one. While identified with the enemy during the Cold War, atheists were now in a position to assert that religion, not atheism, constituted the greatest threat to world order. Bullivant suggests that the New Atheism may have been more palatable in America precisely because it was a "patriotic atheism" that, at least with respect to Christopher Hitchens and Sam Harris, offered outspoken support for the wars in Iraq and Afghanistan and defended the use of torture in interrogating terrorism suspects.[3] This is somewhat paradoxical when considered in relation to the other major factor in the rise of the New Atheism, which is the surging power and influence of the Christian Right during the presidency of George W. Bush. All the New Atheists were united in opposition to this movement, Harris and Hitchens for explicitly political reasons, while Dawkins and Daniel Dennett were ostensibly opposed primarily to the attack on evolutionary biology by young-Earth creationists, who advocated for teaching intelligent design in public-school science classes. Christian government representatives around the United States in recent years have argued that schools should "teach the controversy," referring to an alleged rift within the scientific community on the matter of intelligent design versus natural selection as the engine of creation. The New Atheists vociferously retorted that for respectable scientists evolution is simply a fact and that the controversy was manufactured by the evangelical lobby.

There is a contradiction in the "patriotic atheism" theory of the New Atheism's popularity in the United States. Some of these thinkers did support the "Bush doctrine" of preemptive war against Muslim societies, but at the same time they all opposed the evangelical movement—which was largely responsible for putting Bush in the White House—because of its rejection of scientific authority. The destruction of the World Trade Center and the rise of the Christian Right are certainly factors in the impact of the New Atheism, but these factors must be supplemented with perhaps the most important one: the generational shift downward in religiosity in America. While America still rates very high in religiosity among Western nations, there has been a discernible shift in the younger demographic away from organized religion, which is conventionally understood to coincide with the rise of what is called the "nones," the group of people who answer "None" to the question of religious affiliation in surveys and censuses.[4] While "nones" are not necessarily atheists—in fact, few identify with the term and most express religious beliefs of some kind or claim to be "spiritual"—the move away from organized religion among this demographic is very significant, and may point to an increasingly critical position toward the institution of religion and a greater interest in critiques of this institution and fundamentalist forms of belief like that offered by the New Atheism.

This generational shift is particularly important in explaining atheism in Canada, where "patriotic atheism" and resistance to the Christian Right cannot be expected to be as important as in the United States, though Canadian culture is so permeated by American media that many Canadians are knowledgeable and concerned about American issues. The global concern about Islamism also affects Canada, and this along with the decreasing religiosity (at least in terms of institutional affiliation and active practice) of Canadians establishes a climate receptive to the New Atheism. It is also likely that the series of sexual abuse scandals involving Catholic priests, and the attempts to cover them up by church authorities, fostered antagonism toward religious institutions and their claims to being arbiters of morality in Canada and around the world. And yet, all of these explanations—9/11, the Christian Right, the rise of the "nones," sexual abuse scandals—do not add up to a completely satisfactory answer to Bullivant's questions: Why here and why now? In this book, I hope to shed some more light on this subject, though at some level it must finally be considered the sort of historical contingency that cannot be predicted or explained with absolute certainty. But first we need to address the most basic question: Who, and what, is the New Atheism?

The Four Horsemen

The Atheist Alliance International (AAI)'s convention in September 2007 was a watershed event in the recent history of atheism. It was the first time that the four writers who would collectively come to represent an intellectual wave known as the New Atheism—Dawkins, Harris, Dennett, and Hitchens—appeared at the same event. This was the New Atheism as its wave of popularity was cresting, with Hitchens publishing his entry in the canon that year and the three others releasing titles the year prior. The event was co-organized by Dawkins' Foundation for Reason and Science, and Dawkins took the opportunity of their appearances at the convention to bring all these writers together in a more informal setting to talk about their views on religion, atheism, and critical responses to their work. This conversation was released on DVD by Dawkins' Foundation under the title *The Four Horsemen*, referring to the infamous Four Horsemen of the Apocalypse of the book of Revelation.

The New Atheists would be at home in the Victorian context from which scientific atheism emerged. The two most famous New Atheists (Dawkins and Hitchens) are British, and the social and intellectual roots of the movement are found in nineteenth-century England and the debates concerning Darwin's theory of evolution. Their arguments differ from those of their nineteenth-century predecessors mainly in the sophistication brought to the theory of evolution by the modern synthesis that united Darwinian natural selection with genetics and molecular biology, and more importantly in the addition of theories derived from the emerging fields of evolutionary psychology and neuroscience.[5] Drawing on these new sciences, the New Atheists craft a vision of religion not only as a prescientific explanation of material reality—what Dawkins refers to as the "God Hypothesis"[6]—but also as itself a "natural" phenomenon. This means that religion is produced by natural forces that can be understood by recourse to evolutionary theory, applied to both culture and individual psychology. The evolutionistic theories of the New Atheists treat religion strictly as belief, with no accounting of the social nature of religious practice. Even in treating it as belief, the approach is severely limited because it restricts the analysis to some version of the God Hypothesis (that is, an attempt at explaining the nature and origin of the cosmos), with little regard for the concerns and questions raised by humanistic atheism.

Harris had the distinction of publishing the first New Atheism text, *The End of Faith*, in 2004, following it up in 2006 with *Letter to a Christian Nation*, addressed specifically to American Christian fundamentalists. These books are a call to arms for what Harris believes is an unavoidable battle, science and reason versus the forces of faith and superstition, with devastating consequences should the former fail. *The End of Faith* today reads very much like a fevered response to 9/11 in its discussions of the West's engagement with Islam as a clash of civilizations, with one representing Enlightenment and moral progress and the other representing barbarism. At the time it was published Harris held a bachelor's degree in philosophy from Stanford University but no other significant credentials, though he has since completed a PhD in neuroscience at UCLA. The book defied expectations for a critical work on religion from an unknown author by achieving bestseller status and winning the PEN award for nonfiction.

Harris tapped into post-9/11 anxiety concerning Islam and the West's relationship with the Middle East directly and effectively, which perhaps accounts for the unexpected and overwhelming success of the book. A good example of his approach is a passage in which he warns that, should an Islamist regime gain control of nuclear weapons, "the only thing likely to ensure our survival may be a nuclear first strike of our own."[7] The apocalyptic fervor with which Harris prognosticates on such scenarios was no doubt a source of his appeal in a historical and cultural milieu that stoked the flames of Islamophobia. Harris is also a polished writer who is skilled at crafting seductive arguments for a mass audience amenable to his point of view. He employs limit-case examples of religious extremism as his primary rhetorical technique, exploiting his audience's fears while ostensibly appealing to their rational faculties. His success is therefore not accidental or incomprehensible, though had he written the book a decade earlier it likely would have slipped silently into the cracks of bookstore shelves. Despite his skill at mass entertainment and his apparent desire to be seen as a philosopher and general intellectual, Harris is not taken seriously by scholars. He has used this fact as a marketing device, portraying himself as an iconoclast who need not refer to the work of peers, who reject him because they are evidently threatened by his radical ideas and the power of his thought. After his book *The Moral Landscape*—which argues for a scientific and materialist basis for ethics, an idea that has been rejected in philosophy since Hume—was ravaged by any professional philosopher who looked at it, Harris insisted on his blog that he had not encountered any review that would compel him to alter any of his arguments. Even his fellow New Atheist Dennett, who Harris refers to as a friend, wrote a trenchant review of his book *Free Will*. Harris characteristically responded by shrugging off all of his friend's carefully considered criticisms.

Despite being the first text in the New Atheism "canon" and a bestseller and PEN award winner, *The End of Faith* is not the most important text in this canon and on its own would likely not have initiated the atheist movement we know today. That distinction clearly belongs to Dawkins' *The God Delusion*, a phenomenal bestseller that launched a period of unprecedented mass media attention devoted to atheist commentators. Dawkins is the de facto leader of the New Atheism. Before becoming the world's most famous and vocal atheist he was an evolutionary biologist who held a professorship in zoology at Berkeley in the late 1960s before taking a position as lecturer, and later reader, at Oxford. Dawkins garnered international recognition both inside and outside the academy with the publication of *The Selfish Gene* in 1976, in which he sought to explain his gene-centered theory of evolution by natural selection to a mass audience. His ability to clearly convey complicated scientific principles to a general audience made him a successful author of popular science, and in 1995 he was awarded the first Simonyi Professorship for the Public Understanding of Science at Oxford University, a position he retired from in 2008.

Dawkins' reputation as a public intellectual, then, was established well before he embarked on his new career as an advocate for atheism. He rather suddenly went from a mostly gentle defender of science to a fierce critic of religion with the broadcast of a two-part television documentary in 2006 called *Root of All Evil?*[8] The film follows Dawkins in conversation with Islamists and Orthodox Jews in Jerusalem; attending a clandestine gathering of atheists in Colorado; and interviewing Ted Haggard, president of the National Association of Evangelicals, shortly before his highly publicized resignation after a male prostitute claimed that he had sold Haggard methamphetamine and that they had regular sex for three years.[9] It was followed by the publication of *The God Delusion*, the success of which ignited a heated public debate about the place of religion in the West and made Dawkins a true star as a public intellectual. The book was not an unforeseeable move for Dawkins, who had already made attacking "intelligent design" (the "scientific" version of Biblical creationism) a priority in his public lectures and writings, notably in *The Blind Watchmaker*.[10] A book attacking religion, the foundation of intelligent design, was a logical step given his trajectory. It stands as the key text of the contemporary atheist movement and was a significant cultural event in its own right. As of January 2010 the book had sold over two million copies in English alone, with many more sold throughout Europe (Dawkins himself reported on his website that the German edition had sold over 260,000 copies).

The God Delusion is primarily a sustained argument that "God almost certainly does not exist," while also exploring the topics of religion's harmful social and psychological effects and a Darwinian theory of the origin and purpose of religious belief. Dawkins treats God as a natural entity amenable to scientific investigation, precisely because he adopts a position of scientific materialism, or the view that "everything that exists (life, mind, morality, religion, and so on) can be completely explained in terms of matter or physical nature."[11] That is, Dawkins believes that anything that exists must exist within nature and that there is no object of inquiry that lies outside the boundaries of science. What is ostensibly an examination of the nature of religious belief, then, is actually a polemic on the merits of the scientific method and its universal applicability.

In general, the most important theme in Dawkins' many writings, lectures, and films about religion actually has little to do with religion itself; rather, his most pressing issue is his vigorous promotion of science and particularly evolutionary theory, with natural selection serving as his "god of the gaps." The theme of the 2009 AAI convention, presented in conjunction with Dawkins' Foundation, was "Darwin's Legacy," and the presentations as a whole paid little attention to religion and instead were geared almost exclusively toward highlighting science's capacity to produce knowledge as well as a sense of wonder and a profound connection to nature (or as Freud would put it, the "oceanic feeling," a distinctly religious sentiment). Dawkins insists that the natural sciences are and must be capable of explaining *everything*. He sets religion up as the opponent of science in the tradition of his nineteenth-century Darwinist forebears and then attempts to use science to discredit religious beliefs in his "crusade to use Darwinism as a means of dissolving all traditional belief in a purposeful universe."[12] The goal is ultimately not to clear the way for secularization as such but to clear the way for the continuing scientization of secular spheres and to increase the influence of Darwinism in politics and culture.

Dawkins spelled these intentions out quite clearly in a talk given in 2002 at the annual TED lecture series. Here, several years before writing *The God Delusion*, he reveals his true purpose, which is to attack creationism, a direct opponent of evolution: "My approach to attacking creationism is, unlike the evolution lobby . . . to attack religion as a whole."[13] His engagement with religion is in essence an attack on creationism as a rival to evolutionary biology's account of the origins of life. There is nothing inherently wrong with an attack on creationism using Darwinian theory, since creationism and Biblical literalism are, in fact, in conflict with the scientific knowledge on the issue. Taking this approach, however, means that his critiques of religion really only address the most literal and fundamentalist kinds of faith; more nuanced (and pragmatic) faith does not have the same built-in incompatibility with scientific explanations of nature. The salient point to be gleaned here is that it is not really religion per se that Dawkins is interested in. Rather, it is opposition to Darwinism that concerns him, and it just so happens that the strongest opposition to Darwinism comes from religious fundamentalism (notably in the United States). To combat his true enemy, creationism, Dawkins uses evolutionary theory, and science more generally, in an attempt to undermine the foundations of religious belief as a whole. More recently, Dawkins' attention has turned to Islam. He has joined a growing chorus of xenophobia and ethnic nationalism in Europe, tweeting endlessly about "Muslim barbarians" to his over one million followers. The significance of this has not been fully appreciated in scholarship on atheism, and I will deal with it in detail in Chapter 3.

Dawkins is joined in his battle against creationism by his colleague Dennett, Professor of Philosophy and Co-Director of the Center for Cognitive Studies at Tufts University. Before becoming known for his atheism, Dennett had achieved some success as a public intellectual with such works as *Darwin's Dangerous Idea* and *Consciousness Explained*. His foray into the philosophy of religion, *Breaking the Spell: Religion as a Natural Phenomenon*, makes the simple argument that religious claims should be subject to scrutiny just like any other. Hence, "breaking the spell" of insulation to criticism that religion has cast upon us is his major goal. This would be a very reasonable request but that Dennett adds that religion must be understood as a *natural phenomenon* and thus, crucially, *not* a social phenomenon. Dennett writes, "The spell that I say must be broken is the taboo against a forthright, scientific, no-holds-barred investigation of religion as one natural phenomenon among many."[14] Like Dawkins, Dennett's understanding of religion, and culture more generally, is firmly rooted in the natural sciences (particularly Darwinism), explicitly rejecting sociological approaches.

Dennett is the least significant among the Four Horsemen in terms of prominence within the New Atheism movement, and he did not achieve the level of fame enjoyed by his colleagues (though *Breaking the Spell* was also a bestseller). This is perhaps because his entry in the canon is the least impassioned and most carefully measured, reflecting the more prudently detached reasoning of a philosopher. Among this group, his book is easily the best and most nuanced reflection on religion and its relationship to science. Unsurprisingly, it is also the one that has received the least attention, offering none of the easy answers or bombastic claims that generate mass appeal.

Dennett stands in stark contrast to the last of the Four Horsemen, Hitchens, whose aggressive attack on religion resonated much more strongly with atheists. Hitchens is something of an outlier in this group, being neither a scientist nor philosopher of science. He was primarily a journalist covering politics, though he was also a general critic who wrote on a vast array of topics, from Thomas Paine to Mother Teresa.[15] As a columnist for major publications like *Vanity Fair* and *The Atlantic* (among many others) and a regular presence on television talk shows, Hitchens was a public intellectual with a significant presence well before the publication of *God Is Not Great* brought him to new heights of international celebrity. The book catalogues many of the standard arguments against religion and covers such familiar themes as interfaith violence, religion's allegedly intractable conflict with science and reason, and the barbaric morality and inconsistencies contained within the major monotheistic texts. Hitchens described himself as an "antitheist,"[16] believing not only that religious myths are untrue but that their truth is undesirable because it would mean that we are all under surveillance by a "celestial dictator" who may punish us for the private thoughts we hold, referring to the Orwellian notion of "thought crime" in making his case against God. In 2010 Hitchens was diagnosed with esophageal cancer and given a bleak prognosis. Some wondered whether his views on religion would change or if there might even be a deathbed conversion. Instead, he claimed that "the special pleading for salvation, redemption and supernatural deliverance appears even more hollow and artificial to me than it did before."[17] He succumbed to the illness in 2011, and whatever one thinks of this love-him-or-hate-him figure, his departure robbed the New Atheism movement of a significant amount of energy and charisma.

The Second Wave

Along with Dawkins, Harris, Hitchens, and Dennett, there is an extensive supporting cast of writers, academics, and public intellectuals who advocate the scientific atheist worldview. While they do not feature prominently in this book's analysis, it is worth noting some of the second-tier figures in the movement and how their ideas support the claims of the New Atheism (in fact, Harvard evolutionary psychologist Steven Pinker and physicist Lawrence Krauss have come to replace Harris and Dennett in the first tier). In the United Kingdom the most significant of these is A. C. Grayling, who was formerly professor of philosophy at Birkbeck College, University of London. Grayling is a prominent public intellectual in Britain, though his influence in North American atheism is considerably slighter and he is not one of the speakers regularly found on the atheist convention circuit. Though closely allied with Dawkins and Hitchens on questions of religion and science, he is critical of the term "atheist" because it places debate on the ground of theists. He prefers the term "naturalist" to denote "one who takes it that the universe is a natural realm, governed by nature's laws."[18] Grayling has authored numerous books that closely resemble those of the Four Horsemen in theme and tone.[19] He founded and is the Master of the New College of the Humanities, a private undergraduate college in London, which in 2012 began offering courses in economics, English, history, law, and philosophy toward a college diploma and course credit at the University of London. Instructors at the high-priced (approximately $30,000 per year) academy include prominent atheists such as Dawkins (also one of thirteen partners of the college), Pinker, Krauss, and Grayling himself (controversy has already erupted over the revelation that some of these celebrity academics will only actually be giving one lecture per year, leading to charges that their names have been used to draw exorbitant tuition fees). The New College is a nominally secular institution, but critics claim that it is in fact explicitly ideological and elitist, offering training and education in the worldview of scientific atheism and favoring the privileged classes.[20]

Pinker is a respected scholar, a public intellectual, and a writer of popular science. He has spoken on numerous occasions at conferences of atheist and humanist organizations and received the Humanist of the Year award from the American Humanist Association in 2006 and the Richard Dawkins award (given annually to those who raise public consciousness of atheism) from the AAI in 2013. Pinker is one of the principal architects of the new science of human nature known as evolutionary psychology. In *The Blank Slate: The Modern Denial of Human Nature*, he argues against the *"tabula rasa"* theories supposedly advanced by the social sciences that posit that individuals are entirely a product of their environments, instead insisting that human thought and behavior are shaped by Darwinian adaptations. In the more recent *The Better Angels of Our Nature: Why Violence Has Declined*, he turns toward sociobiology, offering a socio-historical analysis of the decline of violence evident in human history. Pinker presents a vast array of statistics that demonstrate a decline in violence and interprets these data as a result of social and cultural forces (including the rise of the nation-state, technology and commerce, and most importantly intellectual progress) that have encouraged good qualities like empathy and reason while tempering our violent and destructive impulses. While dutifully noting that the "New Peace" he identifies as characteristic of the post–Cold War period is partial and tenuous, his position is that the historical trajectory points to a coming age of peace. This is essentially a utopian and teleological theory of science-driven progress. Pinker is not a historian and has no training in sociology, the fields of principal concern in the book. Instead, evolutionary psychology becomes the foundation of socio-historical knowledge and Darwinism the basis for the interpretation of his selected data. It could even be argued that Pinker veers toward Spencerism when he endorses the high incarceration rates in America for drug possession, which as a desirable side effect probably purge some violent individuals from the pool of society. In this view, individuals can be sacrificed for the greater good of progress.

Krauss, another star New College lecturer, is a physicist at Arizona State University specializing in cosmology. He was the first Director of the ASU Origins Initiative, whose website describes it as a "transdisciplinary initiative that nurtures research, energizes teaching, and builds partnerships, offering new possibilities for exploring the most fundamental of questions: who we are and where we came from." Krauss explored the question of cosmic origins in a work of popular science entitled *A Universe from Nothing: Why There Is Something Rather than Nothing*, which features an afterword by Dawkins. It addresses the theological First Cause argument—that is, that something cannot come from nothing, and that therefore the universe needed a creator—by arguing that the laws of physics allow for a universe coming into existence from nothing, without supernatural intervention. He is outspoken on the dangers of creationism and the need to protect science education in America and, like the other figures discussed here, has spoken on numerous occasions at atheist, humanist, and rationalist gatherings. Perhaps most significantly, he and Dawkins were the featured subjects of the 2012 documentary film *The Unbelievers*, which follows the two intellectuals on a speaking tour advocating for science and rationality in a world threatened by religion and superstition.[21] The film's approach of treating its subjects like rock stars on tour underscored the importance of the aura of status and authority in the atheist movement.

Perhaps the most interesting—and problematic—figure associated with the New Atheism is Ayaan Hirsi Ali. Raised as a Muslim in Somalia, she fled an arranged marriage for Holland, where she lost her Islamic faith and eventually became a member of parliament. In 2004 she co-wrote the short film *Submission*, a critique of the repressive nature of Islam (particularly with respect to gender) that instigated a furor among Muslims in Holland that culminated in the murder of director Theo Van Gogh, who was found dead on a street with a knife in his chest and a note attached to it indicating that Ali was next.[22] Not long after this incident she relocated to the United States, where she lives under 24-hour armed guard while writing books, making appearances on television news networks, and acting as an advisor on the religion of Islam and Muslim societies for the American Enterprise Institute, a neoconservative think tank.[23] Ali is a venerated figure among atheists who view Islam as a particularly malevolent faith, and her view of religion as a fountain of ignorance, an instrument of oppression, and the enemy of civilization is directly in line with New Atheist thought. She gave a presentation at the 2007 AAI convention where the Four Horsemen were first assembled, and during the question period Dawkins rose to the microphone to note that he would like to nominate her for the Nobel Peace Prize. As an indication of the esteem she commands within the movement, she took Hitchens' place at the Global Atheist Convention in Melbourne in 2012 in a roundtable discussion that reunited the other three Horsemen, and she was the keynote speaker at the 2015 AAI convention.

While these thinkers are all successful academics and intellectuals who have achieved wide recognition, there are a few other important figures who are not as well known to the general public but are highly regarded within the atheism community. University of Minnesota biologist PZ Myers, author of the popular science blog *Pharyngula*, has a large following of readers and is a mainstay on the atheist convention circuit, though he is a very divisive figure within the movement. Another regular speaker at atheist conventions is physicist Victor Stenger, author of *God: The Failed Hypothesis*, a title that indicates the convergence of his perspective with that of Dawkins in terms of the nature of belief in God. If the connection were not clear enough, he titled his next book simply *The New Atheism*, claiming to speak on behalf of the movement, even though he has had little to do with the much more prominent Four Horsemen. Jerry Coyne is a University of Chicago biologist and author of a book titled *Why Evolution is True*, as well as a blog with the same title that features discussion of science-related topics. Much attention is devoted to debunking intelligent design and engaging in online quarrels with philosophers and other public intellectuals who are critical of science (or, more precisely, scientism). He occasionally also writes for other outlets, for example *New Republic*, where he explicitly declares himself one of the "New Atheists."[24]

There are many others, some of whom will be discussed in the following chapters, but this sampling gives an indication of the type of people associated with the New Atheism as an intellectual movement: scientists and philosophers of science, particularly those in the fields of evolutionary biology and psychology (or in Krauss' case, a scientist concerned with cosmic, rather than biological, origins). The major exception is Ali—not least because she is an African woman in a group dominated by white men—who is renowned for her critical views on Islam grounded in direct experience, rather than a distant scientific perspective on it.

It should also be noted that these figures represent atheism in the English-speaking world; other contexts have their own leading figures. One major example is Michel Onfray, perhaps the most famous atheist intellectual in France, who has also found readers in English for his book *The Atheist Manifesto*, a New Atheist–style assault on the irrationality of religious belief.

Public Impact and Critical Response

The New Atheism has had a tremendous impact on Western society and culture, a fact that has escaped all but a small number of scholars until quite recently. Only now is the significance of this phenomenon beginning to be recognized. During the peak years soon after most of the major texts were published (roughly 2006–2010) the Four Horsemen were highly visible in the mass media, and talk of the New Atheism and the debate it was provoking was common in major news media. This is difficult to quantify, but we should note that New Atheists made multiple appearances on most major American news networks during this time, including CNN and Fox News. In Canada, Dawkins and Hitchens both appeared on the nationally broadcast interview programs *The Hour* (television) and *Q* (radio). In perhaps the greatest sign of Dawkins' fame and status in popular culture in particular, he made a cameo appearance on *The Simpsons* in 2013—as the devil—and was satirized in an episode of *South Park*.

There has been very little quantitative analysis of the media presence and impact of the New Atheism. Cimino and Smith have completed the only study to date of coverage of atheism in major American newspapers, focusing on the *New York Times* and the *Washington Post*.[25] They find a large expansion in coverage after 2006, the year of publication of *The God Delusion*. In terms of the type of coverage, they note that the tone also changed soon after this time. Whereas atheism had previously appeared in editorials as an ideological stance alongside religion, in the new millennium it was increasingly discussed as political identity and lifestyle choice finding a place in a pluralistic society. They attribute these changes to the rise of the New Atheism and the growth and increasing visibility of atheist organizations that accompanied it. This points to what we might consider the greatest measure of the New Atheism's impact: its role as a primary mobilizing force for the emergence of a new social movement (or at least a revitalization of an existing but relatively dormant one), encouraging a previously silent but substantial minority to publicly claim an atheist identity and a collective voice in the public sphere.

While the New Atheism is not in the public eye as much as it was in the late 2000s, it is still alive and well in the secular movement. Dawkins, Harris, Krauss, Ali, and Pinker command large audiences for their books and talks and still regularly appear on the movement's active convention circuit. While there is currently no way of quantifying their influence, we know it is significant given that their books are bestsellers, they lecture at sold-out theaters, and their YouTube interviews and debates draw viewer numbers that reach into the hundreds of thousands. These thinkers and their ideas are also still regularly discussed in major publications such as *The Guardian* and *Salon*, among many others.

At the same time that the New Atheism was achieving massive popularity, an intellectual counterattack arose seeking to discredit its claims, often in defense of religion but sometimes also as a response to what is perceived as an attack on non-Western others. Christian apologists in particular have used the term "atheist fundamentalism" to fight back against attacks by atheists who, they claim, have an unalterable vision and are thus fundamentalists in their own right. The Oxford theologian and historian Alister McGrath is a notable exponent of this view, but the concept is not rigorously examined in his work and there is no theory of fundamentalism, including why it occurs and what it responds to.[26] For McGrath the label "fundamentalist" seems to apply to a general faith in science to reveal the true nature of reality, but this does not address the political nature of fundamentalism as a movement. McGrath's attacks on Dawkins closely resemble the defensive and disrespectful tone used by his target and illustrate the symbiotic relationship between scientific atheism and popular theology. Another theologian who has contributed to this debate is David Bentley Hart, whose book *Atheist Delusions: The Christian Revolution and Its Fashionable Enemies* is another counterpunch to the New Atheism that answers force with force. Hart takes a slightly different approach than McGrath, directing most of his energy toward emphasizing what is good in Christianity and its (generally) positive role in history. Most of the New Atheism's arguments against religion are dismissed without much attention given, often with a sarcastic comment. This disrespectful approach closely resembles the New Atheism's own hostile tone—Hart is the mirror image of Dawkins. Hart also shares McGrath's tactic of calling the New Atheism a fundamentalism and a kind of religion itself, suggesting that Dawkins and the others preach a "Gospel of unbelief." McGrath and Hart are representatives of a theological defense that approaches the New Atheism from a defensive position in claiming that it simply does the same thing that religion does, but worse (this is the same argument made by the New Atheists, but in reverse).

The other major category of response to the New Atheists is in philosophy, where some thinkers have taken a more analytical approach to their arguments. The most significant among these is Alvin Plantinga's *Where the Conflict Really Lies: Science, Religion, and Naturalism*. Plantinga counters the popular notion that religion and science are in conflict by arguing that the conflict is superficial and that there is in fact a "deep concord" between science and theism, while there is conversely only a superficial concord between science and naturalism that masks a deep conflict. Unlike some of the theological responses to the New Atheism, Plantinga does not reject a scientific worldview, but more precisely a naturalistic one. He argues that it is not the science of evolutionary biology that must be rejected but rather the assumption that it is an entirely naturalistic process, which has no scientific grounding. In moving the terms of the debate from one of a conflict between religion and science to one where religion and science are in accord but in conflict with the philosophy of naturalism, Plantinga offers a more novel response to scientific atheism than many of the theologians who have responded to the New Atheism on its own terms. That is, theologians like McGrath counter the attack on religion with an attack on science, while Plantinga steps around this unresolvable conflict by claiming that religion and the scientific method are in concord, while both are in conflict with the philosophy of naturalism.

A more rounded approach comes from theologian Tina Beattie, who mostly avoids the philosophical debates that concern McGrath, Hart, and Plantinga regarding the nature of science and religion and their relationship to each other. Instead, she analyzes the New Atheism in relation to its historical, social, and cultural context and addresses issues such as postmodernism, globalization, and identity politics in seeking an answer to Bullivant's question of why here and why now. The simplest and best answer, in her view, is 9/11. She also raises a key issue missed by others who perceive the New Atheism as a reaction to religion, which is that it is just as much a reaction to relativism and postmodernism.

This idea merits much more attention, and it is addressed in more detail in Terry Eagleton's *Reason, Faith and Revolution: Reflections on the God Debate*. Eagleton spells out a point somehow missed by so many others, which is that the New Atheism is much more than a critique of religious belief: it is a political ideology. He identifies the New Atheists as liberal rationalists, and his main criticism of their thought is that it legitimates the Western social order by making religion the scapegoat for any major problems within it, most importantly violence and racial and sexual oppression (economic oppression is notably absent from the New Atheist discourse). This is the view advanced by David Martin, who considers the New Atheism an ideological narrative of scientific progress and authority that legitimates the social organization of modernity by casting the blame for its failings upon "religion." The most significant aspect of Martin's critique is his emphasis on the status of the social sciences in this ideology, observing that "scorn is poured on all the varieties of observation, representation and truth-telling that do not conform to the natural science model."[27] He argues that Dawkins deploys irrelevant authority derived from his status as a scientist (and a celebrity) to an issue that he knows nothing about in order to advance an ideological narrative.

All of these critics have produced works with merits and contributed to our understanding of the phenomenon, but this work is highly provincial, particularly in the focus on a constructed conflict between theology and scientific materialism by thinkers like McGrath and Hart. What is missing is a sociological examination of the New Atheism not just as an intellectual current but as a social and political phenomenon. Most existing critical responses engage with the New Atheists on their own terms, challenging their arguments and ideas. My sociological approach seeks to understand the New Atheism on another level. The strength, or lack thereof, of their arguments about religion is of little concern to me. Rather, I am interested in what lies beneath these arguments—that is, the political ideology that underwrites all of New Atheist discourse.

Most importantly, I want to stress something that is completely lacking in these other accounts: the New Atheism is as much a social phenomenon as an intellectual one. It is not restricted to a group of elite thinkers; rather, it is an ideology that informs the practices of a burgeoning social movement and a vast and disparate network of secular communities. There is no doubt that the New Atheists galvanized a moribund movement, and their success itself is indicative of a generational turn, with many young skeptics finding in them a voice for the expression of views rarely encountered in the public sphere. Chapter 3 examines their thought in detail, illustrating that the New Atheism, like the historical forms of atheism reviewed in Chapter 1, is much more than a critique of religious belief. It is itself a belief system, or more precisely an ideology, ostensibly concerned with epistemology but essentially political in nature. This ideology is rooted in scientific atheism but updated with respect to developments in science (particularly in the fields of evolutionary psychology and neuroscience) and explicitly tailored to the socio-political circumstances of the twenty-first century.

3

A Light in a Dark Jungle

INSOFAR AS IT can be considered an intellectual current, the New Atheism emerged in the wake of an emerging consensus among social scientists that the secularization thesis, holding as a universal principle that religion declines as scientific modernity advances, is a product of ideology rather than an empirical reality.[1] The New Atheists' strategy of aggressive confrontation with religious ideas is a tacit recognition of this failure of the secularization thesis to come to fruition. That is, rather than waiting for the natural progress of history to unfold, the New Atheists seek to aggressively push history forward.

We can view this development in atheism as a product of—and reaction to—three major events or trends: (1) the rise of young-Earth creationism and intelligent design among anti-evolution Christians in the United States, (2) 9/11 and its cultural aftershocks, and (3) the influence of relativism in two forms falling under the umbrella of "postmodernism," which the New Atheists understand as a combination of epistemic relativism and cultural pluralism, manifest in policies of multiculturalism in liberal democracies. These factors refer us to reactions to two very different kinds of ongoing threats: one "premodern" (in the case of creationism and 9/11, which the New Atheists understand as natural consequences of the persistence of premodern forms of religious fundamentalism) and one "postmodern" (in the case of epistemic and cultural relativism, which the New Atheists consider responsible for a misguided effort toward tolerance that takes the form of multiculturalism). This chapter examines their thought as a response to these perceived threats to modernity, as they strive to bring us out of the "dark jungle" of religion and superstition and toward the highest form of civilization: one shaped by science, the light on the path of progress.[2]

Science, Modernity, and Secularization: The Ideology of New Atheism

The New Atheism, I will argue, is not an absence of belief or a critique of religion but is itself a belief system or, more precisely, an ideology. By this I do not mean ideology in an orthodox Marxian sense of illusory beliefs or false consciousness, but rather a view of ideologies as "coherent and relatively stable sets of beliefs and values" that bracket social cognition and provide "schematically organized complexes of representation and attitudes with regard to certain aspects of the social world."[3] In this view ideology is a schematic or rigid framework of preconceived ideas that shape, and thus potentially distort, understanding.[4] But, as Thompson argues, ideology refers to not only belief systems but also a means of legitimating the authority of this belief system and the group that advances it.[5] Ideology is thus not only about what can be known and what precisely is known, but also about *power.* I thus take ideology to refer to *a stable structure of beliefs and attitudes that determine how knowledge is constructed and interpreted to legitimate a form of authority.*

While Thompson understands ideology as a means to "sustain relations of domination," I take it to apply to any means of legitimating authority that follows certain criteria, regardless of whether and to what extent the group advancing it actually occupies a position of domination (hence ideology can also be a property of subordinate or oppressed groups).[6] I take these criteria from Eagleton, who writes,

> A dominant power may legitimate itself by *promoting* beliefs and values congenial to it; *naturalizing* and *universalizing* such beliefs so as to render them self-evident and apparently inevitable; *denigrating* ideas which might challenge it; *excluding* rival forms of thought, perhaps by some unspoken but systematic logic; and *obscuring* social reality in ways convenient to itself. Such "mystification," as it is commonly known, frequently takes the form of masking or suppressing social conflicts, from which arises the conception of ideology as an imaginary resolution of real contradictions.[7]

Eagleton notes that a problem with this definition is that not all beliefs we might consider ideological are associated with a dominant political power, but again, the "dominant power" part here may be excluded and the definition can then apply to any group seeking to advance its own interests through advancing a belief system legitimated by these means. Crucially, in this understanding of ideology the beliefs that are promoted are not necessarily false or illusory, as in the Marxian version. Rather, any belief system that seeks legitimation by these means may be considered ideological regardless of the question of its "truth."

The New Atheism advances an ideology that meets these criteria. Its goal is the legitimation of scientific authority. It *promotes* a belief system characterized primarily by scientism, which is the grounding of its epistemology, its critique of religion, and its politics. It *naturalizes* and *universalizes* this belief system by equating it with objective science and the pinnacle of human intellectual progress, thus representing it as the only universally valid one, and further, the outcome of a natural and inevitable process of accumulating knowledge and an according restructuring of society. Like all ideologies, it is thus *dehistoricizing* in its denial that this belief system is specific to a particular time, place, and social group. It *denigrates* religion, which is the belief system it considers its direct antagonist. It *excludes* social scientific thought on religion, which it considers a rival to its own Darwinian understanding of the origin and function of religious beliefs, as well as a direct challenge to scientific authority in the form of "postmodernism" and epistemic relativism. Finally, it *obscures* social reality in its insistence that scientific progress is equivalent to social progress and that religion is the cause of the major ills of modernity, including its new forms of conflict, violence, and oppression. The contradiction classically formulated in Horkheimer and Adorno's "dialectic of Enlightenment"[8]—which understands modernity in terms of a tension between the quest for emancipation and the rise of new forms of oppression that replace "Church and King"—is thus resolved by rejecting the idea that such a contradiction exists in the first place and insisting that the only problem with modern society is the stubborn persistence of premodern beliefs and ways of thinking.

The following sections of this chapter explore these elements of the ideology that is "New Atheism," including its critique of religion, its rejection of the social sciences as a rival form of thought, and its political implications with respect to the nature of modern societies and the challenges they face. But first we must outline the belief system it promotes, which can be summarized with one key concept: *scientism*.

For Jurgen Habermas, scientism means that "we no longer understand science as *one* form of possible knowledge, but rather identify knowledge with science."[9] This is to say that scientific knowledge is the only kind of knowledge there is. Mikael Stenmark more precisely outlines a number of different kinds of scientism. The most relevant for my purposes is his definition of "epistemic scientism," which is "The view that the only reality that we can know anything about is the one science has access to," and further, that "what lies beyond the reach of scientists cannot count as knowledge. The only sort of knowledge we have is the scientific kind of knowledge."[10] Like Habermas, Stenmark defines scientism as the reduction of all knowledge to scientific knowledge but adds that scientism is a statement not merely on knowledge, but on the nature of reality. That is, science defines the parameters not only of what can be known but what can be said to exist, or what is real. Something that is not knowable by science cannot be said to exist or to have any basis in reality.

It is important to be precise about what "science" means here. I understand scientism to refer specifically to the extension of the authority of the natural sciences beyond the boundaries of nature. Scientism in this view is "the attempt to apply the methods of natural science to the study of society,"[11] or, more precisely, an attempt to "bring methods, concepts, practices, and attitudes from the investigation of the natural world to bear on human activities and institutions."[12] Richard G. Olson suggests that we can speak of scientism when "scientific attitudes, methods, and modes of thought are extended and applied beyond the domain of natural phenomena to a wide range of cultural issues that involve human interactions and value structures,"[13] thus adding ethics to the purview of science.

Scientism, then, involves two major characteristics: first, the view from Habermas and Stenmark of scientism as a statement on the limits of knowledge and nature of reality; and second, the view from Gorski and Olson that scientism is an extension of the authority of the natural sciences, specifically, to nonnatural or immaterial social and cultural phenomena. I thus define "scientism" as *the view that science is the only legitimate form of knowledge; that the domain of knowledge of the natural sciences encompasses human behavior, institutions, and value structures; and that the theories and methods of the natural sciences are the best approach to the study of society and culture.*

In the case of the New Atheism, where the centrality of Darwinistic ideologies in atheist thought has never been clearer, we can identify a more specific kind of scientism: *evolutionism.* Matthew Flamm, himself an atheist writing in the pages of *Free Inquiry*, the magazine of the Council for Secular Humanism, writes that the New Atheism, "while similar to that of positivists of previous generations in its scientistic, naturalistic rejection of religious claims as knowledge, is grounded in the latest synthesis of multiple scientific areas of study, filed compendiously under the heading of 'evolutionary biology.'"[14] Flamm's point reflects my argument that the New Atheism is scientific atheism updated with recent advances in fields closely related to evolutionary biology, particularly evolutionary psychology and neuroscience. I would further argue, however, that evolution is not only the basis of religious criticism but also a vision of the nature and historical development of human society and culture. The scientistic application of theories and concepts derived from Darwinian evolution to the social world is the basis of the social theory and political science at the heart of the New Atheism. While scientism is the New Atheists' epistemology, then, it is more precisely *evolutionism* that is their ideology. It is a vision of the world that is expressed in their views on religion and science, secularization, and the nature of modernity.

The key idea within this ideology is the evolution of society from the premodern phase of religious superstition to the modern phase characterized by scientism and its application to social and political questions and problems. This involves a teleological vision of human progress, with "premodern" giving way to "modern" ways of thinking and living. That is, enchantment and superstition are replaced by science and reason. From this perspective religion is an obsolete evolutionary adaptation akin to the appendix, a vestigial organ of a premodern ancestor that stubbornly refuses to go away even though it is no longer needed, and, indeed, can cause us great harm. Modernity is that historical period, and social and political structure, that represents the project of universalization of scientism.

The New Atheism, then, should be understood as a vigorous defense of an ideological vision of modernity that is grounded in the notions of progress and civilization, which in turn are characterized primarily by the spread of scientific rationality in social and political institutions, and in the general culture. It rejects what it sees as the premodern ways of thinking and living that are characteristic of religion and of "uncivilized" societies. Just as important, however, is its position on what it considers to be *postmodern* epistemology and politics. The key point is that the New Atheists are responding to what they perceive to be a modern crisis brought on by two very different challenges to the authority of scientific rationality and the sociocultural configuration that is presumed to accompany it: "premodern" religious fundamentalism and "postmodern" cultural pluralism and epistemic relativism. This latter challenge to modernity is a concern for the New Atheists because not only does it reject their claims to universality and objectivity, but in a sense it legitimates the first force ("premodern" fundamentalism) by undermining the rational-scientific grounding of critique.

So while the New Atheism claims to be a reaction against premodern ways of thinking, it is actually more an attempt to deal with a crisis of modernity brought on by what some would call an entry into postmodernity (religious fundamentalism is also in part a response to this crisis, perceiving pluralism and relativism as a threat to traditional values and social structures). The New Atheists battle not only competing epistemologies and faith systems but also history itself in their construction of the Enlightenment as the apex of a teleological process of social evolution that is still playing out and must be protected. Dawkins is a fervent believer in moral progress (or evolution), arguing that there is a steady change in social consciousness in a relatively consistent direction in modern liberal democratic societies.[15] He does admit that there are challenges and interruptions to this progress but nonetheless believes that progress is inevitable: "Of course, the advance is not a smooth incline but a meandering sawtooth. There are local and temporary setbacks . . . But over the longer timescale, the progressive trend is unmistakable and it will continue."[16] Hitchens is more measured in his celebration of the ideals of the Enlightenment and progress than his New Atheist colleagues, noting that

> only the most naive utopian can believe that this new humane civilization will develop, like some dream of 'progress,' in a straight line. We first have to transcend our prehistory, and escape the gnarled hands which reach out to drag us back to the catacombs and the reeking altars and the guilty pleasures of subjection and abjection.[17]

While Hitchens problematizes the notion of "progress" here in a way that Dawkins never does, it is problematic for him only in practice, not in principle. He presents religion as a premodern challenge to be overcome and devotes the final chapter of his treatise on religion to "The Need for a New Enlightenment."[18]

In equating being "modern" with the Enlightenment, however, the New Atheists ignore some of the most important intellectual developments of the intervening period, leaving a bare-boned empiricism bereft of real humanist philosophy and substituting the requirements of scientific progress for politics and democratically determined ethics. It is because of this strict attachment to a subsection of Enlightenment thought and a general commitment to scientism that we should not equate the New Atheism with secular humanism or, for that matter, with secularism. Rather, it is in part a reaction *against* secularism. The New Atheism is an expression of an ideology of radical secularism, which Talal Asad describes as a political doctrine that not only is about removing religion from public life but has "a particular vision of the world."[19] This vision, in New Atheist thought, is a global civilization where cultural differences are eroded by the universalization of the scientific worldview and, more implicitly, where decisions regarding the common good are best made by scientific experts. In this more radical version of secularism, what is advocated is not the separation of religion and public life but, more precisely, the universalization of a scientific worldview and the eradication of any opposition.

To understand the New Atheism, then, we must establish its position on secularization, a concept at the core of its concerns. One understanding of secularization holds that "the religious beliefs of antiquity irreversibly lost their credibility as scientific cosmologies progressively embarrassed them,"[20] and thus attachment to religious beliefs was bound to fade. This idea predates social science and originated in the Enlightenment, which produced the view that modernity necessarily involves a decline of religion, both in society and in the minds of individuals.[21] This refers to two very different processes, and thus the theory of secularization should actually be understood as two separate but related subtheses that posit that secularization is a process characterized by (1) a general decline in religious belief and practice and (2) functional differentiation of religious and secular spheres and a concomitant distinction between private and public dimensions of life.[22] It is clear that subthesis (1) is not necessary for subthesis (2), though in traditional formulations of the secularization paradigm in the sociology of religion these were seen as complementary processes. Charles Taylor has added a third subthesis: the "nova effect,"[23] an explosion in the possibilities of belief and unbelief in late modernity whereby belief in God is just one among many options. Indeed, many prominent scholars in various fields have in recent years weighed in on the secularization debate, resulting in an emerging majority view that the secularization paradigm is effectively moribund and that we must begin to speak of a "postsecular" age where religion continues to exert a strong influence in public life and coexists with other forms of belief.[24]

The New Atheists do not explicitly address the secularization thesis, but an examination of their work reveals that while they obviously support the first subthesis (decline in belief), they are very much at odds with the next two.[25] Taylor's "nova effect" is definitely not the type of secularization the New Atheism would endorse, as it implies that any kind of belief is possible and is thus an affront to the foundational premise of scientific atheism, which is that only beliefs that are supported by empirical evidence are acceptable. The relationship to the second subthesis is complicated because of the "deprivatization of religion"[26] and its emergence as a major political force in the late twentieth century, most clearly exemplified in the Islamic revolution and the rise of the Christian Right, which shook the foundations of the secularization thesis. Even where secularism was an important force, the realization came that "a straightforward narrative of progress from the religious to the secular is no longer acceptable"[27] and that religion was in fact growing stronger in some areas of the world.

This deprivatization—if in fact we can speak of such a thing, as many believe that the retreat of religion to the private sphere was greatly exaggerated[28]—led to a unique situation in the history of atheism. Suddenly atheists were in a certain sense seeking to *reverse* the process of secularization, or at least one aspect of it: the move from public to private. This is because religion, though still considered a private matter of individual choice and belief, was exercising a huge influence in the public sphere. This nominally private status granted it immunity from public reason, and in these conditions it flourished.[29] This is a crisis of conflict between the two primary subtheses of the secularization thesis, which the atheist movement views as a danger and as an opportunity. The New Atheism seeks to counter religion's immunity to critique by bringing it into the public sphere—or at least revealing that it was never effectively private—so that it can be subjected to public reason and thereby eradicated. They want to undermine religious authority through a campaign of scientific-rational critique and enhance the authority of science—the same project undertaken by Victorian Darwinists who exercised a campaign for the authority of science in academic institutions,[30] which has now been expanded to a much larger scale.

There is another understanding of secularization beyond the two (or three) subtheses typically associated with it that is pertinent to my discussion. This approach views it not only as a theory of a social process bound up with modernization but, more importantly, as a political doctrine, rendering its empirical validity irrelevant and pointing us instead to questions pertaining to the origins and consequences of secularization as an ideology.[31] Jose Casanova suggests that "theories of secularization double as empirically descriptive theories of modern social processes and as normatively prescriptive theories of modern societies, and thus serve to legitimize ideologically a particular historical form of institutionalization of modernity."[32] In his view, secularization is a myth perpetuated by Enlightenment thinkers that was taken for granted and never rigorously examined or systematically formulated.[33] In an influential article, Jeffrey Hadden claimed that the doctrine of secularization had achieved the level of a sacred principle within the social sciences.[34] Robert Bellah dissented against this principle at a time when it was broadly accepted, calling secularization a myth that creates a coherent picture of reality based on the idea of progress and universalization.[35] This is also the view favored by Asad, who, as noted above, describes secularization as a straightforward narrative of progress that, upon closer inspection, is more ideology than social process.[36]

The New Atheism might be understood as an expression of this ideology, instituting this narrative of progress as historical reality through its discourses regarding the universal and emancipative nature of modern scientific rationality and its inherent conflict with the premodern force of religion. It thus adopts the ideology of secularization to the extent that it is a normative prescription for the development of modern societies. In the ideology of evolutionistic scientism adopted by the New Atheists, the theory of secularization is ideological support for a political project rather than a theory of an actual socio-historical process. Rather than evidence that the *process* of secularization is indeed proceeding as it was once expected, the New Atheism is a reaction to the fact that the *ideology* of secularization has come under threat by the deprivatization of religion and the influence of postmodernism in Western scholarship, particularly with respect to the social sciences.

These two developments indicate to the New Atheists that the second secularization subthesis—functional differentiation of religious and secular spheres—is untenable. Religion continues to invade the public and political spheres, and criticism of this process is undermined by the current liberal imperative for pluralism. Since religion cannot be sequestered within the private sphere, the only option is to eradicate it completely. The New Atheists thus represent the move to a secular world specifically as a move to a world where religion simply disappears under the light of science. Their project is to hasten this process—in other words, to defend modernity as a process of cultural universalization defined by the authority of scientific rationality in all spheres of life, both public and private, and in individual minds. The strategy is to engage in an ideological struggle against modernity's antagonists, specifically premodern religion and postmodern relativism and pluralism, to ensure that the progress of secularization continues. Modernity, for the New Atheists, is co-terminous with secularization, which in their view is essentially the progressive universalization of scientism. We might in fact say that what the New Atheists want is not so much secularization but the *scientization* of politics and culture. This means scientization with respect to both secularization subtheses—that is, the authority of science within political institutions but, more importantly, the adoption of a scientistic worldview by individuals to such an extent that it becomes culturally dominant.

This view of the nature of secularization takes no account of the social scientific knowledge on the issue. For instance, Elaine Howard Ecklund's study of scientists at elite American universities found no clear relationship between science and atheism. To the contrary, she found that most scientists do not believe that religion and science are mutually incompatible, and that while a vast majority reject the idea of a "personal God," many hold some kind of religious beliefs or claim to be "spiritual."[37] The assumption by the New Atheists that knowledge of science leads to atheism is not supported by the evidence, and the narrative of secularization as a function of the dissemination of scientific knowledge is at best questionable given Ecklund's research.

And yet, the New Atheism's strategy centers on this assumption. While not explicitly addressing a "secularization thesis" as such, we can say that the New Atheism neglects the second secularization subthesis (functional differentiation of secular and religious spheres) in favor of advancing the first (decline of religious belief). In summary, the goal of the New Atheists is not simply to critique religious beliefs; rather, they seek a broad cultural transformation that would see religious belief and all other forms of superstition replaced with scientism. Given this general goal, I argue that the New Atheist movement adopts three central strategies: (1) to discredit claims made by religious texts, institutions, and leaders in areas ranging from social history to natural history, and most importantly on the question of the existence of God, by way of rational-scientific critique; (2) to persuade others to adopt a worldview defined by scientism and, more specifically, evolutionism; and (3) to build a sense of community and a positive collective identity for atheists in order to encourage others to "come out" and to create a hospitable environment for atheism to flourish. These three strategies reflect the dimensions of ideology discussed above. These include promoting a belief system that is naturalized, universalized, and dehistoricized and denigrating and excluding challenging ideas and rival forms of thought.

The first two strategies—that is, the negation of the religious worldview and construction of an alternative scientistic one—are addressed by public intellectuals such as the Four Horsemen. These two strategies are addressed in the following sections, which deal with the New Atheism's response to the two major threats to modernity. The third strategy refers to social movement activism within atheist organizations, which is covered in Chapter 4. Through an analysis of the New Atheists' response to the perceived dual threat to modernity we will arrive at an understanding of the ideology that underwrites their thought, which I argue is in essence a political ideology that advances a particular vision of the nature of the world and a normative prescription for achieving progress toward the highest form of civilization—one where science is dominant in epistemology, politics, and ethics.

This ideology is represented in Table 3.1 as a set of binaries that establish its tenets through negation and opposition. These binaries should be understood in terms of their relationship to the evolutionism at the heart of this ideology, implying a natural and inevitable progression in both the intellectual and social worlds that is driven by science. They serve to distinguish modernity from its "others," equating religion, faith, and barbarism with the premodern and relativism, multiculturalism, and pluralism with the postmodern. Islam is contrasted with modernity in this

Table 3.1 Binaries Constitutive
of the Ideology of New Atheism

Modern	Premodern
Science	Religion
Reason	Faith
Civilization	Barbarism
Modern	Postmodern
Absolutism	Relativism
Secularism	Multiculturalism
Universalism	Particularism

table because, in New Atheist discourse, it embodies both premodern and postmodern otherness. That is, it is a barbaric form of religious faith that threatens Western civilization because relativism, multiculturalism, and pluralism have rendered the West impotent to defend its values against this foreign intruder. These binaries, and the ideology they constitute, are all interrogated in the following analysis of the New Atheism's defense of modernity, beginning with the first strategy of discrediting and denigrating religious beliefs, the premodern threat.

The Scientific Critique of Religion

The New Atheism's critique of religion is predicated on the assumption that the purpose of religion is to explain nature (this assumption is not a result of any kind of empirical inquiry into religious belief and practice but is assumed *a priori* on ideological grounds). Science reveals that it fails in this task, and therefore religious belief is irrational. These irrational beliefs could develop in the first place because ancient people were ignorant of the truths of science and had no alternative explanations. They are maintained in the modern age because of evolutionary processes that have endowed us with brains susceptible to supernatural beliefs. Overcoming these irrational beliefs and the cognitive tendencies that allow them to persist, and taking the step toward a higher form of thinking characterized by scientific rationality is the challenge, and promise, of modernity. This view is expressed in the following passage from Hitchens:

> One must state it plainly. Religion comes from the period of human prehistory where nobody—not even the mighty Democritus who concluded that all matter was made from atoms—had the smallest idea what was going on. It comes from the bawling and fearful infancy of our species, and is a babyish attempt to meet our inescapable demand for knowledge (as well as for comfort, reassurance, and other infantile needs) . . . All attempts to reconcile faith with science and reason are consigned to failure and ridicule for precisely these reasons.[38]

Here we are offered the theory of religion that characterizes scientific atheism—namely, religion as explanation of the mysterious and threatening forces of nature. Other sources of religious belief, such as those offered by the nineteenth-century humanistic atheists (with "comfort, reassurance, and other infantile needs" Hitchens echoes Freud), are relegated to a brief parenthetical aside, despite their obvious and overwhelming importance. Religion is, rather, a relic of the ignorance of the premodern, or prescientific, "period of human prehistory," a view that David Martin notes is "a revival of a nineteenth-century narrative identifying religion with fundamentalist opposition to science, in particular evolutionary biology."[39] This is one major idea shared by all the New Atheists, and it is expressed most clearly in Richard Dawkins' description of God as a pseudoscientific hypothesis.

Dawkins' understanding of religion begins with one simple premise: the "God Hypothesis," or the idea that God is "a scientific hypothesis about the universe, which should be analyzed as skeptically as any other."[40] He formulates it, on behalf of all religions and religious believers, like this: "there exists a superhuman, supernatural intelligence who deliberately designed and created the universe and everything in it, including us."[41] This hypothesis about the origin of the universe can be empirically tested, argues Dawkins: "Either he exists or he doesn't. It's a scientific question; one day we may know the answer, and meanwhile we can say something pretty strong about the probability."[42] Dawkins deems that the probability is exceedingly in favor of nonexistence.

In the history of atheism outlined in the first chapter, I discussed Michael J. Buckley's description of the development of a modern theological conception of God that departed from an emphasis on transcendence and instead described God as a "thing" of definite substance and location with a role in nature.[43] This is clearly the God that Dawkins is talking about, but even if we were to base our understanding of religious faith on the modern conception of God as an immanent force within nature, Dawkins' critique is logically incoherent. This might be explained with reference to one of Dawkins' own rhetorical devices, the notion of the "god of the gaps," or God as the explanation used to fill gaps in our understanding of nature. In this view, modern science has achieved impressive results in solving the mystery of nature, though crevices where explanations are lacking are still filled with God:

Creationists eagerly seek a gap in present-day knowledge or understanding. If an apparent gap is found, it is *assumed* that God, by default, must fill it. What worries thoughtful theologians . . . is that gaps shrink as science advances, and God is threatened with eventually having nothing to do and nowhere to hide.[44]

Dawkins argues that Darwinian evolution forces God out of his last refuge—namely, the origin of life—thereby filling in the last major gap in our understanding.[45] From this follows the conclusion that the God Hypothesis has been "proven" false, leading Dawkins to proclaim that "God almost certainly does not exist."[46] A more appropriate conclusion would be that modern science is in conflict with a literal interpretation of the Biblical account of creation. Dawkins' proof that God does not exist can be valid only if God's existence is tied to the historical accuracy of Genesis.

Nonetheless, Dawkins maintains that science and religion are incommensurable forms of knowledge with respect to the natural world that are characteristic of distinct periods of human history. This brings us to the heart of the matter: the supposed conflict between religion/faith and science/reason, which, he claims, is essentially a conflict between ways of thinking that are characteristic of the premodern and modern world, namely superstition and rationalism, of which religion and science are just particular forms.[47] His major point of emphasis is not that religion is harmful but, rather, that it is an obstacle to truth and the greatest of the "enemies of reason."[48] The harm that religion does is measured by Dawkins not in social but in intellectual terms:

> As a scientist, I am hostile to fundamentalist religion because it actively debauches the scientific enterprise. It teaches us not to change our minds, and not to want to know exciting things that are available to be known. It subverts science and saps the intellect.[49]

Note that Dawkins refers specifically to fundamentalist religion, while his main problem with "moderate" religion is that it is "making the world safe for fundamentalism by teaching children, from their earliest years, that unquestioning faith is a virtue."[50]

Harris takes precisely the same view of faith as Dawkins, claiming that faith is "the license people give themselves to keep believing when reasons fail—faith fills the cracks in the evidence and gaps in logic," and that "faith is nothing more than a willingness to await the evidence—be it the Day of Judgment or some other downpour of corroboration. It is the search for knowledge on the instalment plan: believe now, live an untestable hypothesis until your dying day, and you will discover that you were right."[51] In these two quotations we see both Dawkins' "God Hypothesis" and his idea of the "god of the gaps." Religion for Harris, as for Dawkins, is a false knowledge claim, a prescientific explanation of the inexplicable that fills gaps in understanding with a hypothesis that needs no verification. The remedy to this condition is substituting the true knowledge of science, as if the faithful just do not yet know enough about science to abandon their false religious ideas, or, alternatively, their brains have been wired by evolution to accept the God Hypothesis despite evidence to the contrary.

Harris goes to great lengths to argue for the latter view, namely that religious belief is not only a product of ignorance but also a direct result of physical processes in the brain, which in turn are a product of evolutionary pressures that have selected genes that precondition us for religious belief. Given his interest in neuroscience (or, alternatively, ideological commitment to scientism), it is not surprising that Harris, discussing the nature of religious belief, asks, "What neural events underlie this process? What must a brain do in order to believe that a given statement is *true* or *false*? We currently have no idea."[52] This simple inquiry demonstrates an unwillingness to look outside of the natural sciences for an explanation of faith. He awaits neurological evidence to explain how it is that brains are able to manage the trick of reconciling illogical beliefs with the demands of reason and logical coherence. That is, he wonders how a *brain*—rather than a *person*—manages to combine, or navigate between, these ostensibly incommensurable ways of thinking. The social existence of the person whose head houses this brain is relatively unimportant.

Addressing this question, Harris suggests that religious belief may be indicative of a defect in brain functioning, implying a material distinction between believers and rational atheists. Dawkins suggests as much when he claims that "atheism nearly always indicates . . . a healthy mind."[53] Harris goes so far as to equate faith not only with ignorance but with mental illness:

> We have names for people who have many beliefs for which there is no rational justification. When their beliefs are extremely common we call them "religious"; otherwise, they are likely to be called "mad," "psychotic," or "delusional" . . . it is merely an accident of history that it is considered normal in our society to believe that the Creator of the universe can hear your thoughts, while it is demonstrative of mental illness to believe that he is communicating with you by having the rain tap in Morse code on your bedroom window. And so, while religious people are not generally mad, their core beliefs absolutely are. . . . In fact, it is difficult to imagine a set of

beliefs more suggestive of mental illness than those that lie at the heart of many of our religious traditions.[54]

If beliefs persist despite evidence that renders them illogical, then the only logical explanation for this is that there must be some defect in brain functioning or something resembling mental illness. Social and cultural reasons for believing are not explored, or even mentioned for that matter. Though he does admit that religious people are not "mad," he also suggests that making an exception for religious people in terms of madness is just an "accident of history," implying that religious beliefs are suggestive of some kind of mental illness or deficiency.

Dawkins also grounds his theory of religion in a strictly materialist account of the religious impulse experienced by human brains, thus eschewing human thought, agency, and culture: "Knowing that we are products of Darwinian evolution, we should ask what pressure or pressures exerted by natural selection originally favored the impulse to religion."[55] The point is that any social behavior humans engage in must be explained in evolutionary terms, particularly behavior that has been exhibited by humans everywhere and at all times, such as religion: "Universal features of a species demand a Darwinian explanation."[56] Dawkins' use of the term "species" here, while technically correct, is very revealing of the problem with his approach in general, which is to view the behavior of people the way he would any other animal, as in his pondering of the evolutionary benefit of a medieval cathedral, which "could consume a hundred man-centuries in its construction, yet was never used as a dwelling, or for any recognizably useful purpose. Was it some kind of architectural peacock's tail?"[57] Here Dawkins reduces certain (nonscientific) human cultural developments and artistic achievements to an ostentatious display that might be understood as a kind of "peacock's tail" to the extent that there must be a sensible Darwinian explanation for such apparently nonsensical (i.e., nonadaptive) behavior.

Dawkins claims that human culture "evolves" progressively in precisely the same way that biological entities evolve—that is, by natural selection:

> Fashions in dress and diet, ceremonies and customs, art and architecture, engineering and technology, all evolve in historical time in a way that looks like highly speeded up genetic evolution, but has really nothing to do with genetic evolution. As in genetic evolution, though, the change may be progressive.[58]

The difference is the unit of transmission: in biological evolution it is the gene, while in cultural evolution the "meme" (roughly analogous to "idea") is the unit that is negatively or positively selected and transmitted. Memes are the "new replicators," doing the job of cultural transmission and evolution just as genes do the job of biological evolution.

Dawkins' theory of religion, bearing these guiding principles in mind, proceeds in two steps: biological disposition, followed by memetic transmission. He insists that Darwinism is an "ultimate" explanation of religion, while theories derived from the social sciences are only "proximate" explanations. In his "ultimate," Darwinian view, religion is a byproduct of evolutionary adaptations: "The religious behavior may be a misfiring, an unfortunate byproduct of an underlying psychological propensity which in other circumstances is, or once was, useful."[59] This is most obvious in the case of children, who are hardwired by genetic evolution to trust the words of their elders; this is a useful adaptation for survival, with the unfortunate byproduct being "vulnerability to infection by mind viruses."[60] These "mind viruses" are ideas or beliefs that are transmitted from brain to brain by a process analogous to genetic replication. The most ubiquitous and pernicious of these mind viruses is, of course, the meme for God. Dawkins refers to this as the "God virus,"[61] which has been evolving and infecting brains for thousands of years—much like a measles epidemic in an elementary school, we are led to understand. Those "faith sufferers"[62] infected with the God virus are harmed by it, yet it has "survival value" because of its psychological appeal, which lies in its "superficially plausible answer to deep and troubling questions about existence."[63] That is, it works as *explanation*.

Dennett supports Dawkins' byproduct theory in his emphasis on the importance of the "intentional stance," or an evolutionarily adaptive proclivity to ascribe agency to inanimate objects and natural events.[64] In this theory, humanity's ancestors—or, more precisely, their genes, if we take Dawkins' gene-level view of evolution[65]—were selected for survival because of their tendency to suspect anything and everything of being a potential predator, or at least a thing with intention to bring harm. This tendency induced caution and therefore enhanced the prospects of survival, but as a byproduct it produced organisms that saw consciousness and intention where there was none. This condition, over evolutionary time scales, produced animism among primitive humans, an early precursor to theistic religions. This theory would allow us to make sense of the belief among some American Christian leaders that natural disasters are a result of insufficient faith or God's punishment for sin.[66]

The New Atheists have not only a theory of the evolutionary processes that create psychological preconditions for religious belief but also a mechanism for the development of different forms of religious belief. Faith evolves from an abstract principle into complex belief systems and religious institutions, and Dawkins goes to great pains to argue that these beliefs and institutions must be regarded as the outcome of natural processes rather than human agency:

> Organized religions are organized by people: by priests and bishops, rabbis, imams and ayatollahs. But . . . that doesn't mean they were conceived and designed by people. Even where religions have been exploited and manipulated to the benefit of powerful individuals, the strong possibility remains that the detailed form of each religion has been largely shaped by unconscious evolution. . . . The role of genetic natural selection in the story is to provide the brain . . . the hardware platform and low-level system software which form the background to memetic selection. Given this background, memetic natural selection of some kind seems to me to offer a plausible account of the detailed evolution of particular religions.[67]

Religious memes, then, have evolved independently of human agents and infect our brains, which have achieved a God-ready state by way of a byproduct of the evolutionarily adaptive proclivity of children to trust the authority of their elders and to impute intentionality and design to inanimate objects. He adds the idea of "memeplexes"—"cartels of mutually compatible memes"—to explain the process by which "a religion becomes organized, elaborate and arbitrarily different from other religions."[68] Describing differences among religions as "arbitrary" reveals an indifference to the history of religion and its social and political nature. More importantly, despite Dawkins' reverence for empirical evidence, experimentation, and rigorous research, he does not subject the meme theory to any kind of scientific scrutiny.

Dennett is a champion of Dawkins' meme theory. He applies it in his discussion of the taboo against a rational-scientific investigation of religion, which he suggests can be understood as a kind of evolutionary adaptation. That is, the taboo is really a meme-complex of prohibitions and defenses. For example, we have internalized the idea that it is "impolite" to question a religious person about the nature of his beliefs too strongly, and the religious person in turn has been taught that such questioning is insulting or disrespectful, and possibly even inspired by Satan himself.[69] Though he doesn't explicitly use the term "meme" in this discussion, there is no mistaking what Dennett is talking about when he says of this process, "What a fine protective screen this virus provides—permitting it to shed the antibodies of skepticism so effortlessly!"[70] Using Dawkins' language, Dennett suggests that faith is a "virus" (meme) that has evolved immunity to "antibodies" (rational-scientific skepticism). Dawkins himself simply states that the meme for blind faith "secures its own perpetuation by the simple unconscious expedient of discouraging rational inquiry."[71]

Hitchens, who is not a scientist or philosopher of science, does not seek to advance a materialist explanation of the origins of religious belief derived from evolutionary biology and neuroscience, though he does defend these efforts.[72] For Hitchens, the notion of the ignorance of ancient people is enough to explain where religion comes from. Religion fulfilled a thirst for knowledge that could not otherwise be quenched, until modern science came along and made it, and those whose understanding of the world is based on it, irrelevant in a world characterized by scientific skepticism and constant questioning: "The person who is certain, and who claims divine warrant for his certainty, belongs now to the infancy of our species. It may be a long farewell, but it has begun and, like all farewells, should not be protracted."[73] While Hitchens does not develop a Darwinian theory of religion, then, there is an evolutionistic essence to this argument, which posits that humanity has evolved beyond religion, and that those who claim certainty for their religious beliefs represent a lower stage in our evolution.

In general, the scientific critique of religion advanced in the New Atheism is informed by the ideology of scientism at its core. More specifically, evolutionism provides the foundation of the critique, positing that religion is a vestige of cognitive processes determined by evolution and a premodern, pseudoscientific explanation of nature that continued to fill gaps in our understanding in the modern period, though those gaps are shrinking. The New Atheism's critique is distinguishable from nineteenth-century scientific atheism only in the greater sophistication brought to it by the theories and technologies of the nascent disciplines of evolutionary psychology and neuroscience, which purport to explain the mechanisms that drive religious belief. Further, we find in the case of

Dawkins and Dennett that the critique of religion is motivated principally by a desire to defend Darwinism against its critics, again mirroring the scientific atheism of the nineteenth century, which was driven by a desire to defend evolution against religious critics.

What is perhaps most striking about the New Atheists' critique of religion is the exclusivity of the theories and methods of the natural sciences and the utter indifference toward knowledge on religion developed in the social sciences. William Stahl notes that the New Atheism makes the assumption that "religion can be abstracted and reduced to cognitive beliefs separated from culture. Sociologically, this is a one-dimensional and impoverished understanding of religion . . . Religion also involves experiences, rituals, traditions, and community, which for many groups are far more important than beliefs."[74] The New Atheists, he writes, "accept the fundamentalists' self-understanding and assume that it can adequately describe all religion."[75] The view of religion taken by fundamentalists that Stahl refers to is precisely that of the New Atheists—namely, that religion is an explanation of where the universe came from and how humanity came to be. In taking fundamentalism as the essence of all religion, the New Atheism reduces all religion to beliefs about the nature of reality. This generalization is only possible in willful ignorance of, and ideological opposition to, the vast reserves of empirical and theoretical work on religion in the social sciences and humanities, which demonstrate the centrality of practice, ritual, and community.

The rejection of social scientific understandings of religion is one aspect of the New Atheism's rejection of the social sciences more generally. This rejection is rooted in the scientistic belief that the natural sciences, and specifically Darwinism, are all that is needed to understand the psychology and social world of human beings. Further, the New Atheism tends to equate the social sciences with "postmodernism" and the flourishing of pluralism and relativism in late modern culture. The account of religion discussed here, then, is only one example of an ideological system that includes as one of its goals the institution of sociobiology as a replacement for the social sciences and humanities.

Science and Civilization

The New Atheism's position on the "postmodern" threat is best understood through an examination of its discourse on Islam, the "other" of enlightened modernity. For the New Atheism, Islam represents both types of threats. As a religion founded on faith it is a "premodern" threat to scientific modernity, and it illustrates the progressive evolution of human societies, with Islamic societies representing barbarism and the West representing civilization. But it also represents the "postmodern" threat in the sense that the New Atheists believe that epistemic relativism and cultural pluralism have paradoxically rendered the West incapable of effectively dealing with the threat posed by radical Islam—and religion more generally—to its core liberal values. Islam is also represented as a threat to the West's very existence in Harris's scenario of a "diabolical clockwork" consisting of blind faith in the tenets of an inherently violent religion coupled with the availability of weapons of mass destruction, which together constitute "a recipe for the fall of civilization."[76]

Islam, indeed, is the most important element in the New Atheists' construction of an ideal of Western civilization. This should be understood in light of their nineteenth-century intellectual heritage. I refer in particular to that century's dominant ideas regarding the relationship between evolutionism and social development—in other words, the theory of the progress of *civilization*. We might understand this in terms of the "comparative method" in anthropology, which was the practice of studying how civilization evolves over time by looking at different groups in the present that are at different stages in this process.[77] Study of the cultures of "savages" was believed to offer a window into history, a glimpse of a previous stage of "civilized" European culture, as it was believed that all groups follow a similar path of development since they are determined by a common human nature, a view that predated Darwin but was buttressed by his insights. The concept of "unilinear evolutionary progress whose eventual goal was perfection and whose highest present manifestation was western European society" led to the inference that "the various societies coexisting in the present *represented* the various stages in this sequence."[78] A further and necessary consequence of this theory was the view that "the normal course of human social development . . . in the case of savages had for some reason stopped short,"[79] leading to speculations regarding the reasons for this that in many cases culminated in the construction of cultural and racial hierarchies.

We see precisely the same line of thought in the New Atheism. Consider, for instance, Harris's view that the Islamic world is a "civilization with an arrested history," explaining that "It is as though a portal in time has opened, and fourteenth-century hordes are pouring into our world."[80] His "portal in time" is in no way different from the comparative method of eighteenth- and nineteenth-century anthropologists and their view that social development is unevenly distributed among different cultures and ethnic groups. Stocking notes the importance of the concept of evolution in the construction of European supremacy: "The assumption of white superiority was certainly not original with Victorian evolutionists; yet the interrelation of the theories of cultural and organic evolution, with their implicit hierarchy of race, gave it a new rationale."[81] Dawkins' own amalgam of organic and cultural evolution (the latter represented in his meme theory) reflects these Victorian efforts at establishing the supremacy of European civilization. While not founded in essentialist doctrines of race, Dawkins' cultural evolution implies a hierarchy of civilization with the West on top because it recognizes the epistemic authority of scientific rationality.

For Harris, Islam and the global population of Muslims constitute modernity's other. All those who practice this religion are indicted equally on the basis of the contents of the Koran. Taking the view that "not all cultures are at the same stage of moral development,"[82] Harris concludes that Islam and its followers are in fact frozen in history and that Islamic nations are "societies whose moral and political development . . . lags behind our own."[83] This view is central to the ideology of modernity that the New Atheists embrace, which involves a path of development from barbarism to civilization, represented by the Middle East and the West in the New Atheism's own "comparative method." A teleology of morality is implied here, with all societies evolving toward an ultimate end-state civilization and some stunted in their development.

The subtext is the imperative to shape the world according to Western culture. Harris writes, "We are at war with Islam. . . . It is not merely that we are at war with an otherwise peaceful religion that has been 'hijacked' by extremists. We are at war with precisely the vision of life that is prescribed to all Muslims in the Koran."[84] He seems less inclined to declare war against Christianity or Judaism, which he considers relatively more benign, while he believes that "Islam, more than any other religion human beings have devised, has all the makings of a thoroughgoing cult of death."[85] So completely are Muslims consumed by the Koran, according to Harris, that they willfully accept their own oppression as mandated by it: "At this point in their history, give most Muslims the freedom to vote, and they will freely vote to tear out their political freedoms by the root. We should not for a moment lose sight of the possibility that they would curtail our freedoms as well, if they only had the power to do so."[86]

Harris's taken-for-granted view that Muslims passively accept their own oppression and have no political will was exposed as a product of ignorance in light of massive protests in Iran following the 2009 presidential election, and the Arab Spring.

Dawkins' views on the relationship between "Islam" and "civilization" are made clear from the opening frames of his television documentary *Root Of All Evil?*, which features footage of people being carried into ambulances on stretchers intercut with images of Arab people in military fatigues loading machine guns, with Dawkins' voice-over narration:

> There are would-be murderers all around the world who want to kill you and me, and themselves, because they're motivated by what they think is the highest ideal. Of course politics are important. . . . But as we wake up to this huge challenge to our civilized values, don't let's forget the elephant in the room: an elephant called religion.[87]

While Dawkins does not target Islam specifically in *The God Delusion*, he has addressed this religion in his numerous interviews and public lectures. Perhaps most telling is a controversy that erupted in 2012 over Dawkins' repeated use of the term "barbarians" in comments made about Muslims on Twitter. In one tweet that garnered a great deal of attention, Dawkins revealed in a tweet on March 13, 2013 that he has never read the Koran, and in the next sentence he referred to Islam as the "greatest force for evil today." This drew the attention of commentators in many major media outlets, including *The Guardian*, *Salon*, and *Al Jazeera*, who took the opportunity to draw attention to the rising Islamophobia among the New Atheists, pointing to recent tweets and blog posts indicating that the tone of discourse had become more hostile and the views advanced more intolerant.[88] When a library in Timbuktu was destroyed by Islamic extremists, Dawkins tweeted on January 29, 2013: "Like Alexandria, like Bamiyan, Timbuktu's priceless manuscript heritage destroyed by Islamic barbarians," and subsequently defended his use of the term. Not long after this incident Harris wrote a blog post explaining his support for ethnic and religious profiling by airport security, arguing that "We should profile Muslims, or anyone who looks like he or she could conceivably be Muslim, and we should be honest about it."[89] Comments like these still regularly appear in the Twitter feeds of the people who follow these authors (in Dawkins' case, over one million followers as of January 18, 2015).

Like both Harris and Dawkins, Hitchens believed that religion is a threat to civilization (i.e., the West) and that among all religions none is a greater threat than Islam. Examples of how religion stunts the progress of civilization abound in *God Is Not Great*, along with an analysis of contributing factors. The most important of these is the concept of faith and the imperative that it not be questioned by its practitioners, and that it be respected by those outside the religion. Hitchens explains:

> All religions take care to silence or to execute those who question them. . . . It has, however, been some time since Judaism and Christianity resorted openly to torture and censorship. Not only did Islam begin by condemning all doubters to eternal fire, but it still claims the right to do so in almost all of its dominions, and still preaches that these same dominions can and must be extended by war. There has never been an attempt in any age to challenge or even investigate the claims of Islam that has not been met with extremely harsh and swift repression.[90]

This passage, in striving to demonize Islam by contrasting it with more "civilized" Western monotheism, ignores ongoing attempts at censorship by Christians in the United States who object to the teaching of evolutionary biology and the mere mention of homosexuality in public schools. Hitchens also disingenuously signals that condemning doubters to hellfire is a characteristic unique to Islam, when many Christians focus much of their attention in public discourse on sin, Satan, and final judgment. The idea that no one has ever investigated the claims of Islam without violent reprisal is also an obvious overstatement.

The Muslim world is represented as the other of the modern—and purportedly mostly secular—West. Discussing the reasons that the West is secularizing, Hitchens explains that "The availability and accessibility of well-produced books, cassettes, and DVDs, emphasizing the triumphs of science and reason, is a large part of this success. And so, of course, is the increasingly clear realization, on the part of civilized people, that the main enemy we face is 'faith-based.'"[91] Besides a proud defense of the scientific atheist movement, this is a claim that an escalating clash of civilizations is pushing people to choose a side between "reason" and "faith," which actually seem to be equivalent to "West" and "(Middle) East." That is, "civilized people" here means the white Western world, while the Islamic world is a faith-based "enemy." This dichotomy reflects Hitchens' general tendency to represent global politics in the black-and-white terms of a struggle between courageous heroes and evil villains.

Hitchens explains what he believes to be the major obstacle in this struggle between the forces of reason and faith within the West. Discussing the infamous incident of the publishing of cartoons depicting Muhammad in a newspaper in Denmark and the wave of protest and violence it spawned, resulting in many major news agencies refusing to reproduce the images, Hitchens blames the mass media's capitulation to the protesters on fear and relativism:

> To the ignoble motive of fear one must add the morally lazy practice of relativism: no group of nonreligious people threatening and practicing violence would have been granted such an easy victory, or had their excuses—not that they offered any of their own—made for them.[92]

This is one example among many criticisms in Hitchens' work of a postmodern cultural climate where matters of faith are beyond question.

Here we arrive at the crux of the matter: the New Atheism's rejection of a liberal politics of tolerance, represented by policies of multiculturalism, and in academic circles by a "postmodern" epistemology of relativism. Grace Davie explains the challenge postmodernity introduces to the theory, and doctrine, of secularization:

> . . . the secular certainties (science, rationalism, progress, etc.), the erstwhile competitors of religious truth, are themselves under attack . . . No longer is it assumed that a secular discourse will gradually overcome a recognizable and unified religious alternative. Instead, both secular and religious thinking will evolve, as multiple groups of people find their own ways forward and creeds (both secular and religious) to live by in the early years of the 21st century.[93]

Here Davie expresses the view that Charles Taylor would articulate as the defining characteristic of our "secular age," namely that secularism does not mean the hegemonic triumph of scientific rationality over religion but rather that secular and religious ways of living coexist and evolve into novel forms in late modern society.[94] The New Atheism is a reaction against precisely this kind of secularism, where science loses its footing as the bedrock of secularization, and truth and meaning are permanently contested and socially constructed fields. This kind of secularization is therefore undesirable, and the New Atheism thus advocates not secularization but the scientization of society and culture.

Davie suggests that in Europe there have been two religious responses to the challenge presented by the uncertainty of post/late modernity, two forms of religious life that have been able to prosper: New Age and fundamentalism. New Age spiritualities have "adapted most easily to the flux of late modernity," while fundamentalism involves "tightly bound groups" that "provide havens for those people that find it difficult to live with change and uncertainty (the hallmarks of postmodernism)."[95] The New Atheism is another such response, and the scientistic belief system it promotes answers uncertainty with absolutism. This is the same view advanced by William Stahl, who argues that "both the New Atheism and fundamentalism are attempts to recreate authority in the face of crises of meaning in late modernity"[96] and that both are involved in a "quest for certainty, for an authoritative foundation that can ground a normative order."[97]

The ground for this normative order is scientism. Harris has gone so far as to claim in his book *The Moral Landscape* that the study of ethics falls within the domain of the natural sciences, and advances in evolutionary psychology and particularly neuroscience allow scientists to "determine" proper values. The grounding for this normative order is perceived to be threatened by "postmodernism," which is equated with epistemic relativism, a product of developments in the social sciences and humanities in the late twentieth century. Because the social sciences are perceived as the grounding of relativism—and thus represent a rival form of thought that must be excluded and denigrated, according to Eagleton's definition of ideology—the New Atheism targets this segment of the academy for attack. The strategy is to argue for sociobiology as a replacement for the social sciences, which Darwinism has made redundant. This is the view advanced by Harvard entomologist Edward O. Wilson in his 1975 book *Sociobiology*, which argues that the social sciences should be considered an undeveloped branch of evolutionary biology.

Dawkins enthusiastically agrees. On the very first page of *The Selfish Gene*, Dawkins laments that "Philosophy and the subjects known as 'humanities' are still taught almost as if Darwin had never lived."[98] In another revealing passage, he ponders the potentially limitless scope of natural selection: "The laws of physics are supposed to be true all over the accessible universe. Are there any principles of biology that are likely to have similar universal validity?"[99] This presumed universal validity extends beyond the natural world and into the social world, where Dawkins' meme-based theory of religion emerges as a speculative translation of evolutionary biology into cultural theory. This leap in logic is an extension of the ideological view that "Darwinism is too big a theory to be confined to the narrow context of the gene"[100] and is indicative of his general contempt for the social sciences.

The explanations of religion provided by the social sciences, Dawkins tells us, are "proximate" and not "ultimate" explanations.[101] Only the Darwinian explanation *ultimately* arrives at the truth about where religion comes from, and it involves an application of the theory to two things: our brains and the genetic evolution that gave rise to them, and ideas that exist outside of these brains in a meme-pool that is also subject to the process of natural selection. He does deal very briefly with "proximate" explanations (i.e., those that lie outside of the province of the natural sciences and are therefore inferior to "ultimate" explanations) in the final chapter of *The God Delusion*, where he notes that "Religion has at one time or another been thought to fill four main roles in human life: explanation, exhortation, consolation and inspiration,"[102] but like Hitchens, he considers these minor and relatively insignificant factors.

Dennett is Dawkins' closest ally among the Four Horsemen on the matter of sociobiology (though Steven Pinker has become a much more prominent spokesperson in more recent years). Dennett is even more explicit about his support for Darwinistic interpretations of sociocultural phenomena and his portrayal of the social sciences as an antagonist to scientific truth. This is clear when he writes, "Anyone who tries to bring an evolutionary perspective to bear on any item of human culture, not just religion, can expect rebuffs ranging from howls of outrage to haughty dismissal from the literary, historical, and cultural experts in the humanities and social sciences."[103] Like Dawkins, he dismisses "proximate" explanations of religious belief, which are symptoms of a "disorder often encountered in the humanities and social sciences: premature curiosity satisfaction."[104] This "disorder" is demonstrated when questions regarding origins are "left unexamined by people who lose interest once they have found a *purpose* or *function* for religion that strikes them as plausible."[105] The purposes Dennett cites are comfort, explanation, and cooperation, and with that he perfunctorily summarizes, and dismisses, the social scientific understanding of religion. Instead, Dennett supports Dawkins' evolutionistic theory of religion, explaining its general nature as a byproduct of adaptive characteristics, with meme theory explaining the particularities. Also like Dawkins, Dennett believes that Darwinism is sufficient to explain social and cultural phenomena more generally, claiming that the process of natural selection is in principle "substrate-neutral"[106] and that evolution will occur wherever the conditions of replication, variation, and differential fitness (or competition) are met. In organic evolution the substrate for natural selection is the unit of the gene, organism, or group (Dawkins favors a gene-centered view), and in cultural evolution the substrate is ideas.

The New Atheism, certainly as represented by Dawkins and Dennett, is indicative of a resurgence of sociobiology in recent years. Sociobiologists like Dawkins and Dennett, who invoke evolution by natural selection as a universal explanatory framework, effectively "challenged the basic assumption on which the social sciences of the twentieth century had been built: the rejection of biology as a determinant of human behavior."[107] Sociobiology is a foundational element in the project of scientific hegemony, demanding that "only genetic causes of behavior should be taken seriously, and it is therefore presented in metaphors which rule out human freedom, presenting people, along with other animals and plants, as machines."[108] It thus seeks to render the social sciences redundant.

Dawkins has recently become more assertive in this regard, particularly on social media, where he tends to express his views most frankly. In a May 24, 2013, tweet in response to accusations of racism for comments he made about Muslim "barbarism," Dawkins wrote: "So many people incapable of drawing an elementary distinction: between racism and IN-STITUTIONAL racism. Probably studied sociology." If his contempt for sociology were not clear here, it is abundantly clear in a re-tweet on the same date of a comment made by one of his followers, a sign of a view he supports: "@RichardDawkins be fair, sociology allows McDonald's to get a slightly more educated staff pool." When another Twitter user made the obviously problematic claim that one cannot by definition be racist or sexist against white men because they are the group holding power, Dawkins responded with: "Really? By whose dictionary? Certainly not the Oxford Dictionary. Dictionary of sociology perhaps?" Finally, Dawkins notably offered a blurb for Alan Sokal and Jean Bricmont's *Fashionable Nonsense*, an extended critique of the social sciences and humanities that equates them with postmodernism, relativism, obscurantism, and, of course, general nonsense. This was a follow-up to Sokal's infamous hoax publication in the journal *Social Text* that instigated the "science wars"[109] of the 1990s, where natural scientists defending objectivity and impartiality in scientific method engaged in debate with postmodernist social scientists who viewed scientific knowledge as a social construction. On the back cover Dawkins is found saying that "the hoax was earnestly needed and richly justified." There is no ambiguity with respect to his disdain for sociology, which he equates with relativism and a general distortion of scientific truth. This hostility toward the social sciences is a great irony given research revealing that rates of atheism are higher among social scientists than natural scientists.[110]

The New Atheism has always been in part an extension of these science wars, though recently more explicitly in the wake of an interview[111] Lawrence Krauss gave to *The Atlantic* in 2012, when some prominent atheists suddenly launched a public attack on the discipline of philosophy. The interviewer pressed Krauss on the misleading title of his book *A Universe From Nothing*, which ostensibly argues that quantum field theory reveals that a universe can arise from "nothing," thus purporting to obviate the question of the origin of the universe (the book is partly, if not primarily, a critique of monotheism). Citing a "blistering" review[112] of the book by the philosopher David Albert in the *New York Times*, Krauss was presented with the criticism that quantum fields and the laws that govern them are themselves "something." Krauss was compelled to admit that the book in fact does not and cannot argue that "physics has definitively shown how something could come from nothing" and proceeded to attack the "moronic philosophers" (a term that he uses twice) who contribute nothing to the advancement of science.[113] In his defense of intellectual territory, Krauss considers science and philosophy of science to be essentially the same thing, or at least concerned with the same ends.

At the prompting of Dennett, Krauss offered a public apology for the interview, or at least the language he used, while defending his basic position.[114] Both the interview and the apology prompted a good deal of discussion within the atheist community.[115] Pinker wrote an article in defense of scientism in *New Republic* titled "Science Is Not Your Enemy"[116] that on the surface implored those in the social sciences and humanities to recognize their common interests with science and try to work together, while overtly ridiculing those same disciplines (Pinker's contempt is clear in the article's subtitle, "An impassioned plea to neglected novelists, embattled professors, and tenure-less historians") and arguing that science is the only legitimate source of knowledge. A peripheral New Atheist figure, physicist Neil deGrasse Tyson, created a stir in an interview promoting his

Fox series *Cosmos* (which many Christians viewed as atheist propaganda) when he described philosophy as a "useless" discipline that has nothing to tell us about the natural world.[117] Tyson echoed Krauss' misunderstanding of what philosophy is, seeing it much like religion: as a competitor in the quest for a rigorous understanding of nature and a threat to the authority of science. While these attacks primarily center on philosophy, the territorialism extends to the social sciences as well, particularly among Darwinists who advocate for evolutionary psychology and sociobiology as the basis for a new science of society.

The salient point is that the rejection of the social sciences is more precisely a rejection of relativism. Replacing the social sciences with sociobiology is in fact an endorsement of absolutism, with the natural sciences providing "ultimate" knowledge with respect to questions and issues that, from a sociological standpoint, have no clear answer and are not reducible to a single all-encompassing explanation. The epistemic relativism attributed to the social sciences is an obstacle to the scientific critique of religion. The social sciences are therefore reduced to an undeveloped branch of evolutionary biology, subsumed to what Dawkins considers the "ultimate" theory of natural selection, which Dennett views as a theory of such vast scope that it transcends disciplinary boundaries, "promising to unite and explain just about everything in one magnificent vision."[118] Sociobiology not only undermines the social sciences but also provides a "scientific" theoretical framework for the New Atheism's views on sociocultural evolution, explaining differences between the West and its others as a matter of more or less advanced stages of progress, which is stunted as a function of the relative influence of religion.

The epistemic relativism that threatens the scientific critique of religion is intimately wedded to cultural relativism, the primary object of the New Atheism's political critique. We see the two converge in Dawkins' analysis of the main obstacle to the critique of religion: the cultural imperative to respect individual beliefs, no matter how they accord with science or reason. The two sources of this imperative are the demand for respect for private faith, which is supported by a climate of epistemic relativism, and the development of a political culture that has abandoned the universal as a guiding principle in favor of multiculturalism and cultural relativism, which embraces diversity in pluralistic societies. These are both grounded in the same general principle, which is that no one has a monopoly on truth and morality, a position Dawkins attributes to a general tendency to embrace a diversity of perspectives and to accept all cultures, ways of thinking, and ways of living as equally valid—in other words, relativism. In the New Atheism discourse these are characteristics of a "postmodern" liberalism that emphasizes pluralism and tolerance of difference. This is in contrast to the "modern" liberalism Dawkins favors, which is essentially an appeal to scientific authority as an absolute foundation for decision-making, regardless of cultural considerations.

Dawkins sees the Western liberal world wading into the waters of relativism, and his concern with religion is more fundamentally a fear that science is losing its place as the pillar of modern society and engine of progress. Further, he seems disturbed that rationalism is being replaced in politics with a pluralistic embrace of diversity to such an extent that it becomes impossible to take a position on anything, with liberalism rendered entirely ineffectual:

> The same tendency to glory in the quaintness of ethnic religious habits, and to justify cruelties in their name, crops up again and again. It is the source of squirming internal conflict in the minds of nice liberal people who, on the one hand, cannot bear suffering and cruelty, but on the other hand have been trained by postmodernists and relativists to respect other cultures no less than their own. Female circumcision is undoubtedly hideously painful . . . and one half of the decent liberal mind wants to abolish the practice. The other half, however, "respects" ethnic cultures and feels that we should not interfere if "they" want to mutilate "their" girls.[119]

Liberals, Dawkins argues, have lost their original guiding impetus of rationalism and empiricism after being "trained" by "postmodernists" to embrace cultural relativism. This makes it difficult to take a firm position on cultural practices such as female genital mutilation, which should naturally offend the liberal mind as a barbaric violation of human health and dignity. Cultural relativism, if it defends irrationalism, is an affront to the notion of universal human rights, and the only answer to this problem is to return to rationalism and empiricism, to reason and scientific evidence, as the basis of politics. Dawkins, then, takes the same position on the "problem of tolerance" that Harris takes: both want to rescue liberalism from a descent into the abyss of relativism, which neutralizes our capacity to respond to the challenge religion poses to civilization. Here the "premodern" and "postmodern" threats to modernity and the project of secularization converge.

The New Atheism's position on this perceived crisis within liberalism and modernity was summarized in a revealing *Los Angeles Times* op-ed by Harris in 2006 entitled "The End of Liberalism." It is worth quoting here in some detail, and I have italicized key words:

> Increasingly, Americans will come to believe that the only people hard-headed enough to fight the religious lunatics of the Muslim world are the religious lunatics of the West. Indeed, it is telling that the people who speak with the greatest *moral clarity* about the current wars in the Middle East are members of the Christian right, whose infatuation with biblical prophecy is nearly as troubling as the ideology of *our enemies*. Religious dogmatism is now playing both sides of the board in a very dangerous game.
>
> While liberals should be the ones pointing the way beyond this Iron Age madness, they are rendering themselves increasingly irrelevant. Being generally reasonable and *tolerant* of *diversity*, liberals should be especially sensitive to the dangers of religious literalism. But they aren't.
>
> The same *failure of liberalism* is evident in Western Europe, where the dogma of *multiculturalism* has left a secular Europe very slow to address the looming problem of religious extremism among its immigrants. The people who speak most sensibly about the threat that Islam poses to Europe are actually fascists.
>
> To say that this does not bode well for liberalism is an understatement: It does not bode well for the future of *civilization*.[120]

Harris's view is that the "dogma of multiculturalism," with its emphasis on tolerance of diversity, constitutes a "failure of liberalism" by rendering it incapable of addressing the threat "our enemies" (i.e., Muslims) pose to "civilization." Perhaps most striking in this passage is that Harris attributes the greatest "moral clarity" on the issue of Islam to European fascists and the Christian Right. These are the people who, by his own admission, share his perspective on how to approach the "looming problem" that immigration of Muslims poses to civilized Europe. In a similar vein, Dawkins, in reference to a ruling by the European court against crucifixes in public school classrooms, wrote on his website, "If I thought the motive was secularist I would indeed welcome it. But are we sure it is not pandering to 'multiculturalism,' which in Europe is code for Islam? And if you think Catholicism is evil."[121] Dawkins interprets the ruling as being motivated by a multiculturalist accommodation of Islam—which is much more "evil" than Catholicism—rather than secularism.

Harris argues that religious "moderates" (i.e., nonfundamentalists) and liberals who preach tolerance and respect of difference "provide the context in which scriptural literalism and religious violence can never be adequately opposed,"[122] a view shared by all the Four Horsemen. Harris insists that science and reason alone can rescue humanity from an accelerating descent into apocalyptic global conflict: "Only openness to evidence and argument will secure a common world for us."[123] This is an implicit rejection of pluralism and the accommodation of cultural diversity. In contrast, Harris advocates a model of politics based on the authority of scientific rationality, where democratic consensus is mediated by science and its "experts." Tolerance of beliefs that contradict scientific knowledge simply does not fit into the worldview of someone who suggests that "Some propositions are so dangerous that it may even be ethical to kill people for believing them."[124]

This is an extreme example of what Asad refers to as "the violence of universalizing reason"[125] at the heart of liberalism. This violence occurs because "to make an enlightened space, the liberal must continually attack the darkness of the outside world that threatens to overwhelm that space."[126] A menacing outside is constructed, against which the enlightened space is contrasted and defended, and they exercise different types of violence: "Violence required by the cultivation of enlightenment is therefore distinguished from the violence of the dark jungle."[127] That is, the former is justifiable in the name of progress, while the latter is the violence of terror and ignorance. This is precisely the logic behind George W. Bush's claims that his wars in Iraq and Afghanistan were necessary to bring justice and peace (in fact, Bush claimed that the wars were ordained by God himself and thus were not only just but holy). Asad argues that liberal violence is not the "necessary unfolding of an Enlightenment essence," but rather it is "just a way some liberals have argued and acted."[128]

The New Atheists are just the kind of liberals he refers to. This liberalism is characterized not by freedom and diversity but by a specific worldview and mode of social organization that its supporters believe they have a duty to bring to others (or impose on them by force, if necessary), justified by the ideals of progress and civilization. In their view, political decisions must be made through a process of deliberation under the auspices of scientific authority. Neither governments nor individuals or groups whose politics are informed by identity or cultural traditions have the right to supersede the authority of science and reason in matters involving the public good. Perhaps the best example of this is Dawkins' view that socialization of children in any religious tradition constitutes child abuse because the child is not yet capable of deciding for himself or herself, through reason, what to believe. Dawkins' version of liberalism clearly would not grant individuals the freedom to practice cultural traditions. In his world freedom would be constrained to beliefs and practices that qualified authorities judge to meet the requirements of rationality and empirical verifiability; anything that lies outside of this realm can be understood as "indoctrination." We should be careful, then, not to interpret the New Atheists' advocacy of liberalism as support for individual freedom and participatory democracy. It is, rather, a statement on the cognitive, moral, and political authority of science and its expert practitioners, who are called on to provide a beacon of light within the dark jungle.

Fundamentalism and Culture

There is a corollary between the New Atheism and the rise to prominence of fundamentalist forms of religion in the late twentieth century. Terry Eagleton suggests that

> The recent religious resurgence is distinctive not just because it is everywhere on the rise, but because it often takes a *political* form . . . postmodernity is the era in which religion goes public and collective once again, but more as a substitute for classical politics than a reassertion of it.[129]

Fundamentalist forms of religion, Eagleton argues, set out to transform the world rather than take refuge from it. They are political, or "antipolitical," in their desire to substitute politics with "culturalism" taking the form of religion.[130] This is exemplified by the Islamic revolution, which instituted the Koran as the unquestionable source of political authority, leaving no room for democratic deliberations. The Christian Right is also effectively antipolitical to the extent that political and ethical principles are derived exclusively from the Bible, which is interpreted by religious authorities, leaving no room for democratic deliberations among citizens.[131]

The New Atheists are similarly antipolitical, but rather than substituting culture for politics, they wish to substitute science for politics (of course, "science" in this case may be understood as a form of culture).

In so doing they reject deliberative democracy, which is subject to nonscientific cultural influences, in favor of scientific authority. The sociobiology that informs the New Atheism's understanding of religion, culture, and the social world is in essence a political program for enhancing the power and influence of science. This is the view expressed by biologist Richard Lewontin in his critique of Edward O. Wilson's *Sociobiology*, in which he sees

> a vision of neurobiologists and sociobiologists as the technocrats of the near future who will provide the necessary knowledge for ethical and political decisions in the planned society. . . . Sociobiology is basically a political science whose results may be used, eventually, as the scientific tools of "correct" social organization.[132]

Lewontin's critique of Wilson effectively captures the political science at the heart of the New Atheism. Sociobiology is an approach to politics and social problems that is effectively depoliticized to the extent that it is presented as an objective science, and thus it stands outside the realm of democratic deliberations because its prescriptions do not rely on consensus of opinion but simply scientific fact. The New Atheism, then, is effectively a political ideology disguised as disinterested scientific inquiry, which in turn is how the views of the New Atheists are naturalized and universalized. Its attack on religion, and on the social sciences and humanities, is effectively a statement on the nature of modern society and a defense of an evolutionistic vision of progress. Its Darwinistic "social theory" carries an imperative for the correct mode of social organization and appropriate systems of belief. While Asad describes secularism as a "political doctrine"[133] that sets up the conditions for a secular democracy, the New Atheism's ideology of scientism and secularization is essentially antidemocratic and authoritarian in its insistence on relegating not just cognitive but also moral and political authority to science and its practitioners.

The New Atheism is much more than an assault on religion. Indeed, this assault is only one element of an ideology with the goal of legitimating scientific authority. Returning to the dimensions of ideology identified above, the New Atheism promotes its own belief system (scientism/evolutionism) that is essentially political in nature, naturalizes and universalizes these beliefs by equating them with objective science and "natural" laws determining the course of history, denigrates challenging ideas (religion), excludes rival forms of thought (social sciences and humanities), and obscures social reality by making religion a scapegoat for social problems at the expense of a careful examination of the structure of modern society, insisting instead that submission to the authority of science is the solution to these problems and the only path to civilization. David Martin similarly argues that the New Atheism is an ideological narrative of religion's intrinsic implication with violence that is similar to other Enlightenment narratives that "load the 'blame' onto religion for what is built into the exigencies of social organization under various constraints."[134]

The belief system the New Atheism promotes is different from nineteenth-century scientific atheism only in the greater sophistication brought to evolutionism by the nascent disciplines of evolutionary psychology and neuroscience. Like other thinkers in this tradition, the scientific critique of religion is only one element in the promotion of a vision of the world, how it should be, how we determine how it should be, and who has the authority to say so. For the New Atheism, this vision is, in a word, *scientism*. The nineteenth-century split in atheism is represented today by a group that has appropriated the term "atheism" as a synonym for scientism and a Darwinian view of human nature and society. This is an extension of the view of some Victorian Darwinists who manufactured the idea of an inevitable and eternal struggle between religion and science to provide a pretext for a challenge to religious control over all levels of education.[135] This false notion of the enduring and intractable conflict between the epistemologies and institutions of religion and science— referred to by some historians of science and religion simply as the "conflict myth"[136]—is today wielded by the Four Horsemen for the polemical purpose of advancing the nineteenth-century view that modern people, who by definition possess science, must therefore reject religion, and that this is a natural and inevitable cultural evolution.[137]

The New Atheism's critique of religion is a manifestation of its defense of a teleological vision of modernity as the unfolding of history from prescientific barbarism to scientific civilization. This, again, is tied to a politicized understanding of evolution as a social process, with all cultures at various stages of evolution toward a singular civilization driven and defined by scientific rationality. This view of social evolution as a progressive scientization of socio-political institutions is thus an instance of secularization as political doctrine, in which modernity is understood as a project of universalizing scientism and the emerging authority of scientific experts. These views on the nature of modernity and civilization arise most clearly in the New Atheist discourse on Islam, with Islamic societies represented as "backward" and "uncivilized" and the presence of Muslims in the West a threat to progress. Islamic civilizations serve as the "other" of enlightened modernity, a notion employed in portraying the advanced status of Western secular-liberal society.

In its uncritical celebration of modernity and the project of universalizing science, the New Atheism is essentially a politics of complacency. In its defense of the status quo there is no room for radical questioning of systemic structural inequalities, but only an effort to purge modernity of religion, and thereby purify it so it can be fully realized. Pinker has argued that violence is decreasing everywhere, largely as a result of intellectual and scientific progress.[138] The glimmering portrait of the modern project that he and other New Atheists have constructed bears little resemblance to the stark realities of looming environmental and economic catastrophe, or the tremors of political violence currently being felt in Europe. With no critical perspective on destructive forces within the existing social structure, they argue that only religion can bring civilization down, and only science can save it.

The New Atheism is an ideological defense of a modern utopia against its perceived antagonists: religion and relativism. It takes shape as a cultural movement that seeks to universalize this ideology by converting the masses to scientism and asserting scientific authority in all spheres of life. As both a utopian belief system and a social movement that advances a political program for maintaining the structural arrangement of modern society, it can be understood as a secular fundamentalism, as opposed to religious fundamentalisms that are antimodern.[139] Like all fundamentalisms, New Atheism is totalizing. Just as communists claimed to have a scientific understanding of the laws of motion of history and thus legitimated the centralized management of society by experts,[140] the New Atheists see a law of evolution guiding history on its natural course toward civilization—that is, a society administered by scientific authorities. The evolution of society, in this view, is driven by the evolution of atheism.

PART 2

Atheism as a Social Movement

4

The Secular Movement

THE SECULAR MOVEMENT's history has been cyclical rather than progressive, characterized by an ongoing internal struggle between groups motivated by distinct political views. This struggle produces variations on a few basic forms of thought and action that have persisted since the movement's very beginning: the founding of the National Secular Society (NSS; originally called the Central Secular Society) in Great Britain in the mid-nineteenth century. Colin Campbell's account of the formation and early development of the NSS—which is generally regarded as the first secularist association in the Western world and the origin of the term "secularism"—addresses intra-associational tensions and debates that are essentially the same as those currently shaping movement dynamics.[1] The precise nature of these debates, their outcomes, and the transformations in movement leadership and structure that they resulted in are similar to the situation of recent years.

These tensions that recur throughout the history of the secular movement reflect the ideological tension at the heart of atheism: that between scientism and humanism. This chapter examines the history of the secular movement and the place of the New Atheism within it and establishes a theoretical framework for analyzing contemporary developments with respect to changing goals and strategies. Most importantly, it identifies internal disputes that threaten to fragment the movement into distinct spheres, with the New Atheism's ambitious project of cultural universalization compromised by deep political and ethical divisions.

Foundations of a Movement

While sociological studies of atheism and secularism as social movements are still rare, there have been some significant—though until recently mostly unheeded—attempts at forging this field of scholarship. My approach is informed by two such previous treatments: Colin Campbell's *Toward a Sociology of Irreligion* and Christian Smith's collection of essays entitled *The Secular Revolution*. Campbell's book, published in 1971, was a call to sociologists to attend to a grossly neglected phenomenon: those who have no religion. His book focused specifically on nonreligious organizations and a history of the secular movement. Viewed in light of recent events, Campbell's historical analysis of the beginnings of the movement in the late nineteenth and early twentieth centuries is uncannily prescient, translating almost seamlessly to the present day. In particular, the tensions, debates, and subsequent change of leadership that occurred in the early years of the NSS, the first secularist organization in the Western world, were repeated in recent years almost exactly in the Center for Inquiry, one of the most important organizations in the movement today. A review of the origins of the movement will enlighten the contemporary situation, as the ideological tensions and dynamics of movement structure and action that shaped its early development still do so today.

As with the history of ideology, for the history of atheism and secularism as a social movement the key period is the mid- to late nineteenth century, a golden age of flourishing secularism and antireligious thought and action. The movement went mostly dormant for much of the twentieth century (in America this is typically attributed to the rise of communism, when atheism was associated with the enemy) before being resuscitated at the dawn of the twenty-first century by the 9/11 terrorist attacks. The secular movement was born in Britain when the Central Secular Society was established in 1851 by George Jacob Holyoake, a lecturer and organizer who published periodicals arguing for "secularism," a term he coined. Holyoake defined the founding principle of the society as the "recognition of the Secular sphere as the province of man" and issued a statement outlining its aims, which included establishing the proposition that science is "the sole Providence of man" and that morals are independent of Christianity, to "encourage men to trust Reason throughout, and to trust nothing that Reason does not establish," to promote open discussion and debate as "the highest guarantee of public truth," and to claim the right to the "fullest liberty of thought and action compatible of like liberty by every other person."[2] In addition to these familiar Enlightenment dictums regarding liberty of consciousness and the legitimacy of science and reason as the basis of knowledge and ethics—which should remind us of the characteristics of scientific atheism—Holyoake added one more aim to his list that stood apart from the others:

> To maintain that, from the uncertainty as to whether the inequalities of human condition will be compensated for in another life—it is the business of intelligence to rectify them in this world; and consequently, that instead of indulging in speculative worship of supposed superior beings, a generous man will devote himself to the patient service of known inferior natures, and the mitigation of harsh destiny so that the ignorant may be enlightened and the low elevated.[3]

This last aim is the most critical for our understanding of Holyoake's position. He wanted to enlighten the ignorant, but the implication here is that this is not possible without first the "mitigation of harsh destiny" and rectification of the "inequalities of human condition." This aim, then, is not primarily for scientific rationalism but for social justice and the mitigation of suffering. In this sense, Holyoake recognizes the major insight of humanistic atheism: that religion is not strictly a cognitive operation relating to the nature of material reality, but a response to the experience of social existence. For him, atheism and secularism were fundamentally, and necessarily, related to improving the conditions of life for all of humanity.

Holyoake's position on religion is not surprising given his political activism. An advocate for socialism, he published several freethought periodicals aimed at working-class readers that addressed issues of labor, exploitation, and forms of resistance to capitalism. The working class also provided the bulk of the support for the Central Secular Society at its beginning, with much of the membership drawn through the readership of Holyoake's periodicals. In a strategic calculation Holyoake later softened the radical political approach of the organization and sought alliances with middle-class unbelievers, particularly members of the intelligentsia. This was the first move away from secularism's original working-class foundations and toward a relationship with eminent middle-class unbelievers and prominent intellectuals. Most important among these were leading advocates of evolutionary theory, including Thomas Huxley and Herbert Spencer, with whom Holyoake partnered in an effort to establish the hegemony of scientific naturalism (he evidently chose to overlook Spencer's political views to meet him on the common ground of defending science). Evolutionary science was thus an important element of the secular movement from its earliest days.[4]

Though Holyoake advocated for naturalism and scientific rationality, he was not as vehemently antitheistic as some other radical secularists of the day. His conciliatory and accommodating position on religion attracted liberal theists who united with skeptics under the broad tent of secularism, helping to expand the movement beyond the restricted sphere of unbelievers by emphasizing common values and underlying political concerns.[5] But he was criticized for his policy of seeking common ground with Christians by a group led by Charles Bradlaugh, who felt that such alliances betrayed the very purposes of the movement. Conflicts over this issue culminated in Bradlaugh taking over as leader of the organization in 1866, when he renamed it the NSS, the name it still goes by today.[6]

Campbell describes this situation as one where "the constructive and destructive sides of Secularism were in a fundamental state of tension."[7] In working for secular political and social reform, it was "tactically advisable to work with all those, regardless of their beliefs, who were prepared to assist,"[8] though on the other hand many secularists felt they had a duty to attack superstitious beliefs, which were an impediment to these goals. Both aims were regarded as desirable, but there was no agreement about which was of greater priority, or how one could be achieved without having a negative impact on the progress of the other. Holyoake and Bradlaugh engaged in public debates in 1870 where they presented their policy for the movement.[9] The debates included the question of whether secularism necessarily implies atheism, with Holyoake saying no and Bradlaugh yes. In terms of strategies, these two promoted "substitutionism" and "abolitionism." Bradlaugh believed that no change was possible until religious belief was "abolished" through criticism, while Holyoake advocated the more pragmatic approach of seeking alliances with liberal religious thinkers and disassociating from the question of atheism. Rather than trying to destroy religion through rational critique, he favored replacing religion through secularist reform. Holyoake, roughly speaking, took a humanistic approach, while Bradlaugh was more in line with the scientific approach. Notably, Bradlaugh was an outspoken critic of socialism, as opposed to Holyoake's support for unionization and working-class mobilization, a contrast that parallels the ideologies of scientific and humanistic atheism and their associated political positions.

Campbell offers a quote from Sidney Warren's *American Freethought, 1860–1914* that illustrates the same tension within the secular movement in the United States:

> The essential difference between the socialist and the "organizational" freethinker was that the former viewed religion in the context of a whole social pattern and not as an isolated phenomenon. The socialist was anti-religious in so far as religion in his eyes was a bulwark of that system which he endeavored to destroy. The "dogmatic" freethinker, on the other hand, condemned religion, not because it was an impediment to the achievement of any specific political and economic system, but because it resulted in the enslavement of man's mind. In short, the one possessed an integrated view of life based upon a clearly defined analysis of society of which anti-religion was one facet. The other was interested in the struggle against religion as the be-all and end-all of his ideological crusade.[10]

Campbell adds: "When the free-thinker and the Socialist agreed in their condemnation of religion, therefore, this was despite a difference in premises."[11] This is precisely the difference that I have conceptualized in terms of scientific and humanistic forms of atheism, which are premised on very different conceptions of the nature of religion and its consequences for the individual and for society. For the liberal scientific atheist, religion is ignorance and a natural enemy of science, the freedom of individual consciousness, and social progress. For humanistic atheists, religion was a symptom of the larger problem of an unjust social arrangement, both an expression of suffering and alienation and a legitimation of it.

Campbell's history of "irreligious movements" extends to the United States, where his analysis of the Ethical Culture movement and the Rationalist Press Association unearths tensions similar to those in Britain. Felix Adler, professor first at Cornell and then of Social and Political Ethics at Columbia University, founded the Society for Ethical Culture in New York in 1876, with more branches soon arising in several other major American cities. The purpose of the organization was to advance the idea that moral truth exists independently of subjective interpretation or religious doctrine. That is, Adler believed that moral law was absolute and could be discovered through reason. Though embracing science and rationalism, the society did not endorse or refute atheism or theism but instead regarded these metaphysical doctrines as outside its purview, which was restricted to constructing an ethical approach to living in the world independently of theology. To this extent the society was more interested in public service and charitable volunteer activities than promoting a worldview, so this was a form of secularism that was more about practice than belief. Though a part of a broadly conceived secular movement, it was committed to improving the condition of humanity rather than reducing the power and influence of religion. The Ethical Culture movement was essentially a form of secular humanism, concerned principally with morality while removing itself from theological debates.

Campbell argues that the rise of Ethical Culture and other humanist groups brought out a tension between the political and cultural goals of the secular movement. Political action was considered necessary to address the discrimination and oppression that the irreligious were subjected to and to secularize the education system. But at the same time, many activists considered this type of activity incidental to the primary aim of the movement, which was the spread of an intellectual culture. An excessive focus on political activity, some felt, might compromise the more important cultural goal. In this view, the emphasis in Ethical Culture on making practical improvements to the conditions of life was a foray into politics that distracted attention from the cultural objective of promoting a naturalistic worldview based on science and reason. The Rationalist Press Association, for example, explicitly claimed it had no political or party allegiance, stating that "the great principle of Rationalism must not be compromised by identification with opinions which are shared only by certain sections of liberal thinkers as the main objects of the Association are philosophical, ethical, and educative."[12] Political differences were considered to be irrelevant to the work of the association, which was to promote rationalism and freethinking, and it always appeared that the majority of members supported the policy and complained if they saw any hint of political bias in its publications. By contrast, Ethical Culture and other humanist organizations have as their mandate not conversion to a particular worldview but moral guidance for the improvement of the conditions of humanity, and they focus more on action than on developing creed. Campbell writes, "Unlike the secular movement, the ethicist's concern with socio-political action was not the privileges accorded to religion, but the application of a liberal, ethical and humanitarian ideal to all spheres of social life."[13]

Tension between the cultural and political dimensions of the secular movement persists today. Humanists and humanistic atheists, whose central concerns are about social justice and human welfare, are more interested in politics. "New" or scientific atheists, whose central concerns are the ideological legitimation of authority, act more as a cultural movement that avoids party allegiance or an explicit political platform (at least beyond the civil rights of atheists) because it advances a universalistic worldview that should encompass everyone. These atheists argue that the movement is only about promoting scientific rationalism over religion, and that atheists have no common political allegiance. Other atheists, particularly an emergent group arguing that the movement should focus more on issues of social justice, see their atheism and secular activism as an inherently political activity that is a natural extension of their more basic political goals and values. This essential disagreement over the meaning of atheism and the beliefs and priorities that come with it gives rise to tensions with respect to the goals of the movement and the best strategies for achieving them. The New Atheism's primarily "cultural" or ideological goal, and its strategies for achieving it, are a current manifestation of an old project of secularization that Christian Smith describes as a "secular revolution."[14]

Smith offers an original and compelling account of secularization in America that challenges the basic assumption of the traditional secularization paradigm, namely that it is part and parcel of the larger social process of modernization. His account begins in the mid-nineteenth century, when many American social institutions—most importantly education and mass media—were controlled by a Protestant establishment. Science was also guided by a Christian worldview, with scientific discoveries considered to work in tandem with theology to authenticate Christian truth. In the late 1800s, however, a secularization of science and education took place that saw religion moved to the private sphere, where it was removed from "core institutions of socially legitimate knowledge production and distribution."[15] This secularization of science and education set the stage for further movements of secularization in the following decades, including reforms in the legal system and new cultural authorities in the social sciences, journalism, and Hollywood, who replaced the "moralizers and pastoral opinion makers" of the Protestant establishment and ended its cultural hegemony.[16]

Smith argues that the old paradigm that explains secularization as an inevitable byproduct of modernization fails to recognize the crucial dimensions of culture and agency, and that secularization in America was not a passive result of natural social changes but rather the result of an active and revolutionary struggle for control over cultural structures and social and political institutions. In his account a "rebel insurgency"[17] developed among a group of intellectual elites and members of the American knowledge class. In the late nineteenth and early twentieth century these "secularizing activists" launched a successful political struggle to wrest control over socially legitimate knowledge from a Protestant establishment. As such, "the secularization of American public life was in fact something much more like a contested revolutionary struggle than a natural evolutionary progression."[18] The secular activists, according to Smith, were motivated by antipathy to religion and a "quasi-religious vision of secular progress, prosperity, and higher civilization,"[19] but, more importantly, the material gain to be derived from the professionalization of the field of science. As religion was excluded from this field and relegated to the private sphere, the cultural authority of scientists would be greatly enhanced, as they would become the only legitimate producers of knowledge. This agent-oriented account that emphasizes ideology and self-interest is very different from the traditional narrative of secularization as a natural and inevitable social process bound up with modernization. It is also pertinent to the contemporary secular movement, especially the New Atheism, which is a kind of secular revolution much like that Smith describes in nineteenth-century America.

The cultural character of the secular revolution in America is crucial to the story. While it was in essence a political struggle for control of social institutions, in practice it was manifest primarily as a "cultural revolution which transformed cultural codes and structures of thought, expectations, and practices."[20] That is to say that while the secular activists' aims were essentially political, their strategy was cultural. They strived to transform the popular conception of science as compatible with theism (indeed, at the service of theism) to one where these were mutually exclusive forms of knowledge, one true and based in reality, and one false and based in myth and superstition. Religion was represented as an impediment to true knowledge and an obstacle to scientific progress. These secular activists thus perpetuated a myth of a historical conflict between science and religion, which is less a historical reality than an ideological frame promoted by late-Victorian academics, not only in America but, as seen in the opening chapter, by defenders of evolutionary theory in Britain.[21] Smith suggests that promoting the conflict myth was an ideological strategy of late-nineteenth-century activist secularizers. It was designed to disguise a political struggle for status and institutional control between identifiable social groups as an inherent logical warfare between religion and science. The secularizing knowledge elites thus fostered the conflict thesis as a strategy to displace the authority of Protestantism and advance their own position as new cultural authorities.

Smith turns to Pierre Bourdieu for theoretical support. Bourdieu's work on knowledge production and the intellectual field captures the idea behind Smith's thesis of a secular revolution, and also my own thesis regarding the New Atheists' ideological legitimation of scientific authority, which is also the advancement of their own authority. Bourdieu claims that academic activity is also political activity:

> The theories, methods, and concepts that appear as simple contributions to the progress of science are *also* always 'political' maneuvers that attempt to establish, restore, reinforce, protect, or reverse a determined structure of relations of symbolic domination.[22]

Far from neutral or objective, Bourdieu argues that academic and scientific discourse is inseparable from structures of domination. While he describes these structures as "symbolic," there is a material consequence of such domination, since the group whose discourse is dominant enjoys a privileged institutional position. Symbolic domination, then, translates into material benefit and enhanced social standing. Bourdieu points out this relationship when he describes intellectual activity as a strategy for gaining power:

> Intellectual, artistic, or scientific stances are also always unconscious or semi-conscious *strategies* in a game where the stakes are the conquest of cultural legitimation or in other terms for the monopoly of the legitimate production, reproduction, and manipulation of symbolic goods and the correlative legitimating power.[23]

The group that holds a monopoly on the legitimate production of symbolic goods holds a "legitimating power" that is akin to the "cultural authority" sought by the activists in the secular revolution described by Smith.

The New Atheists' goal is precisely the same as that of the secular revolutionaries: advancing their own cultural authority by advancing a legitimate form of knowledge (science) against a pernicious false one (religion). The difference is that while the nineteenth-century activists were engaged in a "revolution" to the extent that they sought to overthrow an established authority, the New Atheism is a defense of an existing authority. The secular revolution in the intellectual sphere was complete long ago. Outside of some self-contained spheres of scholars at religious institutions engaged in defending certain pseudoscientific doctrines (intelligent design, for example), religion today holds no claim to authority in the academic world. But as Bourdieu says in the quote above, science as political activity is about not only reversing structures and relations of symbolic domination, but also reinforcing and protecting already established structures. For the New Atheism this means defending the cultural authority of science in the public sphere, not only against religion but also against social science, which it equates with the advancement of relativism, and thus considers a threat to science's claim to exclusive authority in the production of knowledge.

The New Atheism, then, fights against a confluence of challenges to an *already established cultural authority*. These challenges come from religion but also another secular challenger within the intellectual sphere itself that presents an alternative to, and critique of, sociobiological understandings of the world of humans. The response to this latter challenge has been to make an even stronger claim to authority and to counterattack this rival form of secular knowledge with the ideology of scientism. The social sciences are the major alternative to normative authority that the New Atheists consider themselves in competition with. They therefore attempt to undermine that normative authority by undermining the status of social science as a whole, declaring it a bastion of relativism and proposing a true social science of sociobiology to replace it. Today this new social science goes by the name of evolutionary psychology, an attempt to gain distance from the stigmatized term "sociobiology." This is another instance where the New Atheism has mirrored Christian fundamentalism, which made a similar move for legitimacy by replacing "creationism" with "intelligent design theory."

It would be unfair to suggest that the New Atheists are motivated only by a desire for the material gain to be derived from the cultural authority of science. They are clearly motivated also by a very sincere belief in the ideals of the Enlightenment (this was particularly true for Hitchens, who did not himself stand to gain from an advanced standing for scientific experts, and argued that it is not science per se but more precisely reason that should guide us). Smith notes that the American knowledge elites responsible for the secular revolution were heavily influenced by the Enlightenment and the idea that scientific experts will lead the advance of civilization.[24] The New Atheists are influenced by precisely the same ideas.

Dawkins more than anyone else associated with the New Atheism fits into Smith's narrative of the secular revolution, being an evolutionary biologist, the branch of science most significant to the secularization of the academic sphere in the nineteenth century. Dawkins is ever mindful of this history and positions himself as heir to Huxley's position as chief public defender of Darwinism. He is himself a product of the emancipation of science from church control, and he takes up the responsibility to defend this reversal in status and authority. The major difference between the New Atheism and the movement Smith describes is that the intellectuals in his account were critics of their societies and often called the very social order and political structure into question. He notes that historically that has been true of intellectuals, who have generally played the role of social critics. The New Atheism is different in that is actually defends a social order that it identifies with—liberal capitalism, a social system friendly to scientific and technological innovation—against others who they perceive to be seeking a revolutionary transformation in that order. These are religious fundamentalists and radical postmodernists, who seek to undermine the authority of science and its claim to absolute truth, and thereby undermine the hegemonic status that grants it its legitimate power.

In New Atheist discourse this is represented as essentially the reversal of the secular revolution Smith describes, with an established scientific order perceived to be facing an insurgency by intellectual revolutionaries who contest its symbolic domination and cultural authority by challenging its monopoly on the production of knowledge. The New Atheism is a movement to reinforce this established order through ideological action and public engagement. It appears not just in the writings of public intellectuals but in an emerging and growing social movement, and its particular goals, strategies, and ideological premises have brought out tensions within the movement that have persisted since the birth of the NSS. The movement's radical change in direction toward cultural and universalizing aspirations that came with the rise of the New Atheism lasted only a short while. Old divisions have arisen and are giving shape to new forms of discourse and new subgroups that directly challenge the dominance of the New Atheism and propel the movement in new directions. To understand these processes we require a framework by which to analyze the development of the movement.

Atheism and Identity: The New Structure of the Secular Movement

The history of the secular movement since the time of Campbell's study is marked by a shift toward identity politics that began in the 1960s, which was led by American Atheists, a group founded by Madalyn Murray O'Hair in 1963 in the wake of her constitutional challenge to religious instruction in public schools.[25] At its inception American Atheists was concerned with church–state separation and protection of atheists from discrimination in a widely theistic society; to this day it is "dedicated to working for the civil rights of atheists, promoting separation of state and church, and providing information about atheism"[26] and thus is still guided by conspicuously political goals. American Atheists was a product of its time, framing its discourse and activism within the narrative of the emerging civil rights movement in representing atheists as another persecuted minority that required legal protection. It was the first organization to explicitly advance the interests of atheists and atheism, which had been implicit in earlier organizations defined by secularism, rationalism, and humanism. It was therefore the true beginning of a movement for atheism in the contemporary sense, with activism largely framed by minority discourse, and a clear entry into the political sphere.

The founding of American Atheists was a decisive turn in a new direction from the movement for secularization as it had existed previously, which was grounded in ideological atheism and the universalization of the authority of secular science. It introduced a new tension within the movement between its totalizing tendencies and a strategic approach based on minority discourse, while maintaining the basic secularist goal of functional differentiation of religious (private) and political (public) spheres. Other secular organizations have adopted similar political goals, particularly with respect to minority identity. The Secular Coalition for America says that its mission is "to increase the visibility of and respect for nontheistic viewpoints in the United States, and to protect and strengthen the secular character of our government as the best guarantee of freedom for all."[27] The Freedom From Religion Foundation, an American secularist group founded in 1976, aims "to promote the constitutional principle of separation of state and church, and to educate the public on matters relating to nontheism."[28] The former, explicitly political goal involves lobbying efforts and lawsuits against government agencies and public institutions. The secular movement in its recent history has had clear political goals and has essentially acted as a movement for secularism as differentiation (i.e., the first subthesis) and to promote the civil rights of atheists, who in their view constitute a marginalized and even oppressed segment of American society.

Cimino and Smith consider the adoption of minority discourse and an "outsider" status by atheist groups a strategy akin to that of American evangelicals.[29] They draw on Christian Smith's study of evangelicals and his explanation of the persistence and strength of religiosity in America using his "subcultural identity theory."[30] Smith begins with the premise that groups construct collective identities by drawing symbolic boundaries between themselves and outgroups.[31] This importance of boundaries and distinction to what Smith calls "subcultures" is equally recognized in social movement theory, where the construction and maintenance of boundaries is considered essential to collective identity construction. For instance, Taylor and Whittier argue that the first and most important factor in collective identity construction is the establishment of "social, political, economic, and cultural boundaries [that] accentuate the differences between [the dominant group] and minority populations."[32] Smith further argues that evangelicalism

is strong not because it is shielded against, but because it is—or at least perceives itself to be—embattled with forces that seem to oppose or threaten it. Indeed, evangelicalism, we suggest, *thrives* on distinction, engagement, tension, conflict, and threat. Without these, evangelicalism would lose its identity and purpose and grow languid and aimless.[33]

The symbolic boundaries that mark insiders and outsiders, and that construct a perception of threat from outside, are essential to identity construction and the strength of the bonds that unite the in-group. Subcultures or movements, in this view, will purposefully maintain a tension with society to strengthen and reinforce their worldview.[34]

Cimino and Smith apply the same perspective to the case of the secular movement, which they suggest actually constitutes a subculture more so than a political movement.[35] In later work they came to regard it fully as a cultural movement.[36] They found that

secular humanists and atheists have assumed a position in American society that stresses maintaining boundaries and reinforcing group identity in the face of a larger external threat. That is, like evangelicals, secular humanists and atheists feel "embattled" by a persistently religious society.[37]

This perception of being "embattled," and even persecuted (particularly in the United States), has strengthened the movement, and the authors note the parallels to Smith's study of evangelicals. For each of these groups, increasing tensions and oppositions with the other has had a "tonic" effect on their own identity.[38] It has always been the case that the secular movement has grown in response to tensions with its adversary. In his review of the history of the NSS, Campbell notes that from the very beginning it was clear that clerical opposition was the greatest stimulus to growth of the movement.[39]

Groups of evangelicals and secularists, according to this theory, have each become stronger because of the threat they perceive from each other. For each group the source of the greatest perceived threat is in fact the "tonic" that gives them strength. The early modern science–religion dialectic outlined by Buckley[40] survives today in this form: while ostensibly dichotomous, these groups rely heavily on each other, and indeed their self-definitions come in good measure from their interactions. The New Atheism is a logical outcome of this dialectic. It is one side of a coin, with religious fundamentalism on the other—these groups each perceive themselves to be competing for followers to their vision of truth. John Gray writes that for Christianity, as opposed to polytheism, religion is a matter of true belief and that "the long-delayed consequence of Christian faith was an idolatry of truth that found its most complete expression in atheism."[41] The New Atheism is just such an expression, advancing a totalizing ideology and argument for authority not only in public advocacy but through the structure of social movement organizations.

The rise of the New Atheism within the secular movement challenged the political-minority approach that had dominated the movement for decades. For the New Atheists, minority discourse and identity politics are a tacit admission that secularization as a project of cultural universalization has failed and they want to return to the secular revolution and extend it outside the academy and to all of society. Dawkins, Harris, and Hitchens all frequently noted that there are far more unbelievers than anyone realizes and their numbers are growing. Dawkins has announced on many occasions, in his writings and on Twitter, that religion is in its "death throes," heralding an imminent mass cultural conversion to scientific atheism. Opposed to the strategy of retreating from the revolutionary cultural ambitions by adopting a minority identity, New Atheists insist that atheists are the emerging mainstream. They do not want atheists to find a place within an existing socio-cultural structure, but a revolutionary transformation in that structure, which they believe is already in process and needs to be protected and reinforced. The New Atheism's stunning publishing successes and public visibility granted a great deal of legitimacy to their "cultural package"[42]—or the ideology and identity they promote—which came to dominate movement discourse for a brief period. But soon old tensions arose, and the emphasis returned to minority discourse, as the movement made a conscious effort to mimic the strategies of the LGBT movement, with which it closely identifies.

Analyzing the New Atheism as a social movement is complicated by the fact that it has arisen within an already existing movement. It is a movement subgroup that intersects with ideologies, organizations, and grassroots activists under the broad umbrella of the secular movement that differ from it in significant ways. These differences include disagreements over tactics and strategy, which point to more fundamental differences in the ultimate goals and purposes of the movement and the beliefs and political ideologies that inform them. But at the same time they also overlap and cooperate in a number of ways, so that analyzing the movement is necessarily a process of analyzing a number of ideological and organizational vectors in states of tension that intersect in some general points of common concern—namely, opposition to religious influence in public life. I believe that it is possible, however, to identify various distinctions regarding goals, strategies, and ideology that compel us to recognize at least three subgroups as relatively distinct elements within the secular movement: secular humanists, atheists, and libertarian rationalists. My primary task is to understand the phenomenon of the New Atheism, so I will emphasize this ideological subset of the movement in my analysis, but this phenomenon can only be understood in relation to other groups that oppose it in some important ways.

The New Atheism emerged within the structure of existing organizations, such as the Council for Secular Humanism; its parent organization, the Center for Inquiry; and Atheist Alliance International. While I will refer to other organizations in this analysis, I concentrate on these because they are the organizations the New Atheists have been most active in. Table 4.1 lists some major organizations that make up the secular movement. There are many more, but these are the ones that are specifically addressed in this work. Some receive much more attention

Table 4.1 Major Movement Organizations

Atheist	Secularist	Humanist	Rationalist
Atheist Alliance International	Freedom From Religion Foundation (U.S.)	American Humanist Association	Center for Inquiry (U.S.)
Atheist Alliance of America	Secular Student Alliance (U.S.)	Humanist Canada	Centre for Inquiry Canada
American Atheists	Canadian Secular Alliance		Richard Dawkins Foundation (International)
Military Association of Atheists and Freethinkers (U.S.)	Secular Coalition for America		

than others. For example, the Center for Inquiry is a major focus of this book, while Humanist Canada is included in the table because it was a co-organizer of an Atheist Alliance International convention where I conducted some research, though the organization itself was not a target of my research. The organizations are divided in the table according to their major focus: atheism, secularism, humanism, or rationalism. Note that these categories are not rigid and there is much overlap. In some cases an organization may be nominally in one category but more properly belongs in another. The most obvious case is the Council for Secular Humanism, a division of the Center for Inquiry, which is ostensibly a humanist organization but today might be more accurately described as advocating a worldview of atheistic individualism. Of course, this may be considered a kind of humanistic philosophy, but the Council for Secular Humanism is now much more an organization interested in promoting political libertarianism than humanistic ethics, which was the concern of its founder, Paul Kurtz. This shift in direction from Kurtz's vision of secular humanism toward radical individualism and aggressive atheism is an important aspect of the story of the movement that unfolds in the following chapters.

The secular movement since the 1960s has addressed one element of the secularization thesis, while the New Atheism addresses the other. These two subtheses posit that secularization is a process characterized by (1) the differentiation of religious and secular spheres and the concomitant distinction between private and public dimensions of life and

(2) a general decline in religious belief and practice.[43] In its emphasis on church–state separation (in recent years manifest most conspicuously in legal battles regarding creationism vs. evolution in public education), civil liberties, and protection for atheists from discrimination, the secular movement has traditionally addressed the first subthesis through instrumental political action that can take the form of lobbying government, organized protests and demonstrations, and lawsuits.[44]

The New Atheists' effort to convince others of the superiority of their particular system of belief places attention on the second secularization subthesis (encouraging the abandonment of religious belief) and exhibits greater concern with cultural beliefs and values than politics (the first secularization subthesis, differentiation of public/secular and private/religious spheres, is more clearly a political process). They therefore eschew instrumental legal and public political pursuits and focus attention on the second secularization subthesis. Toward this end, they pursue a goal of broad cultural transformation, arguing that religion cannot be simply pushed to the private sphere, but rather, religious beliefs must be destroyed and replaced with scientific rationality in the name of progress. We can thus distinguish the New Atheism from the broader secular movement, as the former is primarily a *cultural* movement while the latter is a *political* movement.

I have already alluded to this distinction, but understanding its relationship to movement dynamics and ideologies requires greater analytical precision. I draw primarily on Alberto Melucci's pioneering work on contemporary movements that direct action outside the formal political system and adopt "cultural" goals like collectively constructing identity, transforming representations of cultural groups and minorities, and challenging dominant values.[45] The "new" social movements in question— primarily identity-based ones such as the women's movement and the gay rights movement—involved actors sharing a common identity but no common structural location.[46] Melucci argued that the locus of social conflict has shifted from class to questions of meaning and identity, and that state-centered approaches could not sufficiently account for the distinctly nonpolitical goals and targets of emerging forms of collective action. These new movements did not express themselves through political action but rather "raised cultural challenges to the dominant language."[47]

Melucci defines the political (in relation to social movements) narrowly as interaction between actors within the formal political system of governance and state authority. Much action in cultural and identity-based movements is not "political" in this sense, even if it clearly has political implications in a more expansive understanding of the concept, since the social and cultural problems addressed by this action cannot be resolved at the level of the state. But groups with no clear political goals (i.e., influencing government authorities) can be considered social movement actors on the basis of strictly cultural goals, such as promoting a particular idea or worldview. Perhaps most significantly, movements can transform cultural representations and social norms in terms of how groups see themselves and how they are seen by others.[48] A signature example is the gay rights movement, which succeeded in bringing about cultural transformation by constructing and promoting identity and challenging conventional assumptions and biases *outside* of the formal political system by addressing homophobia in society. Successful movement outcomes are therefore not limited to legislative and policy changes achieved through direct interaction with the state; rather, cultural impacts on their own can be considered successful outcomes, regardless of whether they result in state action, and identity may be a worthwhile goal in itself.[49]

I will refer to these identity- and ideology-based movements as "cultural" movements, while I understand "political" movements as those that engage in action within the formal political system that is directed toward state authorities (following Melucci's formulation of the political). I do not mean to make a rigid distinction between cultural and political spheres of social life and action, but rather these terms distinguish different types of social movement goals and activity for analytical purposes. I thus offer the following definitions:

- *Political movements involve instrumental action aimed at the state with the goal of legislative and policy change.*
- *Cultural movements involve constructing and defending shared identities, as well as ideological action aimed at society with the goal of transforming beliefs and values.*

I distinguish these two types of movements in relation to Melucci's model of the three dimensions of movement activity that together make up its "action system," with collective identity emerging from the process of negotiating tensions regarding orientation to this system.[50] A collective actor, then, is defined in terms of a common orientation to an action system, which includes three elements: the desired goals of the action (ends), the strategies by which they might be realized (means), and the

Table 4.2 Characteristics of Political and Cultural Movements

	Political Movements	Cultural Movements
General Orientation	formal and restrictive	informal and expansive
Goals (Ends)	legal and policy change	change values and beliefs
Strategy (Means)	instrumental action	ideological action
Target (Field)	state	civil society

environment or field within which the action is carried out, and where and to whom it is directed (i.e., the target of the action). Table 4.2 outlines a distinction between general orientations to the action system in political and cultural movements. Political movements are more formal and restrictive in their approach: their goals involve specific legal and policy changes, they take an instrumental approach to realizing these goals, and the target of action is the state, with action aimed within the formal political system. Negotiation of the action system within a political movement will involve different approaches to these specific dimensions of the action system—that is, differences in terms of what specific laws or policies should be instituted or challenged, what type of instrumental action is required (e.g., a protest, a lawsuit), and what specific state authorities should be targeted—but they will concur in terms of the general political orientation. Cultural movements, meanwhile, are more informal and expansive: their goals involve changing norms, values, and beliefs in society in general, and their means of doing so involve ideological action through public advocacy and promotion (e.g., protests, books, videos, websites). Again, while there will be debate on specifics, a cultural movement will agree on the general orientation to the action system. In the event that a failure occurs in the process of negotiating tensions between different elements of the action system, Melucci argues, the construction of the collective actor also fails, and action becomes impossible. In the worst case the movement may fragment or break down entirely.

This perspective requires a more expansive definition of social movements than those of the political process and mobilization school. David Snow provides one, writing that social movements are

> collectivities acting with some degree of organization and continuity outside of institutional or organizational channels for the purpose of challenging or defending extant authority, whether it is

institutionally or culturally based, in the group, organization, society, culture, or world order of which they are a part.[51]

The key concept here is *authority*—both cultural and political movements involve challenges to authority, whether institutionalized (e.g., in the state) or based in dominant cultural norms, beliefs, and values. Armstrong and Bernstein argue that we need such an expansive definition because domination is not organized around one source of power (i.e., the state), but rather there are multiple sources of power in society, both material and symbolic.[52] In this view, collective actors need not challenge the state to be considered a social movement; rather, sustained challenges to cultural systems of oppression and authority can be understood as movement activity.[53] These authors propose a "multi-institutional politics" approach that recognizes both political and cultural dimensions of social movements that challenge power and authority from multiple sources. They thus support Melucci's critique of state-centered models and his expanded framework for analyzing movements with nonpolitical goals and targets.

I want to argue that the secular movement, and more specifically the New Atheism, can be understood within this framework. The New Atheism was a novel development within the secular movement, which had focused on the political goals of secularism and civil rights for atheists before the Four Horsemen came forward with a radical program of public attacks on religion and a substitute worldview defined by scientism. The New Atheism challenges the moral authority of religion by attacking its intellectual authority, arguing for the epistemic superiority of science over "religious" forms of knowledge. The conflict between groups advocating for scientific rationality as a form of authority on the one hand and those advocating for religious and traditional authority on the other is a political conflict that is being played out in the cultural arena as a dispute over "true" knowledge and values. The New Atheism positions its ideology of scientism as an alternative to religion, which is represented as a cultural system of oppression and authority. It might therefore be considered a social movement, following the definitions of Melucci, Snow, and Armstrong and Bernstein. More precisely, it is a cultural movement that targets civil society, with the goal of changing beliefs and values, and uses a strategy of ideological action that takes the form of public advocacy and science education. It is thus an example of the type of movement that challenges dominant cultural "codes" rather than state authorities, institutions, or policies.[54]

The shift in focus from instrumental legal-political action to general cultural transformation that came with the influence of the New Atheism can be understood in terms of Melucci's notion of a "latency" period that characterizes the emergence of some new social movements.[55] This is the period before a movement becomes visible or highly organized and politically active, defined by the development of ideology and collective identity. An example of this is Christian Smith's study of the Latin American liberation theology movement, which he argues is different from traditional social movements (e.g., labor) in that "its first task and goal was the institutionalization of novel symbolic and ideological forms in a relatively inhospitable, self-reproducing institutional structure,"[56] the institutional structure referred to here being the Catholic Church. In this phase of movement emergence, dialogue is directed internally, with the priorities being ideological development and finding a structural location within which the movement can grow. In the liberation theology movement, this location was the church, an obviously natural development given its origins.

The parallels between the liberation theology and New Atheist movements in their latency phase are evident in Smith's description of the initial task of the former:

> The first analytic problem faced by the liberation theology activists . . . was not the mobilization of a powerless, excluded group for noninstitutionalized methods of political action. Rather, the first problem was essentially that of organizational takeover and validation of a new worldview. The original problem was not how, as excluded ones, to constrain the state, but how to develop, diffuse, and institutionalize a new form of consciousness in the Church.[57]

Similarly, the New Atheism had to first succeed as a movement-within-a-movement, promoting its own specific ideology within the established institutional framework. It found a home within secularist organizations such as the Center for Inquiry and Atheist Alliance International. These organizations, of course, were not exactly hostile to this new movement, but the rise of the New Atheism was also not uniformly welcomed, and there was considerable debate within the pages of *Free Inquiry* (the Center for Inquiry's flagship periodical) regarding its merits and potential impacts on the movement. Center for Inquiry founder and former chair Paul Kurtz was critical of the New Atheists' "militant" approach, which he felt undermined the goal of promoting humanist ethics that constituted his vision for the organization.[58] Nonetheless, the New Atheists' phenomenal publishing successes, intellectual capital, and celebrity status, as well as the public debate they initiated, empowered and mobilized atheists and spurned a period of tremendous growth and activity.[59] This influence allowed them to establish scientific atheism and the aggressive confrontation of religious truth with the alternative vision of scientism as the dominant ideology within the secular movement.

Figure 4.1 presents a model of movement development. It begins with the latency phase, characterized by the development of ideology and collective identity construction. The result of this period was the establishment of the New Atheism as the dominant discourse within the movement and a new emphasis on its cultural goal (relating to the first secularization subthesis) of disseminating the scientific atheist worldview. However, this did not completely erase the movement's more traditional political goals (relating to the second secularization subthesis) of

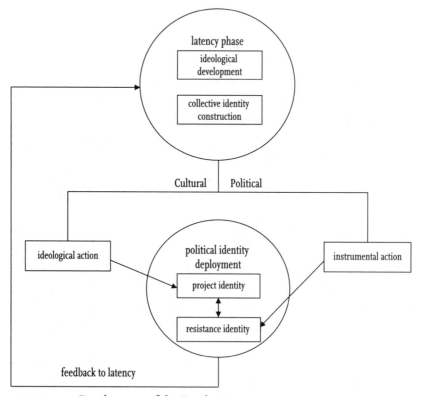

FIGURE 4.1 Development of the Secular Movement

functional differentiation of religious and public spheres, and civil rights for atheists, even if this goal received less attention after the success of the New Atheism made the movement more ambitious in believing broad cultural transformation was possible. The result of this latency period was a division of the movement into two streams, represented in Figure 4.1 as a division in terms of cultural and political goals.

These two streams are a product of different responses to the perceived failure of secularization: one responds by more aggressively attacking religion and fighting for cultural transformation, while the other seeks to carve out a niche within that culture using instrumental legal-political strategies aimed at protecting civil rights, as well as maintaining established political secularism. The two responses are represented in Figure 4.1 as strategies based on ideological action and instrumental action, respectively. Relating these responses to the three dimensions of a movement's action system (represented in Table 4.2), the cultural side of the movement employs the ideological strategy of public advocacy, the target of which is civil society, toward the goal of ideological validation and universalization. For the cultural element of the secular movement, ideological action is aimed primarily at its own validation rather than toward other instrumental purposes. This can cross over into political goals, which the New Atheism has done in also embracing the goal of functional secularism, but the more substantive goal of transforming beliefs and values is the heart of this movement. The political side of the movement, meanwhile, employs instrumental strategies (e.g., protests, rallies, petitions, legal action) aimed at the state with the primary goal of maintaining established functional secularism. There are therefore two distinct orientations with respect to the action system within the secular movement, which are represented by its cultural and political dimensions.

While the goal of the New Atheism may be primarily a cultural one, in practice it intersects with more political and instrumental dimensions of the secular movement. This should be expected given that cultural and political goals are not mutually exclusive or isolatable categories. These categories are ideal-types that do not correspond absolutely to any particular movement, and identity and cultural processes are always involved to some extent in strategy, interest, and politics.[60] While the creation of a collective identity is a significant cultural impact in its own right, then, it may also contribute to political goals. Mary Bernstein argues that collective identity construction may be just an initial phase of movement activity, and once established identity is often "deployed" as a strategy for instrumental political purposes.[61] In Bernstein's "political identity" model, identity is not strictly a cultural matter or a tool for recruitment, but rather "expressions of identity can be deployed at the collective level as a political strategy, which can be aimed at cultural and/or instrumental political goals."[62] Both the "cultural" and "political" dimensions of the secular movement deploy a political identity, but disputes concerning the nature of this identity, and the goals toward which it is deployed, reveal deep divisions.

Bernstein's concept of "political identity" is a general approach to understanding the strategic deployment of identity toward particular ends. I add two more specific categories of political identity, which are represented in Figure 4.1 as distinct categories within the sphere of political identity strategy. These are "resistance identity" and "project identity," concepts drawn from Manuel Castells' work on contemporary or "new" social movements (i.e., identity-based movements) that emerge in the information age.[63] Castells' categories of identity can be understood as distinct political identity strategies that reflect different kinds of movements or movement goals. Resistance identity is

> generated by those actors who are in positions/conditions devalued and/or stigmatized by the logic of domination, thus building trenches of resistance and survival on the basis of principles different from, or opposed to, those permeating the institutions of society.[64]

Identities for resistance emphasize the formation of communities and forms of collective resistance against oppression. Project identity is "when social actors, on the basis of whatever cultural materials are available to them, build a new identity that redefines their position in society and, by so doing, seek the transformation of overall social structure."[65]

One example Castells gives to illustrate the difference is when feminism moved from resistance against oppression and protecting women's rights to challenging patriarchy, and thus the entire structure of society. This was in effect a transition from a resistance identity to a project identity, or from defending a marginalized group's place within society to challenging the structure of the society that produces this marginalization. The other major example Castells discusses is religious fundamentalism and the evangelistic drive to convert the entire world to a particular faith, which involves the construction (and deployment, in Bernstein's terms) of a collective identity "expanding toward the transformation of society as the prolongation of this project of identity."[66] This second example obviously resembles the New Atheist movement and the desire to eliminate supernaturalism and convert the world to scientism. The New Atheism, then, is in effect a project identity that mirrors the Christian Right in some respects, while providing its own alternative vision of the new science-based society it wants to build.

Identity deployment as movement strategy is not necessarily the same thing as identity politics, which Teemu Taira defines in the context of the New Atheism as "empowering strategies and procedures which are based on differentiating a group from others on the basis of their socially constructed identity."[67] This kind of identity politics involves self-representation as a marginalized or oppressed minority, and this is precisely where the matter becomes contentious in the case of the secular movement. The New Atheism favors a goal of cultural universalism and therefore represents atheism as the emergent mainstream position, as opposed to atheists as a group that must be differentiated from the rest of society. Their approach is to emphasize how atheism is a "positive" worldview and that atheists are good, moral people. Hence, the "political identity" the New Atheists construct is not based on minority status but rather the view that atheists are representative of an emerging cultural transformation that will reach all sectors of society—indeed, this is demanded and expected by the evolutionistic ideology of progress they ascribe to. Political identity in this approach is a strategy for changing the dominant culture's perception of atheism, which in turn is a step toward ideological validation, which is also an effort to persuade others to adopt their ideological perspective.

The New Atheism therefore involves construction of a project identity, which is a political identity strategy aimed at broad cultural transformation. However, another group within the movement that takes a more political approach favors identity politics as a strategy aimed at improving the status of atheists within society, with the idea being that gaining recognition as an excluded minority is a pathway to political influence, mirroring the strategies and demands of the LGBT and civil rights movements. The group within the movement that emphasizes the political goals of combating oppression of atheists and resisting organized religion's infiltration of the political system—that is, the movement as it was structured before the New Atheism emerged—therefore adopts an identity of resistance that seeks to strengthen the place of nonbelievers within society's institutions rather than seeking a cultural transformation.

To New Atheists who desire universalization of the scientific atheist worldview, the engagement in identity politics necessarily condemns atheists to the fringes, a permanent minority rather than the presumptive heir to hegemonic authority. Harris and Hitchens have been vocal critics of this strategy. Harris objects even to the use of the term "atheist" to describe their movement, as he feels that theirs should be the default position, and that it is "supernaturalists" who require a term to denote their deviation from it. Hitchens frequently expressed his opinion that self-representation as an oppressed minority is both a tactical error and a misrepresentation of the trend of history, which points to secularization. Identity and the issue of minority discourse, then, are where the cultural and political dimensions of the movement clash.

Even among those who are not opposed to engaging in identity politics, there are tensions regarding what shape it should take. This tension is expressed in the ongoing debate regarding strategies of "confrontation" versus "accommodation," with advocates of the former seeking to mark clear lines of difference between themselves and religious groups and individuals, and the latter willing to overlook differences on the question of God in order to cooperate with those who share the ultimate goals of secularism, the emancipation of science from religious and political spheres, and basic social justice concerns. I will argue that this tension exists primarily between atheists and secular humanists and results from the influence of the scientific and humanistic types of atheism that were discussed in Chapter 1.

It is not only atheists and secular humanists who are sometimes at odds, since the matter is complicated by the rise of another group in its latent phase: the libertarian rationalists. They embrace the New Atheism's confrontational stance as well as an emphasis on difference rather than assimilation when it comes to identity construction. Their goals, however, are political rather than cultural: they supplant the New Atheism's goal of ideological universalization with the political goal of secularism and supplant the New Atheism's liberalism with radical individualism and economic libertarianism. These libertarians appear at least as concerned with separation of economy and state as they are with separation of church and state. The New Atheist movement, then, is caught between two subgroups in the secular movement it resides in: secular humanists who seek assimilation and cooperation with groups sharing similar basic values, and libertarian rationalists who are more interested in individual and economic liberty than promoting the growth of scientific atheism (though they do share most of the key features of that ideology). There is a further tension within the category of atheists between New Atheists and their cultural goal of ideological universalization, and a grassroots movement to frame atheism as a political movement for social justice. How tensions between these groups can be resolved, or at least managed, is the major question facing the secular movement in the coming years.

To understand the implications of these developments we should return to Melucci's model. For Melucci, the collective is socially constructed through negotiation of the action system, which includes goals, strategies, and the target of action (as outlined in Table 4.2). That is, collective identity for a social movement actor is the expression of a negotiated construction of the action system. He writes, "Collective identity takes the form of a field containing a system of vectors in tension."[68] I would alternatively say that collective identity is a dynamic field of tensions relating to the action system. In situations of crisis or intense conflict these tensions may become too strong to negotiate a common orientation to the action system, which means that the collective actor cannot define itself or its purposes, and must restructure its action according to new orientations. This is the current situation of the secular movement, where a complex field of mutual tensions with respect to the action system involving three major groups is threatening a failure in collective identity construction. I refer to these groups as New Atheists, secular humanists, and libertarian rationalists. I do not want to suggest that individuals within the movement can be clearly distinguished along these lines, but I do argue that these are the three major ideological groupings in the movement, and that leaders in particular can be positioned more or less within these categories, with overlap in some cases.

Table 4.3 outlines the defining characteristics of these three groups, including the type of atheism and their goals and strategies. It also includes the nature of the political identity they work to construct, which is categorized according to either "deconstructive" or "category-supportive" approaches,[69] or alternatively "distinction" and "assimilation."[70] Finally, the groups are categorized in terms of their politics and their basic ideological grounding, which I will argue is the ultimate source of the divisions— manifest in identity and strategy debates—that are compelling a restructuring of the action system and threaten a failure or breakdown of the movement. Armstrong and Bernstein argue that once we recognize that

Table 4.3 Characteristics of Movement Subgroups

	Atheists	Secular Humanists	Libertarian Rationalists
Atheism Goals Strategy	scientific cultural ideological	scientific/humanistic cultural/political ideological/ instrumental	scientific political instrumental
Political Identity	category-supportive	deconstructive	category-supportive
Politics Ideology	liberal scientism	liberal secularism	libertarian individualism

not all movements target the state or seek entry into a single polity, questions about why actors make the decisions they do about targets, goals, and strategies—that is, orientation to the action system—become more interesting.[71] These questions are especially interesting for nonpolitical movements or those that combine political and cultural elements. In the case of the secular movement, I argue that the answer to these questions lies in ideology, which is the basic motivation for action and its structuring logic.

My analysis of the ideologies at work in the secular movement proceeds in two steps. In Melucci's model collective identity is the expression of a collectively negotiated orientation to the action system, including the three orders of orientations outlined in Table 4.2. This negotiation is informed by the motivating ideologies and tensions between the three major groups shaping movement dynamics. These tensions, manifest in the debates on identity, can be understood through debates on strategy, since strategy choices and debates are also statements about identity.[72] An analysis of strategy debates further reveals distinct underlying ideological motivations. My analytical approach is to begin with examining processes and projects of collective identity construction and then work backward to see what this reveals about orientation to the action system in terms of strategy and goals, which in turn allows us to identify the distinct ideological groupings that give rise to these different approaches.

Chapter 5 therefore deals with identity construction and movement strategy. It includes an analysis of current dynamics shaping movement development, and the possibility of a failure or breakdown, as groups united only by their lack of religious belief struggle to maintain cohesion in the face of deep divisions in their politics. I argue that the ideological tensions at the heart of the movement, represented in the distinct approaches to political identity and expressed in debates on strategy and minority discourse, are much more than simply a division between cultural and political approaches. The libertarian rationalists—the major element of what I call the atheist Right—make consensus even more difficult because they differ from both the New Atheists and secular humanists with respect to the action system and ideological grounding. The response to the atheist Right on the part of another emerging group of atheists expressing a desire to direct movement activity toward social justice introduces another layer of complexity.

These developments are driving another latency period, which is why Figure 4.1 is represented as a feedback loop. The new latency period, characterized by intense and diversifying ideological conflicts, may lead to restructuring or to movement failure or fragmentation. Many movements face the problem of "identity correspondence"—the alignment of individual and collective identities—particularly those where members cannot be expected to share an extant collective identity derived from being commonly situated structurally.[73] Atheists share no common structural location and are united only by ideology, so the movement is particularly vulnerable to fission produced by ideological disparities, but the outcome of these processes remains unclear. However, the secular movement has dealt with these tensions since its beginning over a century and a half ago, and it will likely survive the recent developments, which for the most part are familiar and recurring forms of thought and action. The exception is the revelation of an atheist Right, an ideological group that was until recently latent and implicit within movement discourse but has since become more bold in making its claim to authority. The relationship between the cultural and political dimensions of the movement, the move to a minority political identity as major movement strategy, and the rise of the atheist Right are examined in the chapters that follow.

5

The Moral Minority

IN THE LATE 1970s, Christian political activist Jerry Falwell founded the Moral Majority, a lobby group whose name referred to his belief that the majority of Americans who were conservative Christians should speak up and demand that their values guide the political establishment. The secular movement, largely in response to the stigma associated with atheism in American culture and the prevailing identification of religiosity with morality that Falwell's group alluded to, is engaged in an effort to construct a representation of itself as a "moral minority." The individuals who make up this minority group are, according to a popular slogan, "good without God." Those promoting minority discourse argue that this new moral minority must "come out" and demand recognition, an end to discrimination, and a voice in the political sphere.

Transforming cultural representations and social norms in terms of how the group is seen can itself be a goal of social movements. But constructing collective identity is also a strategy that can be deployed in pursuit of very different goals. This is the case for the secular movement, which is struggling to define the nature of the identity that should be constructed because of a disagreement regarding goals and strategy. This chapter examines processes of collective identity construction within the movement, identifying two major elements: community building and self-representation as a moral minority. These processes are examined through the lens of some major instances of atheist activism, including the Coming Out Campaign, the Atheist Bus Campaign, and the Reason Rally.

Analysis of these campaigns and the debates surrounding them reveals a tension between those who deny that atheists are an oppressed minority and prefer to self-represent as the emerging mainstream (the New Atheists belong to this group, a position that makes sense given the cultural goal of universalism) and those who wish to move in a more political direction, constructing a "political identity"[1] in order to achieve minority recognition. This approach is expected to allow atheists to carve out a distinctive space for themselves in the cultural landscape and to grant them a stronger voice in public affairs. The tension regarding identity and atheists' relationship to society is further expressed in debates regarding strategies of "confrontation" of all forms of religion versus "accommodation" of religious groups that share certain basic values. This disagreement can be understood in terms of the fundamental ideological tension between atheism and humanism that has gripped the secular movement since its birth in the nineteenth century.

Coming Out

Alberto Melucci writes,

> a certain degree of emotional investment, which enables individuals to feel like part of a common unity, is required in the definition of collective identity. Collective identity is never entirely negotiable because participation in collective action is endowed with meaning but cannot be reduced to cost-benefit calculation and always mobilizes emotions as well.[2]

The "common unity" Melucci refers to is simply a more precisely stated version of "community," an essential ingredient of any collective definition of identity and approach to action. Mobilizing actors requires emotional investment in the cause and in the collective one is asked to be part of. For some movement participants, community and a sense of belonging are all they really want. But even for movements with instrumental goals, community is a crucial building block in the construction and later deployment of political identity.[3] Identity, then, can never be purely instrumental or strategic. There must be real emotional investment to mobilize participants to act, particularly in the case of "new" or identity-based movements where participants do not share a structural location and must do more "identity work" to form the bonds of community.[4]

The present analysis of collective identity therefore begins with community-building projects that address precisely the requirement of emotional investment in the definition and construction of identity. In the case of the secular movement, this emotional investment involves addressing alienation and the desire for belonging by emphasizing the potential for atheists to "come out" and find others like themselves with whom they can share their concerns and frustrations. Community-building efforts and other projects of identity construction are at the same time intended to counter the stigma against atheism (particularly in the United States) as an amoral, or immoral, worldview and, by extension, against atheists as people without morality. They thus reject the claim that morality is derived and maintained from religion and emphasize morality in representations of atheists. While intended to create the emotional investment that forms the bonds of community by appealing to atheists' desire for self-validation, they are also an important element of the movement's political identity strategy, which represents atheists specifically as an essentially good but socially marginalized or stigmatized minority.

Community building was the project of two of the largest and most significant single instances of activism in the recent history of the secular movement: the Godless Americans March on Washington on November 2, 2002, and the Reason Rally, also held in Washington, on March 24, 2012. The Godless Americans March was a protest, orchestrated by American Atheists, against the "increasing infringement of religion in governmental affairs."[5] The Reason Rally was sponsored by many of today's most prominent freethought organizations, including the Center for Inquiry and the Richard Dawkins Foundation for Reason and Science.[6] Both of these major events were aimed at the same purpose: bringing a hitherto unrecognized identity group into focus and mobilizing participants for an emerging social movement.

Commenting on the gay and lesbian movement, Suzanne Staggenborg observes that the construction of community and collective identity can be a goal in itself or a step toward more instrumental goals:

> In some instances, activists aim to empower constituents with a sense of collective identity and to create a shared community before they can engage in more instrumental action. In other instances, the goal is to transform the values, categories, and practices of mainstream culture rather than to win specific policy changes, and activists may focus on developing community and collective identity among gays and lesbians by emphasizing their uniqueness and differences from the mainstream culture.[7]

In the case of the secular movement, building community and a positive collective identity are goals in themselves for some; for others they are constructed strategically to be deployed toward instrumental ends. I will here examine some campaigns aimed at building community and identity and the ways in which this identity is being deployed by those with political goals.

The first instance of New Atheist activism was a community-building effort initiated by Dawkins through his foundation. It was called the Out Campaign and was officially announced by the foundation in July 2007.[8] The problem facing the movement, he argued, is that much of the atheist population regrettably remains "in the closet," and thus "a major part of our consciousness-raising effort should be aimed, not at converting the religious but encouraging the non-religious to admit it—to themselves, to their families, and to the world."[9] Exhorting atheists to "come out," then, was the purpose of the Out Campaign, and Dawkins noted that this involved an obvious comparison with the gay community.[10] Dawkins and his collaborators created a website and a campaign logo—a red "A"—that was printed on t-shirts and buttons to be worn by atheists to announce their beliefs and demonstrate to others that "they are not alone."[11]

The most visible and highly publicized community-building effort—or campaign of any kind for that matter—by organized atheists to date was the Atheist Bus Campaign, an excellent example of the scope and significance of the movement. It began in 2008 when Ariane Sherine, a comedian and writer for *The Guardian*, blogged about seeing buses in London carrying a Bible quotation and a link to a webpage that threatened eternal torment in hell for nonbelievers. Concerned about a message "advocating endless pain for atheists," Sherine proposed running an advertisement carrying the slogan, "There's probably no God. Now stop worrying and enjoy your life."[12] Encouraged by the overwhelming response to the idea on her blog, she partnered with the British Humanist Association, which solicited donations and raised £140,000, enough to buy advertisements on eight hundred buses in twenty-six cities and towns throughout the United Kingdom, which went up early in 2009.[13]

The success of the atheist bus campaign was a watershed moment for atheist activism. Hanne Stinson, a representative of the British Humanist Association, offered this rationale for the campaign:

> We all, whether we have religious or non-religious beliefs, have a
> right to be heard, and no one particular set of beliefs has any more

right to influence the public debate than any other. The message isn't aimed at people with religious beliefs—it's aimed at atheists and agnostics.[14]

In other words, the campaign was aimed at nonbelievers in order to tell them that they were not alone, to demonstrate that there is a community of others who share their point of view. Sherine articulated the same sentiment in an interview on the CBC Radio program *Q*:

> I think atheists, because we don't see each other very much, we don't get together, we don't have a community in the same way as religious groups do. You don't really know how many people feel this way [. . .] So it seems to be this kind of underground thing, and then you see all these thousands and thousands of atheists coming out going, you know, 'I'm so relieved that so many people feel the way I do.'[15]

Again, the ideas of community and "coming out" are conveyed here. The atheist bus was an effort toward constructing community and building recognition and legitimacy for the atheist identity, more so than an attempt at conversion to atheism.

The spectacular success of the atheist bus campaign in the United Kingdom inspired freethought groups elsewhere to participate, bringing the campaign to Canada (Toronto was the first city outside of the United Kingdom to adopt it), the United States, Ireland, Spain, Italy, Sweden, Finland, Germany, the Netherlands, Switzerland, New Zealand, and Croatia, where ads were removed after one day as a result of public complaints.[16] The Atheist Foundation of Australia launched a series of bus advertisements to coincide with the 2012 Global Atheist Convention in Melbourne, this time carrying a memorable quote from Woody Allen: "If God exists, I hope he has a good excuse."[17]

The organization of the bus campaign and the growth and development of the secular movement more generally were possible only because of the Internet. Coupled with the attention brought to atheism by the publishing success of the Four Horsemen, it constituted a "cultural opportunity"[18] for the emergence of a new identity group. Atheists have traditionally had little access to mass media, but the Internet allowed geographically dispersed atheists to communicate and organize, as in the case of the bus campaign. Today atheist groups make extensive use of blogs, discussion forums, podcasts, meetups, and so on as a way to build community. There is a social networking website, modeled after Facebook, called Atheist Nexus, which has just under one thousand groups engaged in the project of community building.[19] Given its transnational and geographically dispersed nature, the secular movement is of necessity largely an online community, with local groups often quite small.[20] The Internet adds a dimension of accessibility vastly greater than that offered by traditional print media, and it introduced the Center for Inquiry and other atheist groups to countless more potential members who were inspired to seek them out after the New Atheists made religion, science, and atheism matters of intense public debate.

While virtual communities are crucial to everyday involvement in atheism, periodic physical gatherings continue to serve the important function of affirmation of the collective as well as reinforcing ties that were forged online through face-to-face interaction. Beyond meetings of local chapters of freethought organizations, there are a number of annual conferences and conventions hosted by major organizations. The most significant of these has been the Atheist Alliance International's annual convention, which in 2007 featured the Four Horsemen, a moment that signaled the dawn of a new era in the secular movement. Melbourne, Australia, has become the site of the largest annual gathering of atheists in the world, hosting a Global Atheist Convention in 2010 that attracted over 2,500 people, with the 2012 iteration looking to build on that number. There are also a number of annual celebrations and rituals observed and practiced by many atheist groups. These include, for example, Darwin Day, held on Darwin's birth date of February 12 to celebrate science and humanity by recognizing his contribution to human knowledge.[21] Individuals and local groups are left to celebrate as they wish (normally this involves lectures, discussion, and parties), though the American Humanist Association's website does offer templates of e-cards that can be sent to family and friends to mark the occasion. Carl Sagan Day was created by the Center for Inquiry in 2009 and uses the occasion of Sagan's birthday, November 9, to "honor Carl Sagan and celebrate the beauty and wonder of the cosmos he so eloquently described."[22] The Center for Inquiry also created International Blasphemy Rights Day as an element of its broader Campaign for Free Expression.[23] Since 2009, it has been celebrated annually on September 30 to mark the anniversary of the publication of cartoons depicting Muhammad in the Danish newspaper *Jyllands-Posten* that led to rioting among offended Muslims in

2005.[24] It involves exhibiting explicitly blasphemous contemporary artworks in a celebration of freedom of speech.

Good Without God

To this point, I have examined two elements of the latency phase of social movement emergence: the development of ideology and validation of a worldview (covered in Chapter 4) and community building (the corollary of mobilization in political process theories). Closely related to the latter is the defining characteristic of the latency period: collective identity construction.[25] This involves basic identity-related self-examination, addressing the questions "Who are we?" and "How do we define ourselves?" In the political identity framework that I am employing, however, we must understand these questions and the way they are addressed in terms of their relationship to more instrumental questions like "What are our goals?" and "How do we achieve them?" The Out Campaign is both an exercise in community building and a project of collective identity construction. It is modeled after that of the gay and lesbian movement, which proved successful at bringing LGBT people "out of the closet" and into visible groups where they could feel not only like members of a community but also empowered rather than isolated and vulnerable.[26]

The efforts toward community building and constructing a positive image of atheists that we see in the bus campaign and the Out Campaign reflect the importance of morality in movement recruitment. Pinel and Swann argue that social movement participation is a kind of "self-verification,"[27] a confirmation of a particular conception of self through a collective identity that affirms and verifies it, a process that Snow and McAdam refer to as "identity seeking."[28] Jesse Smith's research on atheist groups in Colorado found that morality is an essential component of individual atheist identity.[29] More specifically, confirmation of the idea that belief in God is not necessary to be a moral person is important to atheists because a common charge against atheism is that it is morally bankrupt and leads to nihilism.[30] Smith also found that morality was central to these atheists' rejection of theism and that emerging atheists

> began to construct a cognitive and symbolic boundary between morality and religion, and asserted themselves as moral individuals against what they increasingly viewed as a false connection between being religious and being moral. They each in some way

observed—and criticized the idea—that people *need* religion to be moral and good.[31]

We should thus expect individual atheists to seek movements and embrace collective identities that verify this self-conception. Crucially, atheists have not advanced a coherent conception of morality on which they agree. That is, precisely what kind of morality they embrace is mostly left unstated, and indeed there is considerable debate within the movement regarding whether being an atheist involves adhering to particular ethical precepts (economic justice is one very contentious issue). What they clearly want to express, and what they can all agree on, is the idea that one can be "good without God"—that is, the idea that religion has no monopoly on morality—even if what exactly constitutes being good is unclear.

Dawkins evidently also recognized the importance of morality and thus initiated the "Non-Believers Giving Aid" campaign in an effort to combat negative stereotypes and construct a positive identity for atheists, particularly those who are just starting to realize that they are atheists and are looking for validation of their rejection of the presumed connection between religion and morality.[32] This is a disaster relief effort that distributes donations to nonreligious humanitarian aid organizations. Spearheaded by Dawkins' Foundation, it involves twenty-two participating organizations, including the Atheist Alliance International, the Freedom From Religion Foundation, and the British Humanist Association. The secular movement, then, provides moral validation for nonbelievers who seek it primarily by constructing a collective identity that emphasizes generosity and altruism.

The "Out" slogan and logo are now entrenched in movement discourse and have reappeared recently in other forms. In October 2010, the Freedom From Religion Foundation launched its "Out of the Closet" campaign. This was an effort to humanize atheists in the United States by demonstrating that "Freethinkers are your friends, neighbors, relatives, colleagues, the person who opens the door for you at your grocery store, a parent at your playground."[33] The foundation designed billboard advertisements that featured a photo of a local atheist along with a "freethought testimonial" that makes "an affirmative statement about being a freethinker"[34] and a short self-description. People were invited to design their own ads through the foundation's website, which provided a template and the opportunity to upload photos. The foundation then selected from among these user-created ads to create the actual billboards, leaving the rest up on the website. There are a number of similar campaigns, including one by the Centre for Inquiry Canada called "Good and Godless." It invites people to submit one-minute videos to the group's YouTube channel *Think Again! TV*, where they explain what they do for charities, nonprofits, or society, and ending with the statement, "That is why I am good without God."

The Out Campaign was Dawkins' first attempt at establishing atheism not just as an intellectual trend but also a social movement. Dawkins encourages the public expression of atheist pride, much in the vein of gay pride, noting that atheists are more numerous than people realize, particularly among the "educated elite."[35] The Out Campaign was thus designed for a practical purpose beyond community building: it was the beginning of a political project. Dawkins emphasized the numbers of "closeted" atheists because he believed that, should they "come out" and organize, they would constitute a powerful political bloc. He gives the example of Jewish influence on American politics to suggest what atheists might be capable of, since atheists are far greater in number, and he argues that atheists should represent themselves as a minority subjected to prejudice and discrimination, citing the example of George W. Bush's infamous declaration that atheists cannot be true patriots and should not even be considered American citizens because America is one nation under God.[36] He thus takes atheism in two directions simultaneously, arguing for cultural transformation (the universalization of the ideology of scientific atheism) while also deploying a political identity toward the instrumental goal of formal recognition by state authorities of atheists' minority status. This presumably would give atheists a stronger voice in legislative and policy decisions but would also undermine the cultural goal of ideological dominance. The development of a minority identity in the United States and elsewhere has been one of the major projects of the secular movement in recent years. Minority discourse in the secular movement is driven by morality and the notion that one can be "good without God."

The movement is evolving, of course, and has expanded its aims. New debates concerning goals and strategies have come with this. After atheists come out and begin constructing a positive, morality-based collective identity, some major questions emerge: What kind of status should they seek? What kind of influence should they exert, and who should be influenced? Do they want to effect broad social change or do they simply want to find their own niche within the existing social structure? Such questions are essential to any social movement (particularly identity-based movements), and in the case of atheism they have proven very contentious. There are some who seek to continue in the footsteps of the LGBT movement by following up on the coming-out and community-building phase—that is, the latency phase—with an effort to construct a minority identity that is recognized by authorities and the general public in order to first gain protection against discrimination, and then reach a step further and use this status to gain influence in the public sphere and over state authorities. We should understand this as an instrumental political identity strategy, with cultural effects of the movement only a step toward political goals.

Community building by the secular movement reached its zenith in the single largest and most significant instance of atheist collective action to date, the Reason Rally, billed as "the largest secular event in world history."[37] An estimated twenty thousand freethinkers[38] gathered at the National Mall in Washington on March 24, 2012, with the intent "to unify, energize, and embolden secular people nationwide, while dispelling the negative opinions held by so much of American society."[39] What was particularly striking about this event was that it signaled a decisive shift in emphasis in atheist discourse, with a lineup of speakers headlined by Dawkins moving away from discussing the moral character of atheists to focusing on the status of atheists in American society. David Silverman, president of American Atheists, declared: "We are here to deliver a message to America. We are here and we will never be silent again."[40] The "come out" message was repeated by a number of speakers, with Silverman offering reassurance to "closeted atheists" that "you are not alone." Fred Dewords, national director of the United Coalition of Reason, borrowed another slogan from the gay movement (substituting "godless" for "queer") in leading the crowd in a chant of "We're here, we're godless, get used to it."[41] The Reason Rally was a clear sign that the secular movement is a sustained and organized movement geared toward establishing a new minority group—or more precisely, recognizing an existing but previously dormant one—in American society. This is a very significant development that so far has eluded the attention of social movements scholars.

The engagement in minority politics is a contentious issue and the idea is rejected by, among others, Harris and Hitchens. Indeed, these authors do not believe that atheists require a social movement at all. In the original filmed Four Horsemen discussion, Hitchens argued for the right of nonbelievers to express being offended by certain religious doctrines while warning against "being self-pitying or representing ourselves as an oppressed minority."[42] At the 2007 Atheist Alliance International convention, Harris criticized the idea of an atheist minority and even the use of the term "atheist" to describe themselves, arguing that "We're consenting to be thought of as a cranky subculture that meets in hotel ballrooms."[43] He thus condemned the movement's employment of a "subcultural identity strategy" that mirrors evangelicals' self-representation as an "embattled minority."[44] He argued, instead, that atheists should consider themselves the mainstream, or at least the emergent mainstream, since skepticism and rationalism should be the default positions, while engaging in minority politics marginalizes the atheist viewpoint. Harris's view here is consistent with the project of cultural transformation that characterizes the New Atheist discourse and distinguishes it from movement subgroups that use minority discourse as a political identity strategy aimed at realizing instrumental goals.

Dawkins, on the other hand, is considerably less discerning in his strategy and supports just about any kind of collective action by atheists. He endorses both minority politics and tackling discrimination while also arguing for the near-universality of the scientific worldview in the modern world.[45] Others in the freethought community are similarly divided on the question of whether atheism simply means a lack of religious belief or involves a set of "positive" beliefs (i.e., affirmation of certain principles rather than strictly negation). For example, D. J. Grothe, formerly host of *Point of Inquiry* and now president of the James Randi Educational Foundation and host of its podcast *For Good Reason*, insists that "atheism" means nothing other than not believing in God; he co-wrote an article in *Free Inquiry* entitled "Atheism Is Not a Civil Rights Issue" that specifically rejected the strategy of minority politics.[46] PZ Myers, on the other hand, defines atheism as "a positive explanation of the world based on scientific thinking . . . When I talk about atheism I'm using a loaded word that has a lot of other content."[47] He exhorts atheists to "take pride in what you do believe, not what you deny."[48]

Despite the disagreements, minority discourse and political action are cemented as a central aspect of the secular movement. This was made abundantly clear at the Reason Rally, where it was the prevailing theme. The claim to being an "oppressed minority" that Hitchens warned against has now been embraced by the movement's mainstream. Despite Hitchens' reservations, many American atheists do report experiencing exclusion and outright discrimination and thus legitimately fear the social consequences of revealing their beliefs.[49] Research on public perception of atheists has consistently found that they are among the least-trusted people in the United States.[50] One major study found that Americans are significantly more accepting of Muslims and homosexuals than they are of atheists, and argued that atheists constitute an "other" in American society, a symbolic boundary setting the terms for cultural membership and morality.[51]

Some recent highly publicized incidents highlight both discrimination against individual atheists and their increasing willingness to speak publicly about it as well as engage in legal action. In 2008 a soldier named Jeremy Hall filed a lawsuit against the U.S. Department of Defense for an unconstitutional violation of his religious freedom—in his case, freedom to have no religion.[52] Hall accused the U.S. military of being a "Christian organization" with a pattern of discrimination against non-Christians. He claimed that he received death threats from other soldiers and that he was denied promotion because of his refusal to participate in group prayer. Hall was joined by another plaintiff, the Military Religious Freedom Foundation, which was founded to protect nonbelieving members of the armed forces from discrimination. In 2012, a sixteen-year-old Rhode Island high-school student named Jessica Ahlquist successfully mounted a legal challenge to have a Christian prayer plaque removed from the wall of her school auditorium on the grounds that it told her, an atheist, "You don't belong here."[53] The heavily Catholic population of her city responded with outrage, sending her online threats and protesting at school board meetings, while a state representative called her an "evil little thing."[54] A representative of the Freedom From Religion Foundation said it had been a long time since she had seen "this level of revilement and ostracism and stigmatizing."[55]

One recent case provided material validation for atheists' claims to suffering discrimination. In 2011 the Center for Inquiry filed suit against Wyndgate Country Club in Rochester Hills, Michigan, after it canceled an event that featured Dawkins as a speaker. The grounds of the suit were breach of contract (CFI had rented the club's convention space) and violation of federal and state civil rights laws. The club's reason for canceling the event was that "the owner does not wish to associate with certain individuals and philosophies," specifically citing Dawkins' recent appearance on *The O'Reilly Factor* and his discussion of atheism and religion on that program. After an out-of-court settlement, CFI claimed that this was "the first time federal and state civil rights statutes have been successfully invoked by nonbelievers in a public accommodations lawsuit," while CEO Ronald Lindsay said, "as this country now rejects discrimination based on race, sexual orientation, and religion, so must we reject just as strongly discrimination against those with no religion."[56] The case appears to indeed have been a landmark legal victory in the movement's quest to establish atheists as a minority group requiring protection under civil rights law.

Discrimination against atheists (or at least a perception of discrimination) is not restricted to the United States. In 2011 the Centre for Inquiry Canada brought its atheist bus campaign to Kelowna, British Columbia. Buses scheduled to carry the advertisements were found in the transit yard with the ads professionally removed, an evident statement of protest from a driver or another transit employee.[57] CFI used this incident to frame its "Good Without God" campaign. Claiming that the Kelowna incident indicated that more needed to be done to "advance the public image of our community," the Good Without God campaign, like the Out campaigns of the Freedom From Religion Foundation and the Richard Dawkins Foundation, combats perceived stigma by emphasizing the moral character of atheists. This incident, then, was taken as a "cultural opportunity"[58] to represent atheists as an "embattled minority," a strategy that has had a "tonic" effect on secularist identity.[59]

The most vocal proponent of minority discourse and identity politics in the secular movement is perhaps *Free Inquiry* editor Tom Flynn, who has argued within the pages of his magazine for several years that the movement should adopt the tactics and discourse of the gay and lesbian movement in an effort to destigmatize atheism. Indeed, he believes that the primary goal of the movement at this point should be to tackle the "antiatheist bigotry"[60] that is analogous to the antigay bigotry exposed and confronted by the LGBT movement. He notes that even if we take the lower estimates of the number of "explicitly secular and nonreligious people" (he offers a figure of 10 percent), that number "will empower us to operate on the same scale as America's most visible and respected activist minorities."[61] Flynn argues that atheists are on the verge of a "breakthrough moment" similar to those experienced by gays and lesbians, and also African Americans and Hispanics, when their populations reached similar numbers.[62] At the Reason Rally, Paul Fidalgo, a spokesman for the Center for Inquiry, echoed these sentiments by stating, "We have the numbers to be taken seriously" and "We're not just a tiny fringe group."[63]

Note in these various statements the comparisons not just to other minorities, but to the discrimination and even persecution experienced by these minorities. The same sentiment is expressed by PZ Myers, who, in an article on the Dawkins Foundation's website, declares that "we are staking out a place in the public discourse and openly discussing our concerns, rather than hiding in fear of that old Puritan scowl. We will not go back in the closet."[64] Several atheist organizations make minority discourse their primary concern. The Military Association of Atheists and Freethinkers represents nonbelievers serving in the U.S. military, a sphere where atheists are particularly stigmatized, even by American standards. The group's webpage asserts in its introductory message that "nontheists are the last unprotected minority."[65] American Atheists' mission statement reads: "Supporting Civil Rights for Atheists and the Separation of Church and State."[66] The organization demanded a public apology from Billy Ray Cyrus for his "bigoted slur" against atheists in an interview in *GQ* magazine.[67] Greg Epstein, humanist chaplain at Harvard University and author of the book *Good Without God: What a Billion Nonreligious People Do Believe*, emphasizes the positive features of humanist beliefs rather than the negative, or negating, approach of scientific atheism. Yet he also notes pervasive discrimination and prejudice against nonbelievers in America and argues that nonbelievers should start to think about themselves as part of a "movement capable of improving perceptions of them."[68]

Despite the clear differences in attitudes toward atheism in Canada versus that of the highly religious United States, Canadian atheism has also embraced minority politics and the discourse of persecution. In March 2013 the Centre for Inquiry Canada released an Internet video[69] addressing the Canadian government's announcement of the new Office of Religious Freedom. In the video, CFI Canada spokesperson Justin Trottier asks the Office of Religious Freedom to include atheists in their mandate, arguing that "all over the world, atheists, agnostics, rationalists, and secularists are subject to hatred, intolerance, and persecution for their minority religious identity." While Trottier's discussion was focused primarily on persecution of atheists in non-Western contexts—particularly Islamic countries—the claim that atheism constitutes a *minority religious identity* was advanced in no uncertain terms. The video includes a clip of Canadian Minister of Foreign Affairs John Baird speaking about the office and its position that "we don't see agnosticism or atheism as being in need of defense the same way persecuted religious minorities are," underscoring Trottier's argument that atheists in Canada need to make a stronger claim for recognition as a minority in need of protection.

Many atheist groups, then, encourage self-representation as a minority excluded by mainstream society and become an in-group that finds its identity not in traits they share internally, but in the perception of discrimination and a common enemy. This is in contrast to the New Atheists' view of a group of enlightened individuals united by a scientistic worldview, as well as to the humanist movement's traditional concern of uniting people according to a common ethical position. These trends support Cimino and Smith's argument that the failure of naturalism and scientific thought to become dominant over supernatural explanations of reality—which was assumed by many "progressive secularists"[70] throughout the twentieth century to be the inevitable course of history—has led these movements to shift their strategy. Rather than assuming that secularization was the inevitable and natural trend of history, atheist and secular humanists now faced the question of how secularism can survive and even thrive in a religious society.[71] The new strategy, in answer to this pressing question, is the construction of a subcultural identity in order to find a place in American society. Cimino and Smith identify three strategies aimed at realizing this goal: (1) creating a niche for secular humanism among irreligious people, (2) mimicking various aspects of evangelicalism in defining themselves, and (3) making use of minority discourse and engaging in identity politics.[72] The project of ideological universalization, taken for granted for much of the twentieth century as the inevitable course of history, has to a large extent been abandoned in favor of defensive strategies aimed at securing a location in the religious landscape.

This defensive strategy, as I have illustrated, involves an instrumental political identity approach modeled on the gay and lesbian movement. The links to this movement are clear in the examples that I have cited of efforts to combat the perceived stigma associated with the label "atheist" and to foster the notion that atheists constitute a hitherto unrecognized minority subject to similar forms of prejudice and discrimination. The dynamics at work within these identity movements are similar in many ways. The issue within the gay and lesbian movement most pertinent to atheists' current situation is the frequent and ongoing debate over the question of a strategy of "assimilation" versus one of "distinction"[73] or alternatively "separatism."[74] Amin Ghaziani argues that gay politics has generally moved from a very subversive and confrontational style that sought to highlight differences to a more conservative approach that emphasized things like marriage and adoption, serving in the military, and employment discrimination.[75]

These strategic differences indicate a tension between those who seek to maintain boundaries and a clear minority identity, which in turn is their source of political power, and those who want to break down boundaries to demonstrate that these differences are socially constructed rather than essential, and thus that gays should have the same rights and privileges as anyone else.[76] Joshua Gamson refers to these as "category-supportive political strategies" versus "deconstructive cultural strategies."[77] The former emphasizes difference and the power that can come from recognition as a distinct minority that must be protected, while the latter emphasizes assimilation. The secular movement is now faced with similar questions and a similar division, though it is further complicated by a series of divisions or tensions between and within various groups that reflect the dynamics involved in the emergence of a new or latent movement within the structure of an existing movement with its own tensions and internal debates. These tensions are best exemplified by an ongoing debate concerning strategies that are generally referred to as "confrontation" and "accommodation," which are analogous to Gamson's "category-supportive" and "deconstructive" strategies. Examining these tensions regarding goals and strategies will in turn tell us much about the complex and evolving nature of atheist identity, since in the theoretical framework that I have adopted, goals, strategy, and identity are inextricably linked and mutually dependent; indeed, internal disagreements over goals and strategies are in fact statements about identity.[78]

Confrontation Versus Accommodation

The New Atheists' polarizing strategy of aggressive confrontation and ridicule of religious beliefs reflects their view of religion and science as dichotomous terms and the demand for ideological validation. For Dawkins, the strategy is to destroy the "God virus" by injecting our culture with a strong dose of the evolutionism meme. The intention seems mainly to be to mobilize inactive nonbelievers and to address those on the fence who might have some sense of religious belief but not a strong attachment to it by polarizing the two sides and forcing them into choosing one. Moderate positions are increasingly abandoned or viewed as untenable by both atheists and devout Christians, who are bound up in a dialectical relationship that propels them to further polarized extremes. Extreme elements of the religious and nonreligious each portray themselves as an embattled minority set against a dominant other.[79] This is typical of movements that employ a strategy of difference and construct identity by maintaining social, cultural, and political boundaries, emphasizing differences between dominant and minority groups.[80]

This reflects the positions Ghaziani refers to as "us versus them" and "us and them" in relation to the gay rights movement and its debates regarding identity strategies focusing on "distinction" versus "assimilation."[81] A similar tension on questions of strategy and identity exists in the secular movement between secular humanists, who emphasize a positive system of ethics and values, and atheists, who take a more uncompromising position in defending and promoting scientific materialism.[82] New Atheists have an interest in maintaining a tension with society (rather than assimilating into it) in order to strengthen a worldview.[83] The New Atheists are less compelled toward pragmatism precisely because their goals are more cultural than political. That is, the validation of a worldview is in and of itself the goal of the New Atheism, and maintaining a tension with outside perspectives is thus crucial to their strategy. Philosopher and humanist Matthew Flamm writes in the pages of *Free Inquiry* that "the new atheists engage contemporary religious sensibilities after the manner of glib scientists, less interested that such engagement produces in dissenters the urge for dialogue than in the fact that it clearly lays down lines of difference."[84]

For the secularists engaged in a political struggle for the differentiation of religious (private) and secular (public) spheres, meanwhile, a pragmatic approach that involves building political power is paramount. The New Atheists, as scientific atheists, ascribe to a worldview where science *and only science* can provide the foundations of knowledge and social organization, and thus any competing claims (or "memes") must be discredited and discarded from the pool of ideas. For other atheists who are more concerned with protecting the rights of individual atheists than promoting a worldview, minority politics and maintaining strict lines of difference are key. Accordingly, these groups adopt the strategy of "confrontation." Those who ascribe to a worldview closer to secular humanism than atheism are less inclined to attack religious beliefs and more interested in issues like education, inequality, and environmental sustainability. They are open to forging pragmatic alliances with other groups—including religious ones—that share similar views on these issues. They thus adopt the strategy of "accommodation." While confrontation and accommodation are instrumental approaches to achieving particular goals, they are also statements about identity, constituting "identity strategies."[85]

The tension between the two major strategic positions was articulated in a panel discussion called "Science and Religion: Confrontation or Accommodation?"[86] at the Council of Secular Humanism's 2010 conference. Four speakers, two arguing for each side, discussed their views on the relationship between science and religion and how atheists should engage with religion in the public sphere. The speakers on the "confrontation" side were biologist and blogger PZ Myers and physicist Victor Stenger. Arguing for the "accommodation" viewpoint were Eugenie Scott, director of the nonprofit National Center for Science Education, and Chris Mooney, a science journalist and regular host of *Point of Inquiry*.

Myers' blog, *Pharyngula*, is known for attacking not only religion but almost equally proponents of "a more accommodating atheism."[87] He treats all religions as a set of truth claims that are vulnerable to competing scientific claims. Myers set the confrontational tone at the beginning of his presentation by declaring that "this is a real battle that we're fighting in this country." He clearly identified himself as a New Atheist and accepted the reputation for militancy that comes with the label while claiming that they "didn't start the war" and that blame should be laid "on the backs of the religious zealots who have been poisoning the minds of the young for a long, long time." His entire presentation rested on the premise that the existence of God is a falsifiable scientific hypothesis, which serves as a useful marker to erect boundaries between the in-group and out-groups. Myers' primary goal seemed to be establishing and maintaining a strong and clear sense of identity: "what I personally feel is an important goal is for atheists to acquire an identity, that one of the things we have to do as a group is recognize that we're all in this together . . . We cannot cooperate and work with other groups if we do not have our own identity as a unique group." Myers represents a group seeking to maintain a clear boundary and reinforce difference and conflict, a manifestation of the scientific atheist commitment to the notion of religion and science as dichotomous terms as well as a strategic choice based on the assumption that an aggressive tone is effective in attracting new members and that a distinct minority identity is a path to political power. Stenger essentially reiterated similar arguments and ventured to offer hope that science can win the war against religion in the near future and that "in perhaps another generation Americans will have joined Europe and the rest of the developed world in shucking off the rusty chains of ancient superstition," a comment that drew vigorous applause from the audience and remains in line with the New Atheists' evolutionary view of history and its relationship to scientific progress.

Eugenie Scott offered a very different perspective. She explained that in her role as director of the National Center for Science Education, her goal is promoting science, not attacking religion, which can actually be an impediment to this goal. This is a sharp departure from the scientific atheist position, which she said fails to engage in the kind of cross-cultural critique of religion that would offer greater understanding. These reductionist accounts of religion, she argued, mistakenly posit that religion is essentially a pseudoscience (i.e., the "God Hypothesis") and fail to appreciate that "because Christianity is not primarily about explaining the natural world it is not necessarily antithetical to science." Her position that religion is not pseudoscience but rather addresses everyday concerns people have related to survival and suffering that cannot be addressed by science is tantamount to humanistic atheism.

Chris Mooney expressed similar concerns about the reductionist theories and aggressive tactics employed by Myers, repeating arguments he had previously made in a number of writings and conference presentations about a view of religion as a social and psychological phenomenon intimately associated with identity and politics. He began by claiming that the confrontational approach is exemplified by the New Atheists, whom he has compared to religious fundamentalists in setting up a "false dichotomy" that alienates many "moderate" believers who might otherwise be sympathetic to science and secular values, which in his view are really what the movement should be about.[88] He therefore advocates abandoning an aggressive strategy of confrontation and argumentation in favor of mobilizing the "pro-science moderates" and supporting religious scientists as chief messengers for reaching out to the "anti-evolution crowd." The New Atheism, he suggests, "flies in the face of this, since it is often about attacking and alienating the religious moderates."[89] He offered the example of Francis Collins, an evangelical Christian who is also an eminent scientist and advocate of evolution and stem cell research, as someone atheists should support. Myers' response was to refer to Collins as a "clown" because of his religious beliefs. It is revealing that the audience responded much more to the contempt and ridicule offered by Myers and Stenger than the decidedly more measured presentations given by Mooney and Scott. The "clown" remark drew applause and cheering, while the response to Mooney's discussion of survey research and reasoned strategic positions was tepid in comparison.

The Center for Inquiry is not the only organization where the "accommodation versus confrontation" debate has emerged. In July 2011, American Atheists filed a lawsuit against the World Trade Center Memorial Foundation, New York City, Mayor Michael Bloomberg, and New Jersey Governor Chris Christie, among others, for displaying a seventeen-foot-tall cross of steel beams at the National September 11 Memorial and Museum on the grounds that it violated the U.S. Constitution and civil rights law.[90] In an apparent response to criticism for their position on this sensitive issue, the group issued a statement on their website titled "Now Is Not The Time For Atheists to Back Down:"

> There are those who are adamant that we should be non-aggressive, respectful and tolerant of those who hold religious beliefs and that we should not be outspoken . . . While some may choose to remain silent or non-confrontational, there are a growing number of us who have decided that the time has come to no longer sit back and let the theocrats run the show.[91]

This statement implicitly addresses the confrontation/accommodation debate—and, further, a division within the movement—by referring to two groups divided in terms of their focus on "tolerance" or being "outspoken" and "confrontational." In November 2010, Chris Mooney and David Silverman, president of American Atheists, debated the future of the movement in terms that essentially mirrored the division of the Council for Secular Humanism conference panel.[92] When the moderator raised the question of "moderate" or "live-and-let-live" atheism versus a more "militant" approach, Mooney explicitly referenced the "accommodationist" position and made essentially the same points he would later make at the Council for Secular Humanism conference. Silverman became noticeably agitated at several points when responding to Mooney. He endorsed the "confrontational" strategy without naming it as such, raising his voice in anger several times, and argued that religious belief is like being addicted to heroin.

Atheism Versus Humanism

These debates point to the tension between atheism and secular humanism within the movement, with some humanists dismayed by the ascendency of "militant" atheism.[93] As early as 2006, the year of publication of

The God Delusion, there were concerns about both the tone and content of the emerging discourse. For example, *Free Inquiry* columnist Julian Baggini argued for a more moderate approach in an article entitled "Toward a More Mannerly Secularism."[94] Another *Free Inquiry* columnist criticized the idea that religion is an "outmoded method of explanation" that can be eradicated by presenting people with better theories, sardonically dismissing this view in arguing that "Megachurches will not empty out when the faithful learn the secrets of the atom."[95]

The most vocal critic of the New Atheism within the Center for Inquiry has been the organization's founder, Paul Kurtz, a philosopher and self-described secular humanist who was a major figure in organized secularism until his passing in 2012. In 2010 Kurtz resigned from his positions as chair of the Council for Secular Humanism and editor-in-chief of *Free Inquiry*, posts he had occupied for thirty years. By his account he was effectively terminated by the board of directors in a "palace coup"[96]—an event precipitated by a period of publicly criticizing the direction the organization was taking under the influence of "militant atheists."[97] Kurtz used the terms "atheist fundamentalists" and "true unbelievers" to refer to hardline new atheists as a secular corollary to religious fanaticism.[98] He rejected the notion that atheism is synonymous with secularism, arguing that "one does not have to be a nonbeliever to accept the separation principle"[99] and that religious believers can also be secularists, which is precisely the position that he claims led to his ousting from CFI. Even more troubling to him was the equation of atheism with his philosophical understanding of secular humanism. Kurtz's views on the matter fueled a debate with Tom Flynn in an episode of *Point of Inquiry* titled "Secular Humanism Versus . . . Atheism?"[100] The interview involved a discussion of the supposed rift within the movement between secular humanists and atheists, and the idea that some who identify as secular humanists and want to advance the cause of reason, science, and church–state separation want to avoid the label "atheist." Flynn denied any tension between the two and sought to reconcile the positions by arguing that atheism is an essential starting point, or basic epistemological foundation, for secular humanism. Kurtz, by contrast, insisted that "you can be a secular humanist and not an atheist," and he made a distinction between secular humanism, which is a "positive" philosophy, and atheism, which is "negative."[101]

Myers addressed Kurtz's criticisms—namely, that atheism is a strictly negative position and that those characterizing themselves as atheists "lack a positive center" that they stand for—in his defense of confrontation at the Council for Secular Humanism panel debate. Myers argued (ostensibly to the contrary but in fact reinforcing Kurtz's point in a certain sense) that atheists believe in reason, evidence, science, and appreciation of nature. Note his focus on *nature* in the abstract, and methods of understanding it, with no mention of *humanity*, which is precisely what Kurtz was addressing. Myers is actually correct that, historically speaking, scientific atheism is not only negation but also a belief system characterized by scientism, Darwinism/evolutionism, and liberalism. Myers also criticized Kurtz's accommodationism, arguing that the purpose of the movement is precisely to attack religious beliefs: "we're in the business of telling believers that their most cherished fantasies are lies."[102] He therefore favors the evangelical approach of promoting scientific atheism by attacking the irrationality of faith, forgoing Kurtz's emphasis on humanist ethics or on secularism as a project of social differentiation.

The position advanced by Myers and Flynn is essentially that humanism begins with atheism and that atheism requires confrontation and eventual elimination of religious belief. In these views humanism is essentially a meaningless and unnecessary addition—the term is defined by atheism and antagonism to religion. Contrast this with a group that takes humanism on its own terms, such as the Humanist Community at Harvard, which has grown under the leadership of Greg Epstein, the first humanist chaplain at Harvard University. In his book *Good Without God*, Epstein defines humanism as "a cohesive world *movement* based on the creation of good lives and communities, without God."[103] Creating good lives and communities without God does not necessarily mean that this cannot be done *with* God, a crucial distinction from the atheist worldview. Epstein also favors accommodation. Similar to Mooney's comments about not alienating religious believers who accept science, Epstein says that for humanists, "to the extent that Catholics and other religious groups accept that we have reliable evidence for evolution, they are our allies and our friends."[104] He explicitly rejects dogmatic confrontation of religion in all its forms, arguing that metaphysical differences are subordinate to political correspondences: "I have no desire to offend my liberal religious allies."[105] Another member of the Humanist Community at Harvard, Chris Stedman, authored a book detailing his conversion from religion and his view that religious and nonreligious people who share basic values must learn to respect each other's beliefs on the question of God, a prerequisite for working together to improve the world.[106] At the time of writing Stedman had become the first executive director of the Yale Humanist Community.

The goals and strategies of these humanist groups are at odds with those of atheist organizations, and humanist groups and ideas have been peripheral to the secular movement during the recent period character-ized by the dominance of the New Atheism. Kurtz fought a losing battle against the rising tide of confrontational atheism within his organization. The issue put him at odds with the man who would become his succes-sor at the Center for Inquiry, Ronald Lindsay. Lindsay used his first *Free Inquiry* editorial after assuming the position of CEO as an opportunity to mark his differences with Kurtz with respect to the latter's plea for a "Kinder, Gentler Humanism" in response to the increasingly vitriolic tone of movement discourse in the wake of the New Atheism.[107] One of the major points of contention between Lindsay and Kurtz was the intro-duction of Blasphemy Rights Day, when works of art in various media ridiculing religion are displayed and celebrated in an ostensible defense of the right to freedom of expression. The most infamous work to come out of this celebration is the painting "Jesus Does His Nails" by Dana Ellyn, a submission to the 2009 Blasphemy Day exhibit that depicts Jesus apply-ing nail polish to nails driven through his hands. In a similar vein, the Centre for Inquiry Canada's Toronto branch hosts a monthly "God-Awful Comedy Show" where local comedians invoke the spirit of George Carlin and Bill Hicks to ridicule religious belief. Kurtz was a vocal opponent of Blasphemy Day, which he viewed as needlessly divisive and antagonistic and having nothing to do with the goal of promoting rationalism and humanism (and would likely similarly oppose the God-Awful Comedy Show). Lindsay, meanwhile, argues that ridicule is a valid form of expres-sion and, further, that

> Our first duty is to the truth, and if well-grounded facts or logic contradict the beliefs of a religious person, we should be able to express our criticism of those religious beliefs without regard to whether the religious person will be offended by our criticism.[108]

For Lindsay and others taking the confrontation approach, Blasphemy Rights Day is both a manifestation of duty to the truth and a celebration of freedom of expression. Individual freedom is indeed of increasing impor-tance in movement discourse as the political ideology of libertarianism has become more influential in recent years. This has produced new tensions, dividing the movement not just between atheists and secular humanists, or confrontationists and accommodationists, but a further and explicitly political division has emerged between right-wing advocates of radical individualism and others who connect their activism to social justice.

These tensions and debates, and the scenario by which Kurtz lost control of the Center for Inquiry, bear a striking resemblance to the events of the early years of the National Secular Society (NSS). The accommodation and confrontation debate and the disagreements over the meaning of atheism and humanism and their place in the secular movement are only the most recent manifestations of tensions that have existed since the debates between George Holyoake and Charles Bradlaugh over the direction of NSS in the 1860s. Holyoake proposed a strategy of seeking common ground with liberal Christians to advance a broad secular agenda, while Bradlaugh insisted that religion must be aggressively critiqued and marginalized if it were to be displaced from its privileged position in culture and in social institutions. The positions advanced by these leaders were termed "substitutionism" and "abolitionism," which Campbell describes as a "constructive" approach of developing an alternative belief system and a plan for social transformation as a substitute for theocratic authority, versus a "destructive" approach aimed at eradicating religious belief.[109] Michael Rectenwald notes that "Bradlaugh and company insisted on atheism as an essential conviction for the Secularist and bitterly reproached Holyoake and his followers for their conciliation with theists."[110] The debate between Kurtz, advocate of humanism and accommodation, and Flynn and Lindsay, advocates of atheism and confrontation, is a duplication of the early NSS debates about the meaning and purposes of secularism. And like Holyoake, Kurtz lost control of the organization he created to a more radical group that adopted a more militant stance against religion and abandoned the basic humanistic principles these organizations were founded on. It would seem that Campbell was correct when he argued that a clash between positive and negative outlooks is a feature of all irreligious movements.[111]

These debates will never be settled because the movement comprises groups motivated by goals and ideologies that are not only different but in some cases directly opposed to each other. This difference is expressed politically in Holyoake's left-wing sympathy for labor and the working class and Bradlaugh's more individualistic liberalism. The mutual incompatibility of different forms of atheist politics is reflected in the tension today between a conservative and libertarian segment of the movement, and another group who believe that atheism is fundamentally about social justice and equality (though, as we will see, "social justice" for this group refers almost exclusively to identity, while the socialist bent toward class issues that was so important in the founding of the NSS is largely absent from the movement today).

This polarization and the growing visibility of political differences are the most important and intriguing developments in the secular movement's recent history. Susan Jacoby is a well-known secular activist, author, and speaker who once served as program director for the New York branch of the Center for Inquiry. She notes a distinction between "secular humanists" and "secular conservatives" that expresses itself within the movement as a division between "humanists" and people who call themselves "skeptics," with epistemological skepticism carrying none of the moral imperative for the welfare of others that might be claimed by humanism.[112] We might alternatively think about this distinction in the terms outlined in the debate between Flynn and Kurtz and consider what relationship there might be between the division between atheism and humanism, on the one hand, and that between those Jacoby refers to as "secular humanists" and "secular conservatives" on the other. Jacoby's distinction implicitly identifies secular humanism with liberalism. Who, then, are the "secular conservatives" she speaks of? Only she knows precisely who and what she was referring to, but there is an identifiable group who clearly seek to sever the connection among humanism, atheism, and social justice that the secular movement was originally grounded in. These are the libertarians, and they introduce a complication to the divisions between secular humanism and atheism that Kurtz and Flynn discussed. The libertarians combine the New Atheists' confrontational approach with the secular humanists' instrumental goals of political secularism, all while carving out their own ideological space and constructing a version of scientism that includes individualism and free-market economics as central tenets. But the libertarians are only one element of a broader group or set of ideas within the secular movement that I call the atheist Right, which represents the extreme pole of the tension within the movement between individualistic atheism and a form of humanism centered on the notion of social justice. I will return to this topic in the final chapter, but first I will examine some of the debates and issues regarding goals, strategy, and ideology discussed in this chapter through the eyes of some of the members of the movement. In their words we will discover some of the deep tensions at the heart of organized secularism.

6

Purists, Freethinkers, and Bridge Builders: Tensions at the Grassroots

ALAIN TOURAINE WRITES that any social movement features "a changing set of debates, tensions and internal rifts; it is torn between grass-roots opinion and the political projects of its leaders."[1] This chapter examines these tensions and internal rifts between the leaders of the atheist movement and its grassroots members. In interviews with members of American and Canadian atheist organizations, I explore questions such as the extent to which members' beliefs are influenced by the New Atheism, the nature and origin of religious belief as they understand it, their views on the meaning of atheism and the goals of the movement, and areas of disagreement with the official discourse of movement leaders, including the issues and debates with respect to movement goals and strategy discussed in the previous chapter. The views of this small sample of atheists cannot be generalized to the movement as a whole, but detailed investigation of how they understand the movement, and the tensions they experience with various aspects of it, illustrate the tensions I have highlighted as characteristics of the secular movement.

The New Atheists' tendency to judge all believers by the words and actions of religious leaders is as erroneous as Christian leaders' tendency to judge all atheists by the words of Richard Dawkins. Just as some Catholics ignore many of the church's teachings (particularly regarding sexual prohibitions), so atheists who participate in the movement are critical of its most visible and outspoken leaders. As is always the case, closer investigation reveals that no movement is homogeneous or submits entirely to ideology. It is therefore not surprising that there is a great deal of variety in the views held by members of atheist organizations. The members I spoke to expressed significant ambivalence about the debates regarding strategy, and considerably more nuanced views on religion than those of the New Atheists or other more ideologically motivated movement leaders. Nuances in the views of grassroots members, and the tensions between their views and those of some movement leaders, are a challenge for a movement struggling to arrive at a coherent strategic focus. Fundamental ideological differences—the deep root of tensions in the atheist movement—are threatening to fracture the movement into distinct, and even opposed, spheres of thought and action.

The interviews discussed here involve "active atheists," or people who are members of atheist organizations or participate in atheist activism.[2] Respondents ranged in age from twenty-three to fifty-eight years old, with nine females and six males. All had attended university, ranging from one year of undergraduate education to PhD-level study. In terms of religious background, the traditions represented include five Catholics, one Baptist, one United Church, one Hindu, one Buddhist, and one Ismaili Muslim, while five subjects had secular upbringings. Ten were Canadian and five American (one of these was originally from Sweden but had lived in the United States for more than ten years). Canada is clearly overrepresented in this group of atheists, but the discourse of the secular movement is transnational as it is largely based online, and the Canadians in this group frequented the same blogs, websites, and YouTube video collections as their American counterparts. The nature of national differences in the movement is a legitimate question that requires further exploration, but for my purposes—illustration rather than generalization—it is not a significant issue. Women are also overrepresented in this group, as atheist organizations tend to be majority male, though one respect in which the sample does reflect a key characteristic of members of the secular movement is in its high level of education, a finding that emerges in every study on the topic.[3]

Following the Leaders?

Aldon Morris and Suzanne Staggenborg define movement leaders as "strategic decision-makers who inspire and organize others to participate in social movements."[4] There are two dimensions to this definition: leaders make decisions about movement strategy and action, and they are mobilizers. How leaders become leaders in the first place is another question. One approach involves the notion that "followers" impute charisma to leaders, though this view is critiqued for a failure to recognize agency, with followers giving themselves up to charismatic leaders.[5] It may be that charisma is involved in the leaders' ability to inspire and organize, but it is not sufficient to grant them authority as decision-makers and shapers of movement discourse and goals, creating a rift between the two dimensions of leadership in Morris and Staggenborg's definition. This is the case for the atheists I interviewed, many of whom were inspired by the New Atheism and its public visibility to seek out and join atheist organizations. At the same time, however, they reject many specifics of these leaders' views, both on science and religion and on movement goals and strategy.

A good illustration of these differences is the reactions to Dawkins' notion of the "God Hypothesis"—the idea that God is actually an attempt to explain nature, including the origin of life and of the universe, and therefore should be treated as "a scientific hypothesis about the universe, which should be analyzed as skeptically as any other."[6] Subjecting the God Hypothesis to scientific scrutiny, Dawkins concludes that it is false. Of the twelve atheists I asked to comment on the God Hypothesis, seven agreed that the existence of God is essentially a scientific question that can, at least in theory, be answered by scientific methods, and five disagreed. A few on either side were very certain of their answers. For example, Sahani was adamant that "It's impossible to disprove something that is by definition unseeable," while Patrice said, "you cannot prove a negative." Jen conversely said she believed that "it's like any phenomenon in science: you take something, you test your hypothesis, if it doesn't work out then you reject the hypothesis . . . if you treat it like any other scientific phenomenon then you can answer it that way."

Others gave more nuanced responses. For example, Terry's answer was that science cannot say God does not exist, but he also suggested that neuroscience might eventually explain belief in God:

It's like trying to analyze Santa Claus as a scientific question, 'cause it's something that's made up in our imagination . . . I can't remember the part of the brain that lights up, sparks up when we pray, and maybe that's the God part of our brain, right? So maybe through neuroscience we can explain, and I think we are already, this make-believe magic that we need . . . but I don't think we can prove that God doesn't exist by science.

In a similar vein, Phil believed that "The definitive proof of whether God exists is outside the boundaries of science" but added the caveat, "For now, anyways," implying, like Terry, that while the answer right now is "no," science may be on track to reach a point where it is equipped to address the question. Like Patrice, Fahim argued that "you can't be asked to, you know, prove a negative" but added that "science can disprove it to a point where it's negligible, but I would refrain from saying absolute just for the sake of not being arrogant." Diana agreed with the essence of Dawkins' views, saying that "If there's a God, I suppose we could test that empirically," but she also acknowledged the possibility of a supernatural realm outside the boundaries of science: "I suppose if you really want to get into sophisticated philosophical speculations about it there's room for belief in the supernatural, and that's interesting to do, it's an interesting intellectual exercise. But for practical purposes it's probably useful to assume that there's not." While Fahim's argument for near-certainty echoes Dawkins' own position, Diana's openness to the idea of the supernatural is completely out of line with New Atheist materialism.

I also asked respondents why people believe in God and invited them to offer as many reasons as they thought were pertinent, which, along with views on the God Hypothesis, was useful in determining the extent to which their views on religion were primarily in the scientific or humanistic categories of atheism. There was some overlap, but my interpretation is that three respondents fall primarily in the "scientific" category while twelve could roughly be characterized as "humanistic" atheists. Most respondents cited comfort as the most important reason for belief in God, particularly in relation to death. Helen talked about death in relation to losing loved ones:

> I think it's really scary to think that you have, say, eighty years, and then it's done and that's it. And I think it's really hard to believe that when someone you love is gone, they're gone, and you're not going to ever see them again . . . My father had cancer, and so you kind of, it's something to comfort you and to cling to. And it's a nice idea, right, to think that somebody's going to a better place.

Sarah referred to the troubling prospect of her own death: "That's one thing that being an atheist hasn't helped me with, is fear of dying . . . I accept that, I mean, we can never really know, but we can have a pretty good idea. And to me the pretty good idea at this point points to nothing."

Diana, like Sarah, mentioned dealing with the fear of death but said that she does not need help with it: "Comfort, probably. Answers to questions that—I think sometimes people aren't okay with there not being answers to questions. And I'm perfectly comfortable with that for some reason. I know that we don't know what happens after we die, and I'm okay with that." Tim, meanwhile, related to the consolation that religion provides to people who are suffering: "I am a very empathetic person and when I see all the misery and suffering in this world it just, sometimes it just . . . takes you back." Some respondents combined comfort with explanation of the origin of the universe, seeing explanation as itself a kind of comfort.

Respondents also noted the importance of socialization and the impact of culture and social pressures, which was articulated in a number of forms, including "brainwashing of kids," "complacency with one's upbringing," "historical context," and "learned behavior." More substantially, Sahani explained her view that

> if you grow up with something you have to think outside of that frame to understand everything that's wrong with it. And I don't know how I started thinking outside the frame, but if people have gone most of their childhood and adolescence not thinking out of it, and then get to adulthood and they're asked to, I think that it's really easy to consciously choose not to step outside the frame.

Phil was one of very few respondents to focus on the social experience of religion, which he said was an important aspect of his own religious life: "You know, partly I did [believe] because I thought good people believed and it's all in the structure of society and everything and everybody believed in it . . . Because also there's the whole social aspect, the community aspect with the church and so on."

A few respondents invoked the idea that religion serves as explanation, which is the idea that scientific atheism rests on. Michael, for example, offered a line reminiscent of Dawkins: "It's easy. It's a lot easier than doing the work necessary to figure things out." Stacey suggested that

> they need to think there's someone guiding them because they're just not okay with being free in the world, they're not okay with not knowing where we came from. And if they believe that there's someone guiding them and can give them all the answers to everything, then they're just, you know, more grounded.

In other cases explanation was combined with a desire for meaning, control, and comfort, and most respondents mentioned more than one reason for belief in God. Only two respondents mentioned biological factors, though neither assigned them a determinative role. One believed that biological and environmental factors "mingle," while another explained, "I think we're learning more about how the brain operates, and that some of these things we take to be profound experiences are simply a matter of neurons firing or whatever." But this same respondent also suggested that comfort was the most important reason that people believe in God. Even Patrice, whom I consider the closest thing to a "pure" scientific atheist in my sample, rejected genetic and neuroscientific explanations of religious belief. "Religion is not coming from the brain," he said. "It's coming from brainwashing, and the social pressure." The atheists I interviewed were not biological determinists who derive their views on religion from neuroscience, and generally they implicitly adopted sociological or anthropological theories of religious belief rather than claiming, like the New Atheists, that it is a means to fill in the gaps in our understanding.

On the reverse question—namely, why people stop believing in God—the answers given somewhat contradicted the views on why people believe in the first place. While offering "humanistic" explanations for religious belief, the explanations for apostasy were generally "scientific." I categorize answers to this question as indicating either "intellectual" or "moral/political" reasons for nonbelief. Some examples will serve to illustrate the nature of these responses. Jen assumed that most people give up belief for the same reason she did: "science and logical inconsistencies and being unable to reconcile the two." She added, "I think the studies show that people who are more educated tend to be atheist." More bluntly, Stacey confidently suggested that the reason people give up their beliefs is "they think." Helen offered the explanation that "people who are less religious often are more critical thinkers." Fahim made a link between education and religiosity: "it's just no coincidence that in a more educated population that can think rationally, think for themselves, make good decisions, [they] don't need someone to tell them what good morality is." Patrice pointed to social pressures in restricting the individual's thinking about religion:

> It certainly helps when the family, the grasp of the family on that individual, is not too, is not killing, you know, the freedom to think.
> I see some documentary on TV, you know, a girl that was in a very

religious family and she decided no, that doesn't make sense, you know. And then the family rejects her, don't want to talk to her, and all her friends, nobody talks to her. I mean, this is difficult, you have to be a strong-minded individual to go through that.

In taking these positions the respondents embraced the narrative of scientific atheism, which posits that religious belief and science are mutually exclusive, and that for those sufficiently educated the latter will inevitably overwhelm the former, resulting in atheism. This is in contrast with the generally humanistic orientation respondents evidenced on the question of why people believe in God. I interpret this contradiction as a result of a lack of a conceptual scheme that can account for apostasy. While some humanistic reasons for belief are fairly intuitive (e.g., fear of death, comfort), social-scientific explanations for apostasy—focusing on social conditions—are less obvious. The respondents therefore resorted to explanations that view apostasy as a response to the "cognitive critique," one of the three major forms of religious criticism that emerged from the Enlightenment reviewed in Chapter 1. A focus on the cognitive critique, while neglecting the "practical-political" and "moral-subjective" critiques, constitutes the basis of the division between scientific and humanistic atheism.

A few respondents did, however, cite moral or political reasons for nonbelief. Michael said, "If you have to choose between medicine and prayer, and if you have a good social safety net, the medicine, the doctors, are there. If you don't have that, well then you have to rely on prayer." These comments on the standard of living present religion as a political issue. He also gave a moral reason, pointing specifically to "the problem of evil"—one of the oldest conundrums in theology, requiring the reconciliation of an omnipotent and benevolent God with the existence of evil and suffering—as "the thing that drives a lot of people toward atheism." Diana similarly noted that "if something tragic happens you might decide that, you know, God must not care about me or whatever, and I can see people rejecting their religion on that sort of a basis." Sahani declined to explain exactly why people lose their faith, but did refute the notion that apostasy is strictly an intellectual maneuver driven by scientific education, arguing that "you're not going to come to atheism because of scientific thinking on its own."

The New Atheism, surprisingly, was not directly or highly influential on the development of most respondents' views. Of the fifteen atheists

I interviewed, only three had read all four canonical New Atheist texts, while three had not read any of them (though it bears noting that all those who had not read any of these books had at least watched some of the authors' lectures on the Internet). Eleven people had read Dawkins, eight had read Harris, seven had read Hitchens, and only three had read Dennett. Dawkins seemed to be the most important figure, which is not surprising given his prominence and celebrity status within the movement, and the fact that *The God Delusion* was a phenomenal bestseller and is widely considered the key text of the New Atheism. To underscore this point, every subject who had read at least one of the four authors had read Dawkins. In general, only a few younger subjects reported being somewhat to heavily influenced by the New Atheists. They did not seem to be of particular importance among older respondents, and for the people I interviewed who had been involved in the secular movement for a decade or more, the New Atheists were basically irrelevant.

When I asked the respondents whether the New Atheists had changed or significantly affected their beliefs, Helen said, "It more felt like my ideas were being reinforced when I started reading them." Diana suggested that "They're just saying what lots of us have been thinking for a long time." Phil said, "I guess they might have made me more confirmed in my dislike of religion." The notion of a "reinforcement" of ideas—often articulated using this specific word—was a common response, even for respondents who reported being heavily influenced by the New Atheists. A good example is Fahim, who described *The God Delusion* as "the book that put words to my thoughts in a way that I could have never thought that would happen," suggesting that Dawkins did not change his mind so much as give clear expression to views he already held. The best way to describe the influence of the New Atheists as movement leaders, then, would be that they have been very effective in terms of recruitment and mobilization, while not having a large impact on actual beliefs.

While an intellectual interest in the New Atheism may have shown them the way to the movement (many reported learning about the movement by clicking the suggested links after watching YouTube videos featuring Dawkins and others), it was the social satisfactions the movement provided that kept them there. My interviews indicate that the most important function of the atheist movement has been creating an environment where people who are already nonbelievers can experience the benefits of a community of like-minded people and can feel comfortable "coming out." Answers to the question of the purpose of the movement fall into three major categories: community, identity, and political change. The last two categories overlap to the extent that atheist collective identity construction is a project of political identity deployment,[7] but generally these refer to different kinds of goals, with some respondents pointing to instrumental pursuits like church–state separation. In general, respondents considered the atheist movement a project of community and identity building and placed much less attention on political goals than we see in official movement discourse. Some respondents cited purposes that fall in multiple categories, but only two, Stacey and Michael, discussed all three kinds of goals. It is noteworthy that these two respondents are both very active, occupying positions on the executive committees of their organizations. They are therefore familiar with the formal mandates of their organizations and framed their responses in those terms. Some other members who are more casually involved gave more personal responses.

Michael's views on the purpose of the movement amounted to the official purposes of his local organization, of which he is a founding member and has served as president:

> We have three purposes. The first is to provide a community for atheists . . . We have black communities, gay communities, women's groups. We're an atheist group, we provide this community for atheists . . . The second thing is to educate the public about atheism. Now that's to let us define ourselves rather than have Pat Robertson define us . . . Again, it's not to try to convert everyone in the public to an atheist, it's just to say we're atheist, this is what an atheist is, this is the atheist worldview. You know, we're not Satan worshippers, we're not evil, we're not hedonists . . . And then the third purpose we have, and this is something we do try to change people's minds on, is to promote separation of church and state. And that's our third thing because, third in importance because you already have the American Civil Liberties Union out there doing that as well.

The goal of community building is given highest priority here. The related purpose of identity construction is here stated as a project to "define ourselves" and delineate the "atheist worldview," and to show people that "we're not evil," an allusion to the morality-based nature of atheist representations of identity (mentioning evangelical pastor Pat Robertson is important here because it means rejecting the representation of atheists as immoral people). Finally, the least important purpose is promoting separation of church and state, the only political goal he references. Michael's prioritization of the purposes of the movement reflects the trend that emerged in my interviews, with community at the top, identity a close second, and instrumental or political goals a clear third. The New Atheists' goal of ideological universalization is off the radar for these particular atheists. The closest Michael comes to it in his response is in saying that one of the movement's purposes is to educate the public about the atheist worldview, but this is aimed at showing that "we're not evil" or asserting a moral identity—he makes it clear that their purpose is not conversion.

Overall, eleven of the fifteen respondents cited community as a purpose of the movement, and for many of them this was the most important goal. Several said that atheist organizations provide an alternative source of support for those who no longer have a support "system" or "network" to rely on after leaving religion. For example, Tim explained his view that "there's alternative people out there who are reasonable, who desire a better world. And I think there's a lot of people that are probably . . . who don't have a support system to navigate through their feelings, like religions do. So I think this provides that opportunity." A case in point to support Tim's idea is Phil, who suffered from alcoholism and went to Alcoholics Anonymous, which did help him with his drinking, and yet he felt "sort of a distance with the other people that do believe." The religious elements of Alcoholics Anonymous made him feel excluded, and though he still attends their meetings, he feels more of a sense of community with his local atheist organization, which he also sees as a source of support.

Jen's involvement with the Centre for Inquiry was motivated more by social concerns than intellectual ones:

> I originally started up, joined them, because I was in a new country, I didn't know anybody. It was a way to meet friends, and then it ended up taking over my life. But it's something I enjoyed so I was okay with that . . . I'm naturally attracted to these types of people.

Sarah also joined an atheist group to meet people, but for reasons beyond basic friendship. She was looking for a connection to others who shared her point of view:

> I wanted to meet some people . . . that I could discuss this with because I didn't really have anyone. I was looking for a little

stimulation, a little conversation and an outlet for my frustrations with, just, things related to atheism, you know? . . . I'm still in a place where I feel totally overwhelmed by my position in relation to the rest of society on religion. So I'm just starting to make sense of it with them.

Sarah's articulation of feeling "overwhelmed" in relation to society captures the essence of an experience reported by many other respondents: alienation. For a rationalist or simply a nonbeliever, living in a world where those who believe in gods and supernatural miracles are the majority can be a mystifying, lonely, and alienating experience. Alicia described a similar experience when explaining her reaction to watching the 2007 Atheist Alliance International convention, which she stumbled across on Netflix:

Every single speaker talked about things that I had already thought in my mind. I thought I was kind of crazy or something. Or you're not allowed to say that, or that I'm the only person thinking that. But they just laid it out. And it was almost like being born again, I use that expression. I guess being in Texas, everything is just kind of, you know, medieval, at times . . . I was crippled with fear that the world is crazy. And, wow, this ain't never going to work for me, I can't live in this world 'cause they're crazy . . . So they gave me the voice of reason and I could relax.

Surrounded by fervent believers in her Texas town, Alicia's fear that "the world is crazy" is an experience of alienation, or at least a profound disconnection from those around her. The New Atheism, and attending atheist conventions, gave her a perspective that allowed her to make sense of what she was seeing and told her that she was, in fact, not alone in her views on religion and her social experience. She added that attending atheist gatherings was also a way for her to meet men: "I want to meet guys, ok. [Laughs]. That's kind of the human side of it. Because there's not a lot of interesting guys in Texas. I'm never going to meet anybody there. 'Cause it's religious, it feels like it's hard to meet somebody."

Many respondents pointed to the importance of being with "like-minded people" with whom they can freely express their views, and reported feelings of relief and elation when discovering these communities. Marcia explained that "there are those who come because they realize, okay, these are people who I can really talk to about these things. So it's very positive in that aspect because of the camaraderie, because people can feel like they're not alone." Referring to her own experience, discovering the secular movement told her that "there's a name for me, and there are organizations, and there are publications, and there are conventions, and there are groups, and that's when I realized that I wasn't the only one." Elaine also cited the "social aspect" of the movement as its most important function, and like Marcia, expressed elation at discovering in the movement "that connection, that feeling that, oh wow, there's other people out there who think like me." Alicia said she thinks that the movement is important primarily because it provides its members with "a place where they belong—where they're not outcasts, a place where they don't have to lie." She said she likes the fact that, among atheists, "I can say whatever, I don't have to censor anything." Terry said he appreciates being able to "just be with a bunch of atheists," which is "a good thing because you can bitch about religion to each other, and sometimes you can say really awful things and no one cares." Sahani said she has friends who are nonreligious but "even with them I never felt completely comfortable questioning religious practices," so she likes that in her atheist group she can "feel safe to discuss certain things without worrying about offending someone or their mother." These references to atheists as "outcasts" and the importance of having "a place where they belong" and can feel that "they're not alone" were common among my respondents, and point to the experience of alienation that I believe is a much more important motivation for movement participation than identification with an atheistic or scientistic ideology.

The experience of alienation is not limited to the private sphere and personal relationships. In describing what motivates his activity in atheist organizations, Terry articulated a common sentiment: "Well, I think it makes me feel a part of society in a way, like, my voice is a part of society. Because it's growing and we're getting a voice . . . so it makes me feel part of that voice, whereas for too long it was just, you know, an atheist on my own kind of thing, you know?" Through his involvement with the atheist movement, Terry said he feels both a sense of connection to others and political empowerment. Several other respondents referred to the notion of gaining a "voice" through the movement and being encouraged by their experiences to become more "vocal" about their atheism or, in other words, to "come out" and embrace an atheist identity.

While community ranks as the most important purpose of the movement, political goals are the least important, with only five respondents pointing to instrumental pursuits as a desired focus of movement activity. None of these respondents cited political goals alone as the movement's purpose—in all cases they combined political goals with at least one of the other two major types. Two respondents—both American—cited separation of church and state as a primary movement goal. Diana suggested that "upholding human rights" should be a goal of the movement, including the rights of atheists to protection from discrimination. She spoke of her desire for atheism to become a "social justice movement," pointing to birth control and the right to die as social issues that atheists should be fighting for. Two more respondents had no clear idea of what specific political goals should be pursued but said they feel that the atheist movement should have a voice in politics. Phil said, "I'd like to see us try to get more of a political movement, to get more politically involved, to try to have our voice be more included in governance" without elaborating on what exactly that "voice" might say. Patrice, taking the same point of view, explained, "I think that, fuck, I mean, when you stay quiet in the corner, people, they run it in a crazy way, okay? They run the society in a crazy way."

Identity, the second purpose that Michael referred to, was also the second most common answer to the question of movement purpose. Responses in this vein frequently referred to combating a perceived stigma associated with atheism, which is understood as a notion that atheists have no moral foundation. Several respondents echoed Michael's comment implying that religious people might view atheists as "Satan worshippers." Diana said she wants to point out to people that this "makes no sense of course, because if we don't believe in God we're probably not going to believe in the Devil either" and suggests that "atheism maybe could use a PR campaign." Sarah and Stacey both said they think one of the movement's most important purposes is to make it more "socially acceptable" to be an atheist. Stacey and Patrice said they believe that it is important to "come out" in public and become more visible, with the goal of making people more comfortable with atheists.

The imperative to "come out" is a strategy toward the goal of constructing a positive identity and fostering a cultural climate in which atheism is accepted, which, as demonstrated in the previous chapter, is viewed as a necessary step in expanding the movement and pursuing more ambitious goals of cultural and political change. Sahani described just this view in describing her own coming out:

I think that it's a big part of my identity now because I think that religion—I've seen so much more how much of an impact religion has on public policy and things like that. And that's why I think it's more important to sort of be open about your atheism too, so other atheists feel more comfortable too, and we can become more of a force for secularism in our society.

Fahim echoed Sahani's view, describing a similar process of first constructing identity for the purpose of gaining acceptance and recognition, which in turn opens up opportunities for social movement activity: "First of all it has to become acceptable, that's our first step. And once it becomes acceptable, then we have to get people to think about it in a meaningful way, and once it becomes that then you can really start holding the reins and having an impact in politics." Fahim thus endorses a "political identity" strategy.[8] Many other respondents spoke of the importance of coming out in the development of the movement and its goals (precisely nine invoked the phrase "coming out" or "out of the closet"), and like the leaders and organizations discussed in the previous chapter, they seem to feel an affinity with the LGBT movement. For example, Terry spoke of atheists facing a similar challenge of first dealing with stigma:

that's why you say you're an atheist, because once people realize that you're just a regular person then it gets rid of the stereotype. Like the gay movement, right? . . . So CFI [Centre for Inquiry Canada] does that, we're saying it's okay, like the gay movement said it's okay to be queer, we're queer and we're here and we're not going away. It's the same thing now, it's like we're out, we're talking about it.

Like Sahani and Fahim, Terry recognizes the importance of identity as both a strategy and a goal in itself. That is, these atheists view the construction of a positive identity based on morality as a worthwhile goal for atheists who feel stigmatized, but also as a strategic necessity prior to pursuing more instrumental goals. We can therefore see the hierarchy of movement purposes reflected in these interviews as a process of movement development, following the latency model, comprising three elements or stages: community, identity, and instrumental pursuits. For these atheists community is the first and most important purpose of the movement. Identity comes next, with collective expression of identity a tool for building community, as well as a goal in itself. The collective attracts more members by offering an avenue for the expression of individual identities, a process Snow and McAdam refer to as "identity seeking," where "individuals strongly imbued with a particular identity actively search for groups (movements, cults, subcultures) with perspectives and practices consistent with that identity and that allow for its expression."[9] Joining these communities provides atheists with "self-verification"[10] and empowers them to "come out" and embrace the identity shared by the collective. Finally, there are instrumental pursuits such as church–state separation and the less precise goal of gaining a "voice" in politics and governance.

Reflecting the official discourse reviewed in previous chapters, atheists in this sample seem to believe that identity construction is an important step and strategy toward reaching instrumental goals. Bernstein's political identity approach, then, seems appropriate for understanding this process at the levels of leadership and official discourse as well as individual members. At all of these levels, atheists encourage the construction and deployment of identity as a strategy for achieving instrumental goals. There are, however, important differences between these organizations and their members regarding the specific nature of these goals. Respondents are not interested in conversion and therefore do not embrace the New Atheist cultural project of replacing religion with scientific authority (or at least do not view it as a primary goal of movement activity). Rather, they seek to build communities and to carve out their own space in the cultural landscape and assert their claim to self-representation by collectively—and publicly—constructing an atheist identity. Instrumental political goals are also not a high priority for these atheists, and those who did discuss instrumental goals were more inclined to mention social justice and secularism than scientism and individualism. It is therefore not surprising that a grassroots rebellion against established discourse has emerged in the movement given the incongruence between the goals of leaders and the goals of regular members revealed in these interviews (this rebellion is discussed in detail in Chapter 7). I will next address this incongruence by examining respondents' views on the tensions within the movement.

Atheism or Humanism?

In the interviews I asked if there were any contentious issues within the movement or points on which respondents found themselves disagreeing with leaders or other members. In a few cases these questions received little in the way of response, but most subjects referred to some common issues and some offered quite extensive discussions. Most significantly, they spoke of tensions between atheists and humanists, and between those favoring confrontation and accommodation (they did not always use precisely these terms). In a few cases people gave clear answers and felt very certain. For example, Patrice said he favors a confrontational approach to religion in the vein of the New Atheism, a product of his strong view that religion is "a crime against humanity" that must be eliminated. Diana, by contrast, said she feels that "challenging these groups directly" is not worthwhile because "they're not going to listen"; instead, she thinks atheists should try to "prevent more people from being persuaded to that side of things" and suggests encouraging the more "gentle aspects" of religion that make it "positive" for some people. Some others expressed ambivalence on these issues. I have chosen to focus on a few individuals and present some more extended quotations here to let them speak for themselves and to demonstrate the nuances, complexities, and contradictions in their views, which are arrived at through struggle and careful consideration.

Marcia, 38, has been involved with what she calls the "freethought movement" since 2000. She was raised in Florida in a Southern Baptist family and was a "fundamentalist" until she gradually lost her religious beliefs in her early twenties. Some years later she wrote a book about her experiences with religion and becoming a self-described secular humanist, and was invited to speak at a meeting of a freethought group in her hometown. She then became very active in the movement, serving on the executive committee of the Council for Secular Humanism and participating in major events like the Godless Americans March on Washington in 2002. She left her position with Council for Secular Humanism in 2003 and since then has pursued independent projects that she regularly promotes at secular events, such as the Atheist Alliance International convention, where I interviewed her. She offered a number of insights based on her experiences with the movement, including some comments on the tensions within it between secular humanists and those she refers to as "purists":

> Well, you've got different, let's say, factions of freethought. The purists are one part of the spectrum. If you were to compare them between a liberal Christian and a right-wing Christian, the purist would be the right-wing Christian parallel. And I think the secular humanists would be on the other end of the spectrum, they'd be

liberal Christians. The purists, they do not want to hold any notion whatsoever that there should be any doubt that there isn't a God. They assert that there absolutely is no higher power whatsoever, don't even think about the possibility, it just plain isn't. And it's kind of a closed-minded angle, too much so to actually call one a free-thinker from that point of view, in my opinion. The purist doesn't seem very open-minded to me. And they tend to be—I don't want to make a sweeping generalization of purists, but there are many who tend to be antireligion, so I guess that would be part of the New Atheism as well, they're more of a purist, evangelical almost, aspect of it. Me personally, I assert that I don't know and can't know if there's some sort of higher power, but I'm not going to make something up until there's evidence of such. I can suspend my judgment indefinitely, I'm okay with that. Purists, they made their judgment, there's no suspension of judgment, there is no God, period.

Marcia's analogical use of Christianity here posits that "purists" are, in their own way, fundamentalists—in her words, "evangelical"—who are just as dogmatic in their approach to the subject of religion as funda-mentalists of the Christian variety. She noted that the New Atheists are purists of this kind, and opposes purists to secular humanists, whom she identifies with and whom she feels embrace a properly open-minded atti-tude that is skeptical but not certain. The different "factions," as she put it, roughly correspond to two groups I have identified: New Atheists and secular humanists (the libertarians are best understood as a subsection of the atheist group, distinguished by their political orientation and unique view of movement goals). Marcia went on to explain that the "purists" do not speak for everyone within the movement, and that many are opposed to their ideological militancy and insistence on attacking religion:

The religious bashing, it's actually less frequent than you would think. A lot—like I said, there are a lot of freethinkers who are in that agnostic spectrum, and they tend to show how much they dislike the whole bashing aspect of religion . . . I don't hear it a lot in the community, jabs here and there, but overall there's not that much hostility.

Alicia, 35 years old, grew up in Sweden in a secular family and as an adult moved to Texas, where she currently resides. She expressed concerns about the movement that closely reflect Marcia's views on "purists." Discussing an atheist event at which Sam Harris was booed for talking about meditation and spirituality, she pointed to members of the movement who do not embody what she feels atheism is about:

> I guess when I heard that Sam Harris got booed at some, in Washington, when he talked about meditation or something like that, I guess I would be a little afraid of meeting those people that would boo Sam Harris. 'Cause then I would feel the same as, okay, these are religious nuts but on the other end of the spectrum. I guess what I'm now learning is that there's atheists that also have closed their mind on to . . . that there's something going on in the brain that we don't know about. They say, "No, the brain is just the brain. It makes us eat. It makes us fuck." And that's it. Which I find, for me personally, I don't go there. 'Cause that feels like religion to me. 'Cause there's so much that we don't really know . . . And I feel that that's kind of sad because my view of the atheist people would be that they would be scientifically geared and not dogma geared.

These "dogma-geared" atheists, she feels, neglect an important aspect of what it means to be human in focusing only on material, physical processes. This point is revealed in her response to the question of what she thinks is not being sufficiently accounted for in the discourse on religion in the movement:

> I think it's the emotional importance of being a human. Just what Sam Harris is talking about, the feeling of this, you know, godly love that religious organizations have now patented and trademarked and kept to themselves. They have a copyright on that. I think that's the most important thing. 'Cause feelings, in my view, are the things that guide us and I don't think it's addressed, I don't think it's addressed at all, actually.

Alicia's critique of dogmatic materialism among some atheists is only one point of contention. She also has problems with the politics of some atheists:

> I have a problem with—I don't know if this pertains to anything here, but Ayn Rand, I have a problem with that. 'Cause I heard

that there's a lot of atheists who are the Ayn Rand fans, like every man just needs to go and do whatever he needs to be doing right now . . . Well, it don't work, I mean, to me. The U.S., it don't work, it's a Third World country, and it's all about objectivism. Don't help anybody, don't do anything, you know, it's all for me, I'm not gonna pay for anybody, blah. It doesn't work.

As a humanist, Alicia is opposed to the libertarianism in the movement, which does not match her idea of the values of atheism and which, as she notes, often takes the form of Ayn Rand's atheistic individualism. Finally, she also expresses opposition to the strategy of confrontation that dominates official movement discourse. Her preference for accommodation perhaps reflects her general attitude about atheism and the movement. She believes atheists should be "open-minded" and not "dogmatic," and this applies to dealing with believers:

You can't tell people what they don't know. You have to come to that conclusion yourself. You can't tell a religious person or a person on the fence that, hey, that's bullshit, 'cause nobody wants to be wrong. You can't tell people that they're wrong, and you can't try to manipulate them either, 'cause that's not going to be the truth for them.

Fahim, 26, was born in British Columbia to Ismaili parents who emigrated from Africa before he was born. His parents were not only strong believers but very active in the local Ismaili community. He himself was "absolutely" a believer in his childhood and enjoyed going to mosque, where he participated in religious debates, but while attending university he underwent a slow transition to atheism that he attributes to his education. While his views on the nature of religion are largely in line with scientific atheism, he expressed considerable ambivalence on the functions and effects of religion, as well as movement strategy. I interviewed him at an Atheist Alliance International convention, and when I asked if there were any presentations or discussions he had attended there that he found problematic or disagreed with, he responded:

Yeah, there was actually a few things I kind of disagreed with. And they were saying how, you know, religion serves no purpose, or some people made some comments about, you know, religion is completely useless or doesn't serve any purpose, and I think that's just completely false. I've grown up in a religion that's very serving to the people, and very good. It does wonders, I mean we've had families in our house stay from Afghanistan, get them over here. If it wasn't for the religion I probably wouldn't be in a place like Canada today ... So I think some of the unfair bias, because maybe they've had some bad experiences in their life, I can see that there's maybe not, they're not totally objective to that.

Though he is a strong atheist, Fahim nonetheless recognizes some value in religion, and in describing the attitudes of some atheists toward religion as "not totally objective" he takes the same position as Marcia and Alicia, who are dismayed by the "closed-minded" and "dogmatic" approach they see in the movement. Fahim's views on strategy thus take a similar form:

I think we should engage them first, rather than provoke them. But that level of engagement is so much more difficult, and I just know that first-hand having chatted with two levels of extreme, whether it's my parents or a friend. I know that engaging is extremely difficult, but I think that's something we need to continue to do.

Preferring to "engage" with the religious rather than "provoke" them, Fahim clearly favors a strategy of accommodation over confrontation. This position, along with his more nuanced views on the nature and value of religion, sets him apart from the New Atheists and other leaders who craft official discourse.

Michael, 51, was raised in a Catholic family in Minnesota. He framed atheism and humanism as distinct but complementary groups and positions within the freethought movement that need to work together to achieve their goals:

If you think of this as an operation, the whole trying to get religion out of society as an operation, atheism is like the sharp scalpel. You've got to cut out the nonsense. And humanism is like the healing, the bedside manner and the stitches and the recovery. So you need the atheism to go in there and cut out the superstition, but then you've got to follow through with the healing and the alternatives and the healthy lifestyle. So they can work hand in hand, they each have sort of a different mission ... There's a lot of emphasis, there's been more emphasis in atheist groups on going after things in religion that are factually incorrect. Resurrections, miracles, that kind of thing. A more analytical approach. And I think in humanist movements, they're more interested in the emotional stuff. Meaning in life, and trying to create the society that is emotionally fulfilling and replaces the emotional needs, the emotional things that religion supplies. So yeah, the atheists are the more analytical, intellectual thing, and the humanists are the more societal, emotional aspect. And that's where I've been very interested for a number of years now in trying to fuse those two, get those groups to come together. It used to be that a lot of the humanists were afraid in the atheist community, but that's less and less now. So the humanists are not afraid of the atheists, they realize the value of atheists. And I think the atheists are starting to realize that it takes more than bashing religion to be successful, we have to have an alternative life. And so the humanists have been working on that. So we do well together, we can work together, and to really be successful we'll need both parts.

Though he notes a tension, he also believes that each of these groups recognizes that the other has a role to play in the movement and will eventually overcome their differences. What is crucial is that, in his view, they *must* overcome these differences for the movement to be effective. Like Alicia, he notes the importance of the "emotional stuff," which he sees as the province of humanism, while atheism has a more scientific or "analytical" mission. He also pointed out the tension regarding strategy, which he described as one between "hardline" and "friendly" approaches to religion. Given that it directly addresses some of the debates discussed in the preceding chapter, his comments are worth quoting at length:

Well, there is sort of a disagreement in the movement about whether we should be real hard and edgy and ridiculing, that's one camp. And the other camp is friendly and some would call accommodationalist in a derisive way. So some will say, you know, religion wherever we find it is the enemy, we should go after it full force, we should ridicule it. That's, you could call it the hardline atheism. And others would say, look, we've got family and friends who are religious. We don't want to alienate them, especially if they're liberal religious people who might vote with us, and if you start ridiculing the liberal religious people who might otherwise vote with us, you might just drive them into the other camp. But going back to the first group of people, they say, and this is Sam Harris's idea, that any kind of religiosity, even liberal religiosity, gives cover to the more extreme kind. That as long as you give anybody a pass on believing anything supernatural, you're giving an okay to anything, anything supernatural, giving cover to it so we should strike at it wherever we find it. So that's, I think, one of the struggles or disagreements that sometimes exist . . . I used to be totally in the friendly approach because I want to treat other people the way I would want to be treated. I don't want to be ridiculed, so why should I ridicule somebody else? When you ridicule somebody they become defensive, you know, they fold their arms, they back away emotionally. I don't think it's a very good tactic, and I don't think it's very respectful. On the other hand, I did once have a young woman come up to me and say "it was the ridicule of religion that shook me" . . . So I think ridicule has its place, but we've got to separate ridiculing ideas from ridiculing people. I do think we should be respectful toward people, but you know, if someone says the earth is only 6,000 years old, we can say "that's ridiculous because," and you have to get into some evidence.

Some elements of this passage worth highlighting include Michael's summary of the "friendly" (accommodation) position as being rooted in a desire not to alienate "liberal religious people who might vote with us." He indicated that the essence of this position is the view that social issues and politics are of primary concern, whereas for "hardline" (confrontation) atheists religion is an enemy, and the imperative to attack it wherever it is found trumps other concerns. When it comes to his own opinion on which strategy is better, he expressed considerable ambivalence, explaining that he "used to be totally in the friendly approach," indicating that he has wavered. He argued that ridicule is not a good tactic, but then also suggested that ridicule has its place but should be accompanied by respect. The contradictory nature of this statement reflects the ambivalence many atheists feel about the issue.

Another respondent who expressed a similar ambivalence regarding strategy is Terry, a 51-year-old gay man from Ontario who was raised in the United Church. He described his desire to cooperate with liberal religious groups while at the same time trying to balance this strategic choice with a "strong dislike" for religion in general that comes in part from its association with conservative positions on sexuality:

> I want to try to build bridges and be one of those atheists that are, like, building bridges with liberal religious people. It's not possible to do it with fundamentalists, there's too much of a divide . . . You know, you don't want to really piss them off if they're just liberal Christians or whatever or liberal Muslims, and they have some of the same values that we have, for human rights and things like that, women's rights and gay rights, stuff like that . . . I do have to be careful because, like I said, I do have issues with religion. I wouldn't call it hatred, but a very strong dislike . . . I can't let that voice out, and I have to think, maybe you're being a little harsh. You know, maybe, try to balance yourself, you know? Not all religious people are like that. Which is true, so it's good for me to actually go out and meet religious people, and I don't enough because I'm always with atheists, right? So it's good to have that balance because it's easy to get hooked into, when you're in a movement, it's easy to get wrapped up in "Yeah, yeah," you know, that kind of fanaticism. And I'm not really like that, like, I do have a lot of anger about a lot of things about religion, but I also respect people and their right to believe whatever they want to believe. So there's a bit of a fight there in my head.

Like Michael, Terry spoke about building relationships with "liberal religious people" with whom he and other atheists share core values relating to human rights. His concerns are related to questions of social justice rather than a desire to assert the superiority of truths revealed by science. Like Michael, his humanistic values and desire to advance liberal politics take priority over an ideological conflict with religion. Also like Michael, he expressed considerable ambivalence on how to relate to religious people. Taking a "friendly" or "accommodating" approach involves a constant struggle with some deeply felt antagonism toward religion. The ambivalence is even clearer in his comments about which New Atheists he likes most:

> I think actually of all of them I probably like him [Dennett] the best, even though I've read less of him than anyone. He just seems kind of moderate, he's not like, he doesn't have anger. Although I

do like Hitchens. A lot of atheists don't like him 'cause he's too loud and offensive and pisses off religious people, but like, we've been pissed off by religious people a long time, so why not?

Terry at once favors Dennett for his "moderate" approach that comes without "anger" but at the same time likes Hitchens for precisely the opposite reason: because his approach is blatantly combative. In relation to his comments regarding strategy, it seems that Terry favors an accommodating position as a reasoned strategic approach but struggles with his more emotional and reactionary side that responds to aggression and attack.

While struggling on the question of strategy and relating to religious people, Terry is less ambivalent when it comes to the ideological divide between those Marcia calls "purists" (i.e., New Atheists) and the more "open-minded" secular humanists. He referred to this divide while discussing an experience with the Japanese healing art Reiki in which, contrary to his expectations, he found himself convinced of its effectiveness:

> As a very strong atheist, I thought, this is challenging my whole worldview. And time and time again other stuff has happened where it's like, how could that happen? So it gives me sort of an interesting perspective because a lot of people that are atheist, like especially some of the real vocal, loudmouth, angry ones, are like, there's nothing, the way it is is the way it is. And I'm going, no, I don't believe there's any god in the sky and stuff for universal energy, whatever, but there's so much stuff that we don't know, and just accept that, it's a great feeling. And actually a lot of people who are believers would probably not want to do Reiki because they think it's a demon's work or evil. And I'm thinking there's something to it, and one day science will probably show what it is, right? But until then, whatever, and that's the good thing about being an atheist, is that you're not just stuck believing these old stories that are 99.99%, I'm sure, false. It gives you the ability to accept that there's mysteries to be discovered, and it's exciting . . . Because some atheists are skeptics, right? And I'm a skeptic, obviously. But they're almost negative skeptics, they go in saying it's not true, there's nothing rational about it, without actually having an open mind, right? So I guess I'm an open-minded skeptic. There are possible things that we don't understand. And it's like, don't get

worried, skeptics, it's not because of something supernatural, it's a natural explanation that we don't understand yet.

Like Marcia, Alicia, and Fahim, Terry marked his distinction from "vocal, loudmouth, angry" atheists and emphasized the importance of being "open-minded" and avoiding a dogmatic approach that excludes certain questions and approaches. His description of atheists who say "there's nothing, the way it is is the way it is" is very much like Alicia's description of atheists who say "the brain is just the brain," and like her, he countered these views with "there's so much stuff that we don't know."

Sahani, 23 years old, was born in Sri Lanka and moved to Canada with her family when she was a small child. She was raised Hindu, as she describes it, "in a pretty lax way." At the time of our interview she had recently taken on an administrative position with an atheist organization, but after only a few weeks she was already having doubts about her participation in the movement that were related to the same issues raised by other respondents—that is, ideological dogmatism and a confrontational strategy. Her concerns emerged in her discussion of the Centre for Inquiry Canada's "Extraordinary Claims" campaign, another advertising campaign like the Atheist Bus Campaign that asserts that "Extraordinary Claims Require Extraordinary Evidence" and lists among these "claims" Bigfoot, UFOs, Allah, and Jesus:

> I didn't want to read *The God Delusion* because I felt like I had been driven to tears by these people who wanted to convince me that I was wrong, and I never wanted to put anyone else in that position. And I felt that these books and this campaign, Extraordinary Claims, is sort of doing that. They're not sitting in a corner and forcing you to listen to them, but it's such a private, such an intimate part of people's identities, even if they only believe a little bit or if they're on the cusp of switching, it's not going to help to tell them that they're idiots . . . So, like I was saying about the words "the God 'delusion'" and things like that. I think when it's a negative—when it's a campaign that's framed negatively by telling people to question themselves instead of seeing the benefit that comes from the other point of view. I mean, it doesn't seem to say "atheism makes sense," it's more like "religion does not make sense for these reasons," which doesn't give people an incentive to join the atheist movement. Even if I was religious or I was at that stage where I was on the cusp of not being

religious, seeing those ads would not make me want to become atheist. It would make me really angry, and it still makes me really angry
because I think it's the same attitude that a lot of evangelicals have,
where they have a specific frame to put things and their frame makes
sense to them. It's not going to make sense to you, and that rationalist framework that we each come to on our own as atheists does not
apply necessarily to religious people. And it's just—Creating a fence
is not a way to create dialogue . . . I'm not sure I want to stay openly
part of an organization that is doing that campaign right now.

While Sahani enjoys the experience of community provided by her atheist
group, she disagrees with its dogmatically scientistic and confrontational
approach, so much so that she is debating whether she wants to continue
participating. Like Marcia and Alicia, she compares some more dogmatic
atheists to evangelicals and feels that rather than trying to discredit religion, they should be focusing on what is positive about atheism. She
feels that applying a rationalist framework to religion and presenting it to
religious people is a fundamental error in understanding what motivates
religious people—that is, their beliefs are not motivated by reason. A confrontational approach, then, is misguided. She elaborated these views in
her discussion of the New Atheists' aggressive attack on religion:

> I feel like it turns people off more than anything, so it doesn't ac-
> complish what they're trying to do. And then, it doesn't accomplish
> what they're trying to do, and at the same time it makes atheists
> seem like these awful people who are belittling and creating really
> extreme analogies which we accuse the religious people of doing
> about atheists . . . It's when they talk positively about the meaning
> that atheism can bring versus when they talk negatively about what
> God has done to our society that I find more appealing.

> . . . people don't come to God as a scientific hypothesis. They don't
> come to it that way. If they're looking at it that way, they're already
> on the side of Richard Dawkins. So putting it in that framing is
> only really going to convince the people on the fence who are al-
> ready looking at this in that way anyway. I mean, I didn't decide
> that I wasn't going to believe in God because I thought about the
> rationale for it and then realized that, [through] overt, careful, ra-
> tional thinking, that I didn't believe.

Again, Sahani does not believe that rational argumentation and scientific evidence are going to convince people to give up their religious beliefs. She also thinks that the confrontational approach is a style of discourse that atheists criticize in religion and is thus hypocritical. Rather than focusing on the negative attacks, she prefers to focus on doing something positive: "I'd really like them to do more charity work to show that it doesn't have to be churches who do it. Because that's often an argument that comes up, about how we need religion because otherwise who would run the soup kitchens?" In taking this position, Sahani indicates that she would like her group to do some of the "healing" work that Michael described as the job of humanism. Sahani, like many other respondents, may not believe in God, but she is much more a humanist than a New Atheist.

Finally, Sahani made an interesting observation that is no doubt related to her experience of being a member of a minority group. She framed it in the discourse on Christmas and other religious holidays that sometimes comes up in the atheist movement:

> So there's this, I don't want to put a stereotype on this either, but it seems like people who are against Christmas are probably, they get the sense that anything cultural is sort of beneath them because they're not cultural, but they don't realize they're cultural. And it also speaks to somebody who's had a lot of privilege and comes from the majority culture and doesn't see that minority cultures, which include religious cultures, have just as much right to be there.

> But things to address I guess, it would be nice, now that we've talked about it, to talk about the intersection between culture and religion and where to draw the line for what we accept in terms of religion but what we need to accept in terms of culture. Because otherwise we're just, we're being blind and exercising a privilege that we don't have the right to exercise over these oppressed minorities.

Sahani notes a conflict between multiculturalism (or pluralism) and hardline atheism. We might again understand this in terms of ideological tensions between New Atheists and secular humanists, and confrontationists and accommodationists. For ideologically militant New Atheists, multiculturalism and pluralism are out of the question, since the goal is cultural homogenization through scientific hegemony. For secular

humanists who embrace a more accommodating position, multiculturalism is a value to be embraced.

There was discussion among respondents of tensions between atheism and humanism, which emerges in the equation of "hardline" atheism
(represented by those Marcia calls the "purists") with confrontation, while
accommodation is associated with a more "open-minded" approach that
emphasizes underlying values and political ideals rather than an attack on
religion. The latter approach is favored by humanistic atheists, who place
social concerns above ideological opposition to religion. The interviews
thus reflected the ideological division within the secular movement that
is manifest in disagreements concerning strategy and identity. The atheists I spoke to are generally supportive of a more accommodating atheism, with some ambivalence about the issue, because their objection to
religion seems to be a lower priority than liberal political concerns. The
ideological and strategic tensions, and the greater emphasis on advancing
a liberal agenda on social issues than attacking religion, reflect the generally humanistic orientation of the sample, in contrast to the scientific
orientation of the leaders and most of the official discourse. For these
members, social justice is a higher priority than the New Atheism's goal
of advancing scientism and legitimating scientific authority by attacking
religion. Their views on the purposes of the movement, which they feel
is primarily about community and creating a positive identity rather than
defending political secularism or converting the world to scientism, highlight this distinction. For most of the atheists I interviewed, the movement is not about changing the world or enhancing the authority or social
position of any particular group, but providing a sense of community and
belonging as a remedy for alienation. Such a goal sets these atheists apart
from their "leaders," who they do not really follow, and who are struggling
to maintain cohesion and support for cultural and political projects.

The distinction between leaders and members in terms of goals and
strategies can be understood more precisely in terms of a tension between
intellectual elites and grassroots activists. The intellectual elites—the
most important of whom are the New Atheists, but they include some
other figures in leadership positions—are motivated by a desire to continue the "secular revolution" that in the United States and Britain culminated in the displacement of a religious establishment by scientific
authority, which these elites are themselves the producers of. Grassroots
members and activists are motivated by their own interests, which include protection from discrimination, countering stigma, and gaining

a voice in the political sphere, goals that make identity politics a sensible strategy. Rather than a homogeneous group of followers of Richard Dawkins, the presumptive leader of the New Atheism, these members are agents who weigh the views of these leaders against their own ideas and lived experiences, asserting their own positions and goals for the movement. Unlike religious fundamentalisms, atheism has no text that serves as an unquestionable source of authority, so the meaning of atheism is continually constructed and reconstructed by individuals and groups with different views. The New Atheism is only one of these groups, and while *The God Delusion* might anchor a canon, it is not sacred. Perhaps most importantly, these members generally do not share the New Atheism's goal of universalization but instead seek to carve out a space for atheists in a pluralistic cultural landscape.

7

The Atheist Right

WILLIAM STAHL DESCRIBES the New Atheism as socially and politically conservative.[1] This view, stated in 2010, was ahead of its time, and it has mostly been ignored since then. Scholars have preferred to characterize the movement as "liberal."[2] Steven Kettell suggests that the politics of the secular movement are diverse and resistant to categorization.[3] This is true with respect to the movement from a broadly inclusive perspective, since, as we have seen in the previous chapter, movement participants and members of secular organizations have disparate and sometimes contradictory views. Much more research would be required before we could assign a relative weight to any particular ideological or political category in terms of general membership. But in terms of leadership and influential public figures, we can identify some distinct trends. Some of these lend support to Stahl's claim. The New Atheism and the secular movement are too diverse to simply label them liberal or conservative, but a connection to the right wing of the political spectrum emerges in several key areas: security (particularly in terms of the West's relationship with the Muslim world and the role of the state), economics, and gender.

Discourse in these areas underscores the intimate relationship between atheism and Christian fundamentalism, which in some superficial respects are diametrically opposed but in their political essence are far more similar than has yet been recognized. Just as there is a Christian Right, there is also an atheist Right, which is the clearest expression of atheism as a secular fundamentalism and response to the crisis of authority in late modernity. The atheist Right seeks to defend and universalize modern Western society and rejects challenges to its constitutive socioeconomic structure and hierarchy of authority. None of the New Atheists fits neatly into this category, but all of them contribute to the ideology in some respects. For the secular movement more generally, the unexpected emergence of the atheist Right is a further polarization in the tension between atheism and humanism at the heart of the movement.

The State, Security, and the War on Islam

Soon after the emergence of the New Atheism, Paul Kurtz made note of what he considered a disturbing totalitarian undercurrent in their thought. In a 2008 editorial in *Free Inquiry*, he wrote,

> Some recalcitrant foes of secularism insist that it is synonymous with atheism; some militant atheists agree with them. But I think that this is a mistaken view. Far from being secular, some militant atheists have sought to protect their "faith" by abusing the power of the state. Indeed, some totalitarian regimes that embraced atheism as part of their ideology, such as those in the Soviet Union and Cambodia, have persecuted—even exterminated—their religious opposition.[4]

Kurtz is far from the only voice within the secular movement to take exception to the totalitarian agenda of "militant atheists." In a commentary about the New Atheism in *Free Inquiry*, Matthew Flamm writes, "Those overly eager to identify coming theocracies can be expected to harbor preferred visions of the world containing their special idea of a unified State."[5] His point is that the New Atheism's critique of religion is strategic, intended to identify the horrors that would come with religious rule in order to highlight the superior nature of scientific authority, which is presented as the natural alternative. Kurtz and Flamm are correct that the secular movement, and the New Atheism in particular, exhibit some totalitarian tendencies with respect to the use of state power to enforce an ideological program and defend the current structure of power and authority, both within the West and in relation to enemies outside of it. Major intrusions by the state on individual freedoms, as well as imperialist projects, are frequently legitimated ideologically through the rhetoric of security and protection.

A good example that is unrelated to religion, but is revealing of the support for state power in accordance with scientific expertise, is Steven Pinker's support for higher rates of incarceration and harsher penalties as a means to reduce violent crime. This is related to his general thesis in *The Better Angels of Our Nature* that the modern state and its institutions, along with the spread of Enlightenment rationality, are responsible for a decline of violence in the world over the past few centuries. Pinker believes that crime rates have declined because "the Leviathan got bigger, smarter, and more effective."[6] In other words, the state's policing and incarceration apparatus became larger and more efficient and committed itself to stronger penalties. Pinker does criticize escalating rates of imprisonment, which disproportionately affect African-American men, but this is because there is an "optimum rate of incarceration" beyond which there are "diminishing returns" on its effectiveness, since once the most violent individuals are imprisoned, putting more people who are less violent in jail makes a smaller dent in the violence rate.[7] But at the same time, Pinker extends his advocacy for incarceration as a solution to violence to other smaller offenses that, by extension, will reduce violence. Noting that people who commit violent crimes are also more likely to drop out of school, engage in petty theft and vandalism, and abuse drugs, Pinker reasons that "A regime that trawls for drug users or other petty delinquents will net a certain number of violent people as bycatch, further thinning the ranks of the violent people who remain on the streets."[8] In other words, to reduce violence we could imprison not only violent offenders but also those who commit lesser offenses because they are statistically more likely to commit violence in the future. Advocating mass incarceration of drug addicts and the socially disadvantaged as a means to maintain order and security is a decidedly right-wing position.

While calculating the statistical effect of incarceration on rates of violence, Pinker takes no time to consider the obvious relationship between socioeconomic status and criminal behavior. Instead he simply refers to the problem of "violent individuals" who must be pulled off the streets, a dehumanizing view that removes these individuals from their social context and implies that they are by nature defective. This is the essence of the right-wing position on crime—that is, that crime is produced by criminals, not society. Shifting the causes of crime to the nature of the offending individuals absolves the state of any responsibility other than to incarcerate dangerous criminals and thereby protect law-abiding citizens. Pinker's endorsement of the expansion of the state Leviathan is typically neoconservative in that it is restricted to matters of security. On economics (as we will see below) Pinker supports unregulated capitalism which, absent artificial manipulation and state control, trends inexorably toward global prosperity and equality.

Another example that is more pertinent to the New Atheists' position on religion is Richard Dawkins' well-known and frequently stated view that religious socialization is a form of child abuse. He considers religious indoctrination to be much more insidious than the sexual abuse of children by Catholic clergy that has been making headlines periodically for over two decades. In a highly uncharacteristic move, he defended the Catholic Church, which he suggests may have been "unfairly demonized" over the issue of pedophilia because experiences of sexual abuse may be "false memories" concocted by "unscrupulous therapists and mercenary lawyers."[9] Even in legitimate cases, he claims that forcing religious ideas on impressionable young children is *more objectionable* than sexual abuse, which is relatively insignificant compared to the psychological torment of being brought up with Catholic beliefs. To illustrate this point he tells us that he was himself a victim of one of the teachers at his boarding school who "harbored an affection for young boys," an incident he describes as "an embarrassing but otherwise harmless experience."[10] This trivialization of the sexual abuse of children is presumably intended to allow him to argue that the indoctrination of children into religious belief systems is the most injurious form of abuse because it allows faith memes to infect the mind before its immune system (rational-scientific education) is prepared to fight them off. Further, Dawkins suggests that if religion does indeed constitute child abuse, then the state would have a duty to protect children from it, which might include taking custody of them to protect them from the offending parents.

Thus Dawkins, a self-proclaimed champion of freedom of thought, would punish parents who socialize their children in religious communities by forcibly removing those children from those communities. The state, in this situation, would enforce the secular agenda in accordance with the authority of scientific experts. Christopher Hitchens was fond of referring to the "thought police" of Orwell's dystopian totalitarian world when he described God as a mind-reading "celestial dictator" who would punish us for eternity for our private thoughts.[11] But Dawkins' views on child abuse and state-enforced restrictions on what one is permitted to teach one's children—and, crucially, the power that may be legitimately exercised in enforcing these restrictions—are as Orwellian as anything attributed to religion. The desire of the Christian Right to eliminate evolution from public school science curricula is no doubt censorious and repressive, but they do not suggest that parents who tell their children about evolution should have their children taken away from them. These proposed policies on religious indoctrination and child abuse are indicative of an undercurrent in Dawkins' writings advocating intricate social administration by 'expert' authorities who would wield tremendous power.

Other New Atheists have supported Dawkins' view (Hitchens and Harris most forcefully). Lawrence Krauss, normally more measured than his atheist colleagues, referred to religious indoctrination as "child abuse" in a July 22, 2014, tweet. But Krauss has said nothing about what the state should do about it, preferring to take a more neutral political position and focus on the epistemic conflict between science and religion. The same is not true for more militant figures in the movement who advocate for the exercise of state power in accordance with scientific authority. This is most obvious in the New Atheism's discourse on Islam, which is virtually indistinguishable from that of the Christian Right when focused on questions of foreign policy and relations with the Middle East.

This discourse came out clearly in July 2014, as Israel was dropping bombs on civilian targets in Gaza. Much of the world watched in horror as schools were destroyed and children were killed and maimed by mortar shells. For one who had spent years commenting on violence in the Middle East, Harris was conspicuously silent. His career was built on making the case that Islam is unique among religions in its violent aims and its threat to civilization. He describes it as a "cult of death" and claims that "it is only rational, therefore, for Israel to behave as though it is confronted by a cult of religious sociopaths."[12] In late July, in response to many Twitter comments asking him why he had not spoken up to condemn the violence, Harris finally posted an entry on his blog titled "Why Don't I Criticize Israel?" After beginning by saying that this is a "boring question" because he has criticized both Israel and Judaism in the past— presumably indicating his neutrality on the issue—Harris launched into a defense of Israel focusing on "an obvious, undeniable, and hugely consequential moral difference between Israel and her enemies":

> Needless to say, in defending its territory as a Jewish state, the Israeli government and Israelis themselves have had to do terrible things. They have, as they are now, fought wars against the Palestinians that have caused massive losses of innocent life. More civilians have been killed in Gaza in the last few weeks than militants. That's not a surprise because Gaza is one of the most densely populated places on Earth. Occupying it, fighting wars in it, is guaranteed to get women and children and other noncombatants killed. And there's probably little question over the course of fighting multiple

wars that the Israelis have done things that amount to war crimes. They have been brutalized by this process—that is, made brutal by it. But that is largely due to the character of their enemies.[13]

This statement suggests that Palestinians have brought this violence on themselves through their own actions, and that Israel is simply doing what it must do to defend itself, having "been brutalized"—or made to act brutally—by the actions of its aggressors. Harris argues that "Israel is not primarily to blame for all this suffering" and that "the Israelis take great pains not to kill children and other noncombatants." Ignoring the many civilian casualties in Israel's strikes in July 2014, and the fact that many were children, Harris claims that the distinction between the two sides can be understood with respect to the use of human shields:

Who uses human shields? Well, Hamas certainly does. They shoot their rockets from residential neighborhoods, from beside schools, and hospitals, and mosques. Muslims in other recent conflicts, in Iraq and elsewhere, have also used human shields. They have laid their rifles on the shoulders of their own children and shot from behind their bodies.[14]

With these comments Harris for a moment slips from behind his own shield of rationality and allows a glimpse of the true nature of his feelings about Muslims. His words and writings paint a portrait of a group of subhumans whose concern for the lives of their own children is gladly surrendered for the opportunity to quench their thirst for blood. Much of Harris's blog entry focuses on human shields as the marker of a moral imbalance between Israel and Muslims. He does not address the question of whether there is a clear and significant moral imbalance between using a human shield and dropping a bomb on a school. Harris begins his piece with the appropriate comment that both sides bear some responsibility for the ongoing conflict. But he then proceeds to argue precisely the opposite: that Israel is a civilized nation doing only what it must to protect itself from the violent barbarians at its gates.

All of this represents the same position he has held for years. He made similar comments in 2012:

The Israelis are confronting people who will blow themselves up to kill the maximum number of noncombatants and will even use their own children as human shields. They'll launch their missiles from the edge of a hospital or school so that any retaliation will produce the maximum number of innocent casualties. And they do all this secure in the knowledge that their opponents are genuinely worried about killing innocent people . . . And yet within the moral discourse of the liberal West, the Israeli side looks like it's the most egregiously insensitive to the cost of the conflict.[15]

Here Israel is cast as the civilized actor in this conflict, with Muslims to be understood as barbarians who exploit their opponent's greatest weakness, namely that their actions are constrained by a higher morality. The moral binary is clear in Harris's use of human shields as a rhetorical tactic: "There are people who will use human shields on one side, and there are people who will be deterred by other people's use of human shields: They're still worried about killing the children of their enemies. Those are two very different groups of people."[16] This is to be understood as a direct result of the different motivations of these two groups. For Israel, Harris tells us, the motivation is national security and self-defense, while Palestinians are motivated by Islam and the demand to conquer the Holy Land. Harris points to Muslim leaders who call for Israel's blood and for Islamic rule over the territory, while ignoring the existence of rabbis who call for the same approach. This is ideologically rooted in a representation of Israel as civilized and rational, as opposed to barbaric Palestinian Muslims who are "deranged" by their religion. This ethical division serves the purpose of legitimizing Western imperialism and strategic geopolitical interests.

Harris's binary view of moral and cultural differences is the basis of his critique of liberalism. Responding to an interview question on why people in the West consider Israel the "bad guys" in the conflict, Harris says,

I view that as a pathology of liberalism in which people assume that everyone everywhere more or less wants the same thing and ignores the endless supply of people with no obvious political or economic grievance who are willing to devote their lives to jihad.[17]

In the first part of this statement Harris raises a reasonable question about liberalism, but the denial of a legitimate political grievance on the part of Palestinians is an ideological tactic.

Harris has been a staunch supporter of the American military and security apparatus. He called Julian Assange a "creepy bastard" soon after WikiLeaks released thousands of confidential documents containing detailed accounts of espionage, torture, and attacks on civilian targets, and he condemned the organization for revealing information that is "keeping people safe."[18] His support for ethnic profiling in airports is captured in a statement, noted in an earlier chapter, that received a great deal of attention: "We should profile Muslims, or anyone who looks like he or she could conceivably be Muslim, and we should be honest about it."[19] Given that the global population of Muslims is highly geographically dispersed, with large concentrations in areas of the Middle East, South and Southeast Asia, and Africa, it is unclear what Harris feels a Muslim could conceivably look like, unless he simply means people who are not white.

Torture also meets with Harris's approval. He employs the limit case "ticking time bomb" scenario as his rhetorical instrument, but this is just an entry point to his defense of the legitimacy of the euphemistically named "coercive interrogation," which he suggests should be used in a "limited" fashion.[20] He does not specify what the limits are, though in *The End of Faith* he advocated the torture of one specific individual: Khalid Sheikh Mohammed, a suspected Al-Qaeda member in U.S. custody. Harris argued that if Khalid could supply information leading to the "dismantling" of that organization, the information should be obtained by any means necessary.[21]

Harris's support for surveillance, racial profiling, torture, and preemptive warfare, which is grounded in xenophobia and the discourse of security, bears all the hallmarks of neoconservative ideology. It is notable that he also supports gun ownership, which he defends by arguing that "the correlation between guns and violence in the United States is far from straightforward."[22]

Harris is not a lone voice among atheists on these issues. His views are supported by leading New Atheists, most importantly Christopher Hitchens. Once a Marxist and prominent spokesman for the Left, Hitchens shocked many observers with his unflinching support for the second U.S. invasion of Iraq. In his memoir, Hitchens identifies this moment as the end of his days as "a man of the Left" after becoming disillusioned with what he saw as the Left's cowardly response to the growing threat in the Middle East.[23] His support for American imperialism in the Middle East seemed to follow from his views on the nature of Islam and societies that are characterized by high numbers of followers of this religion, though as time passed his position slipped into unabashed defense of American interests and its unilateral exercise of military power. Contrary to other New Atheists who claim to be liberals and implicitly posit a correlation between liberalism and secularity, Hitchens wanted to sever the liberal–atheist connection:

> It is often unconsciously assumed that religious faith is somehow conservative and that atheism or "freethinking" are a part of the liberal tradition. This is for good and sufficient historical reason, having to do with the origins of the American and French revolutions. However, many honorable and intelligent conservatives have rejected "faith" on several grounds.[24]

In his review of Susan Jacoby's book *Freethinkers: A History of American Secularism*, Hitchens supported the idea that the activities of nonbelievers are an important and neglected element of American intellectual and social history, while taking exception to the "near-axiomatic identification of the secular cause with the liberal one."[25] It is not clear whether or to what extent Hitchens' position on economics changed along with his neoconservative shift on war and foreign relations. But it is notable that his Marxist critiques of capitalism all but disappeared in his later years, replaced by Islam as the root of the world's problems.

A similar political shift happened for Ayaan Hirsi Ali, who explains that her turn to the Right was a simple consequence of the fact that her views on Islam were unwelcome in the left-wing political parties she had worked with in the Netherlands. Ali is a distinctive figure within the New Atheism. A woman raised as a Muslim in Somalia, she is an anomaly within a group characterized principally by middle-class white Western male intellectuals. Her direct experience of socialization in a Muslim society—which included genital mutilation, violent physical abuse by male family members, and an arranged marriage that led her to flee to Europe—is the source of a kind of authority that the others do not possess. She thus demands to be taken more seriously, though her criticisms of Islam have brought her into close association with neoconservatives. Ali has long advocated prolonged warfare against "Islam" (precisely what that means is not clear) and derided Barack Obama's decision to scale back military action in Afghanistan as evidence of a "weak America that roars but retreats when the going gets tough"[26] that will embolden its other enemies in the Middle East. She is currently employed as an advisor on Islam by the American Enterprise Institute, a right-wing think tank that has interests well beyond her limited area of Islam, most importantly support for free market capitalism and globalization and opposition to organized labor.

It is an apparent irony that these atheists have found themselves warmly welcomed by conservative interviewers on *Fox News*, which is commonly understood as an ideological mouthpiece for the Christian Right. But this is only an irony if we think of them solely or primarily as atheists. Aside from the question of the existence of God, these atheists and right-wing Christians have much in common. Moving from metaphysics to politics, the line between the groups begins to blur. When Ayaan Hirsi Ali appeared on Glenn Beck's show, he declared that she was "one of the bravest people on the planet today" and repeatedly made note of what an honor it was to have her on the show to give her insider's take on the dangers of Islam. Bill O'Reilly, interviewing Hitchens on the subject of torture of terrorism suspects, referred to his guest as a "level-headed guy" as opposed to the liberals opposed to "any use of coerced interrogation." During Harris's appearance on the program there was a stunning moment when O'Reilly actually attempted to distance himself from Harris's view that most Muslims endorse violence, saying, "I don't necessarily agree that most people who are Muslim agree with blowing up children, I don't think they do. Am I wrong?" Harris then nuanced his position somewhat by saying that "we just don't know" what percentage of Muslims agree with this, but he also noted that the results of polls "have not been encouraging" to indicate that his suspicion was probably justified. In this exchange, O'Reilly was the more moderate voice.

Some other New Atheists are less vocal and not as obviously hawkish on these issues, but their position is nonetheless clear. In a sign of endorsement, Pinker tweeted a link on July 27, 2014, to Harris's "Why Don't I Criticize Israel?" blog post. Dawkins differs from the anti-Islam group of Harris, Hitchens, and Ali in significant ways and notably did not support Britain's participation in the invasion of Iraq. Given how his attention has turned so sharply from Christians who attack evolution to Muslim "barbarians" in recent years, however, it is a fair question whether he would take the same position today. In a July 28, 2014, tweet, he said he was "on the fence" about the Israel–Palestine conflict. Dawkins and Harris are regularly criticized for promoting Islamophobia, a charge they claim is meaningless because they deny that there is such a thing as Islamophobia, a term they suggest was invented to silence criticism.[27] While never directly advocating war or discriminatory social policies,

Dawkins has nevertheless become a leading voice against multicultural-ism and the accommodation of Muslim values in the United Kingdom, where such views are accompanying a rise in support for far-right nation-alist political parties. Dawkins may not support such parties himself, but as an influential public intellectual he is playing a role in fermenting anti-Muslim discourse. He is unapologetic about his views, and in an act of defiance against his critics, he has adopted the habit of including the hashtag "#barbarians" in tweets about Muslims.

Spencerism Versus Darwinism

The New Atheism's totalitarian and neoconservative streak is only one aspect of the growth of the right wing of the secular movement more broadly. Though it is still in an early latent phase, this is a remarkable de-velopment given the movement's historical connection to progressive po-litical movements. It emerges in the subtext of movement discourse, such as a Center for Inquiry blog post by current president and CEO Ronald Lindsay[28] criticizing Chris Mooney's book about the workings of the "Re-publican brain."[29] Lindsay here calls into question our understanding of the terms "liberal" and "conservative," particularly the mutual exclusivity of stereotypically liberal and conservative views. For instance, he takes issue with the presumed correspondence between conservatism and cli-mate change skepticism, thereby critiquing the notion of a tension be-tween conservatism and supporting science, and brings up the trope of Soviet communism[30] to argue that proceeding leftward we also see rejec-tion of science that conflicts with ideology. It is worth noting that atheists notoriously get frustrated by those who point out a connection between atheism and twentieth-century totalitarian political movements, yet Lind-say employs the same tactic in his critique of the Left. He also objects to Mooney's inference that liberals are more "open-minded" than conserva-tives by nature and argues that there is no inconsistency in being an athe-ist or a humanist and a Republican.[31]

Lindsay is opposed to government intervention in the economy to ensure a more egalitarian distribution of wealth because it removes incentives to individuals to "innovate" and "take risks," and he claims that humanism has no problem with "significant disparities in income and wealth."[32] His political views, like those of many libertarians, seem to lie somewhere outside of the traditional Left–Right spectrum. That is, economic libertarians align with the extreme Right on taxation and government regulation of the economy but might adopt progressive positions on social issues like sexuality and gender equality, education policy, and environmental stewardship. What is clear is that Lindsay is not an advocate for the Left, and his writings suggest that movements for economic justice are irrational, while the current system, with its free market and "incentives" for "innovation," is inherently rational and therefore just. His leadership of the Center for Inquiry is the clearest sign of contemporary atheism's departure from its roots in social justice movements and ideologies, with a group emerging that moves away from humanism and embraces something like Ayn Rand's vision of atheistic individualism.

Individual rights concerning free speech are a common theme in *Free Inquiry*. One striking example is regular columnist Wendy Kaminer's critique of the Left and the culture of political correctness for censoring ideas that might be deemed offensive, citing the example of a Harvard law student who was reprimanded for writing in an email that she is open to the possibility that African Americans are, on average, genetically predisposed to be less intelligent.[33] Kaminer points to the left wing of the academy and certain "anti-libertarian trends on campus that are anathema to reason"[34] as the cause of this censorship and the assault on individual liberty and freedom of inquiry.

The rhetoric of "freedom" and "responsibility" is not restricted to free speech and a sense of duty to truth. Economic freedom is also a major topic of conversation in *Free Inquiry*, sometimes overshadowing discussion of science and religion. For example, in an article titled "The Quintessential Secular Institution," Frank Pasquale argues that we should celebrate corporations as the most substantially secular institutions in human history and that we should not overgeneralize in our descriptions of them (i.e., they are not all avaricious and destructive). Tibor Machan argues that "everyone has the inalienable right to private property"[35] and that nobody has the right to make demands on anyone else's property or wealth. He equates state support for victims of natural disasters and illness with "penalizing" or "fining" other individuals, which is a violation of their right to private property. He further argues that the notion of "surplus wealth" is a "myth" because we cannot determine what constitutes a surplus here. His reasoning is that people who have a lot of wealth may be "powerfully enriched, psychologically, by holding onto wealth beyond what others may consider reasonable"[36]—in other words, they enjoy being wealthy. It is notable that Machan, an emeritus member of the Philosophy Department at Auburn University, has described Ayn Rand as "a writer with powerful philosophical ideas" and her novel *The Fountainhead* as "inspiring," "a literary masterpiece," and "*the* American novel of the twentieth century."[37]

Science writer Michael Shermer, publisher of *Skeptic* magazine and monthly columnist for *Scientific American*, makes regular appearances on *Point of Inquiry*. He is a libertarian and a Darwinist who has written books on evolutionary theories of morality and religious belief,[38] as well as "evolutionary economics,"[39] arguing that the free market is a natural reflection of innate human motivations related to economics and justice and concluding that a free market capitalist system has an inherent morality derived from nature. In a 2009 *Point of Inquiry* appearance, he argued for the abolition of state support for the unemployed: "How do I know that they can't actually earn that money? Maybe they just don't want to, they'd rather not work"[40] (it should be noted that he also expressed opposition to the practice of "corporate welfare," or government "bailouts" of private enterprises). In this same interview, he also defended increasing wealth disparity as a symptom of a healthy economy; claimed that individuals in the West are responsible for their own circumstances and that poverty is a result of making poor decisions; and argued that Ayn Rand's contemporary relevance is limited only by her vision of human nature, which is not supported by emerging theories in evolutionary psychology.

Shermer's interviewer, D. J. Groethe (the original host of *Point of Inquiry*), noted during the discussion that many of the "big guns" in the movement are libertarians. For instance, Tom Flynn has compared social welfare programs to Ponzi schemes,[41] and I have already discussed Lindsay's views on atheism's relationship to politics and economics. As Darwinists, they clearly espouse scientific atheism, and, indeed, their views are antithetical to humanistic atheism with its concerns regarding alienation, oppression, suffering, and struggles for social justice. The tension between atheistic individualists and more moderate liberal humanists is evident in a recent issue of *Free Inquiry* centered on the theme of activism in secularist organizations. It featured articles from members of various organizations offering examples of people "who are *living* the values of secular humanism" by collectively engaging in community service and volunteer work and organizations that believe that "secular humanism is a way of living that compels them to stand up and become part of their communities, encourages them to offer their hands to strangers, and inspires them to do what they can to improve the lives of their fellow human beings."[42] The issue comes with a "Note From the Editor," Tom Flynn:

> Several articles in this section take a strong position in favor of shared charitable or social-service work as a platform for secular humanist activism. It is not the intent of *Free Inquiry* or the Council for Secular Humanism to advocate this variety of activism for all. We recognize that some readers will . . . find the idea at odds with their understanding of secularism as an individualistic and cosmopolitan framework that encourages men and women to connect to the highest levels of society as directly as possible, relying on their community of belief for nothing that does not immediately concern their life stance.[43]

The authors in this issue offer stories of how they and others in their respective groups were inspired by humanistic concerns to collectively engage in charitable work to help others. This type of activity is evidently so contentious within the atheist movement that the pieces required a disclaimer noting that they did not represent the official position of the Center for Inquiry. Lindsay's column arguing that being a humanist and being a Republican are not mutually exclusive also appeared in this issue, providing contrast to the pieces arguing for a conception of secular humanism rooted in social justice, as well as refutation of their premise by a figure of authority.

As in the case of foreign relations and the war on Islam, there is a correspondence here between the atheist movement and the Christian Right. Not long after the publication of Flynn's comment comparing social welfare programs to Ponzi schemes, Texas Governor Rick Perry—a devout and very right-wing evangelical Christian supported by the pious Tea Party—garnered some attention for making a similar analogy concerning Social Security during his ill-fated campaign for the Republican presidential nomination.[44] This apparent irony points us to some interesting facts and questions emerging from the rise of libertarianism to a position of power and influence within the atheist movement, which brings new resonance to the comparison between atheists and religious fundamentalists because they share so much politically. In their opposition to state intervention in socioeconomic life (particularly in social welfare), their support for neoliberal capitalism, and their view that individuals bear responsibility for their own problems, these groups are united. While the New

Atheists are fundamentalists to the extent that their worldview is shaped by scientism and they reject all other claims to knowledge, they bear little similarity to the religious variant on the question of economics. The libertarians, on the other hand, have a good deal in common with Christian fundamentalists in terms of their position on the state and the market. Just as there are liberal Christians and a Christian Right, there seem to be both liberal atheists and an atheist Right.

Given the significant degree of correspondence between atheist libertarians and Christian fundamentalists on matters of social justice and inequality, we might ask whether the New Atheists have more in common with libertarian rationalists or with liberal Christians. PZ Myers, for example, describes himself as a "godless liberal."[45] At the 2010 Council for Secular Humanism conference, Sam Harris took pains to make it clear that he is a left-leaning liberal with progressive views on gender equality, gay marriage, economic inequality, and wealth redistribution (his views on immigration and race relations are an entirely different matter). In August 2011 he wrote a blog entry under the heading "How Rich Is Too Rich?" in which he advocated increasing taxes on the wealthy in order to address the economic crisis in the United States.[46] Noting the large amount of negative feedback he received about this post—which he said was "a little crazier than normal" and presumably from atheists—he followed it up with another post discussing the American "quasi-religious abhorrence of 'wealth redistribution'" and suggested that "the conviction that taxation is intrinsically evil has achieved a sadomasochistic fervor in conservative circles," including libertarians who consider it a species of theft.[47] This post included a critique of Ayn Rand's objectivism—which Harris described as "a view that makes a religious fetish of selfishness and disposes of altruism and compassion as character flaws"—in response to libertarians who were "enraged" that he would support taxation in any form.

Other New Atheists have generally avoided direct discussion of these topics, and when they have discussed them, they have not shown the same critical perspective that Harris takes. For one who comments so frequently on so many social issues, Dawkins is conspicuously silent on economics. This silence, accompanied with his relentless attack on religion as the source of social problems, should lead his followers to wonder where exactly he stands on the state of capitalism today. What is clear is that, unlike religious beliefs, libertarian economic views will not draw criticism from Dawkins, who twice refers to his "friend" Matt Ridley in

The God Delusion.[48] Ridley is a journalist and popular science writer who, like Shermer, defends his libertarian political position using the language and conceptual framework of Darwinism, most notably in his book *The Rational Optimist: How Prosperity Evolves*. While Dawkins is quick to ridicule anyone who expresses any religious belief, Ridley's sociobiological theory of unfettered capitalism as the engine of progress goes unmentioned.

Pinker is one New Atheist who has given some indications of his position in this area, though mostly indirectly through promoting pieces written by others. One example is a July 19, 2014, tweet linking to an editorial in the *New York Times* economics section arguing that "global inequality has been falling and that, in this regard, the world is headed in a fundamentally better direction."[49] The author, libertarian[50] economist Tyler Cowen, suggests that we should therefore see neoliberal policies of free trade and market globalization as a positive force from a global perspective: "Although significant economic problems remain, we have been living in equalizing times for the world—a change that has been largely for the good." His view is of "a world that, over all, is becoming wealthier and fairer," and he concludes that "globally minded egalitarians should be more optimistic about recent history, realizing that capitalism and economic growth are continuing their historical roles as the greatest and most effective equalizers the world has ever known."[51] In the tweet, Pinker admonishes "dataphobic journalism" for misleading people about economic inequality, as it does about violence (the topic of *The Better Angels of Our Nature*, which argues that violence is decreasing globally, has been for some time, and can be expected to continue to do so in the future, as we have embarked on a "Long Peace"). Pinker regularly tweets links to articles making similar claims about the positive effects of capitalism on equality at a global level. These articles are usually problematic in a number of ways, most importantly in equating rising wages among the world's poorest citizens in places like India and Africa with a net positive effect of global capitalism. The approval granted to these articles and their claim that capitalism propels us toward greater equality is in keeping with New Atheist ideology, which grants that there may be "local and temporary setbacks" (in Dawkins' description), but over the long term and in a broad perspective, civilization is moving forward and improving.

In another revealing tweet on August 1, 2014, Pinker linked to a *New Republic* article critiquing Thomas Piketty's *Capital in the Twenty-First Century*. The authors argue that Piketty is wrong that the accumulation of wealth over generations by a small number of rich citizens will ultimately lead to economic devastation and political conflict.[52] Rather, they envision a scenario in which the concentration of wealth over generations will in the long term result in the "exponential spread of capital into the hands of many," a notion arrived at through the premise that as the upper class procreates it spreads its wealth to an exponential number of citizens, since all offspring will supposedly not be able to find marriage partners within their own class. The net result is the idea that attempting to control the accumulation of wealth through progressive or hereditary taxation only delays the inevitable "utopia for the masses" that capitalist growth is destined to create. Pinker's endorsement of this idea is consistent with his general view that in the long term the trend of history points to a better world for everyone, and that we should recognize that the conditions are already in place to bring this about—this is the essence of the New Atheism's political position. While utopianism is often connected to politically radical strategies for social transformation that are necessary to realize the utopian dream, in the case of the New Atheism utopia is in progress. It is the end point of a trajectory of social evolution we are already on—the horizon of the realization of modernity.

In approaches such as those endorsed by Pinker, the evolutionary logic is the same as that which guides the New Atheists' view of progress and improvement in modern society. Capitalism is actually pushing us toward greater equality, rather than toward greater inequality, as all outward appearances suggest. This is a pseudo-Darwinian theory of progress. But the libertarian atheists take it much further. Not only is capitalism a force for good and for progress, but any attempts to artificially manipulate the effects of market capitalism are presented as unnatural. These include any state-regulated limits on the capacity of individuals or groups to maximize their own profit, the redistribution of resources for the purposes of minimizing inequality through taxation, and social welfare benefits and institutions to assist the more disadvantaged members of society. The atheists promoting this libertarian ideology are self-proclaimed Darwinists, but their views are actually more in line with Herbert Spencer's than Darwin's, as they distort the theory of evolution and apply it to society to serve a radically individualistic political agenda that is strongly in favor of an unregulated form of capitalism. For example, Shermer's "evolutionary economics,"[53] with its theory of the "invisible hand" of natural selection regulating the market, could be described as evolutionistic neoliberal apologetics. These Spencerians translate Darwinism into ideological legitimation for libertarianism through the rhetoric of freedom, individual rights, and human nature. The Christian Right has similarly translated Christianity into capitalist ideology through essentially the same rhetoric, substituting a religious vision of human nature for a scientific one while holding the same basic tenets. Though the foundational principles (Darwinism vs. Christianity) are different, the ideological upshot is the same, at least with respect to social inequality and the responsibilities of the state.

This correspondence points to a key tension within the secular movement, which targets liberal, left-leaning Christians for attack because of a disagreement on metaphysics, even though their basic political orientations are similar. Secular humanists and liberal Christians may disagree on who created the universe, but on more practical political matters it is reasonable to assume that there is significant agreement (though the political views of members of the secular movement is still not very well understood and demands further study). Libertarians, meanwhile, are inclined to denounce left-wing socioeconomic policies as much as irrational religious dogma. It is, in fact, difficult to determine which they find more objectionable, or indeed, which is of greater interest or more closely related to their goals, given that *Free Inquiry* and *Point of Inquiry* have in recent years featured so many libertarian critiques of taxation and state welfare programs and defenses of corporations and the free market. This puts the libertarians at odds politically with many atheists and secular humanists, and their tendency to emphasize the political dimensions of movement activity and the discourse of civil and individual rights, as opposed to the cultural universalization favored by the New Atheism, is a key distinction between those groups.

These tensions are well illustrated by the change in leadership at the Center for Inquiry. Paul Kurtz, the organization's founder, was highly critical of the excesses of capitalism and wealth concentration. In one *Free Inquiry* editorial he discussed the growth of "plutocracy," which he defined as "government of, for, and by the wealthy class in society."[54] He criticized rising inequality in America and the growing power and influence of corporations and suggested that a new response is needed:

> For more than two decades, we have been deluged by the *libertarian mantra*: that government is evil, that regulation and taxation have stifled the free market, that welfare is abused and needs to be drastically reduced, and that the amassing of wealth is the basic

American virtue . . . Marxism has been virtually defeated, and all too few critics have risen in its place to decry the excesses of capitalist greed or to defend social justice and the principles of fairness.[55]

Kurtz proposed progressive taxation as a solution to rising inequality, the same proposal that Harris made, and was also met with hostility.[56] He also pointed specifically to "radical libertarians" who oppose what he considers to be "common moral decency."[57] While Kurtz did not name anyone or specify that he was talking about libertarians within the movement, these comments indicate that as early as 2006 he was wary about the rise of radical libertarianism within his organization. By his own account, it was a group of militant libertarian atheists who took over the Center for Inquiry and removed him from his position. In the previous chapter, I referred to Kurtz's debate with Flynn about the relationship between atheism and humanism as a sign of a key tension within the movement. But the tension between libertarianism and social justice is a related and equally important tension. The two are inseparable, with Kurtz's views on humanism, accommodation, social justice, and capitalism opposed to another group's focus on atheism, confrontation, and economic libertarianism. The difference of opinion that led to the change in leadership at CFI is not only philosophical or strategic; more precisely, it is political.

This difference is clear in the new mandate set out for the organization under Lindsay's term as president and CEO. In his first *Free Inquiry* editorial, Lindsay marked his differences with Kurtz on movement strategy and the question of accommodation or confrontation: "Our first duty is to the truth, and if well-grounded facts or logic contradict the beliefs of a religious person, we should be able to express our criticism of those religious beliefs without regard to whether the religious person will be offended by our criticism."[58] He disputed Kurtz's view that being aggressive or offensive will not help the movement and argued in favor of multiple forms of expression, which may include slogans, cartoons, and works of art that mock religion, such as those exhibited on Blasphemy Rights Day. The theme of the first issue published during Lindsay's tenure was freedom of speech, and the endorsement of criticism and outright ridicule of religion clearly established the position of the new leadership.

On politics, Lindsay again marks a clear difference with Kurtz's view that secular humanism should lead to a concern for social justice. Lindsay counters: "With respect to many, if not most, questions, secular humanism does not point in any particular direction. Instead, it opens up our horizons so we can assume responsibility for shaping our lives through our personal choices."[59] Note here the notion that individuals are responsible for their circumstances, a tacit rejection of the very idea of structural inequality. Lindsay abandons the collectivist aims and notions of community and social responsibility favored by Kurtz, shifting instead to an emphasis on individualism: "Secular humanists hold that individuals have the responsibility to make use of the freedoms they enjoy. In particular, they should employ critical reasoning in making important decisions."[60] He rejected Kurtz's view that humanism involves particular cultural values, claiming instead that secular humanism involves a commitment to "civil equality and the dignity of the individual" who is not bound to any value system.[61] Lindsay's vision for the Center for Inquiry moves away from Kurtz's philosophy of secular humanism as a set of specific epistemological and moral principles and toward a libertarian ethic of individual freedom. Despite this shift, or perhaps because of it, there has been a resurgence of a discourse of social justice in the secular movement (reactions to Lindsay's public comments have played a prominent role in this resurgence, as we will see). While Kurtz would not live to see it, his view of secular humanism as a philosophy of social justice has taken on new life, and his hope that a group would emerge to counter the atheist Right has been realized, at least partially. What Kurtz probably would not have foreseen was the trigger for this development: a feminist response to sexism and patriarchy in the atheist movement.

The Elevator Incident

While libertarianism and radical individualism are important and fascinating aspects of the secular movement, the area in which the movement has perhaps demonstrated its conservative strain most clearly is in attitudes about gender. It is well known that many feminists who identify as atheists have experienced the culture of atheist groups to be very masculine and sometimes misogynistic, and a project of white men.[62] But it is only recently that this issue has entered the sphere of public debate, following the emergence of a group of feminist atheists who began to speak out about issues like the lack of representation of women at conferences, sexist comments by prominent movement figures, and sexual harassment at movement events and online. These feminists, and the critics who spoke out against them, have highlighted a major tension within the movement between those who want to focus strictly on promoting atheism and rights for atheists and others who feel that their atheism is closely related to other beliefs and concerns, notably regarding social justice. The division between groups with different goals, politics, and understandings of the meaning of atheism is the most important force shaping movement dynamics today. This was essentially the same division that shaped the movement in its earliest years, with current debates reflecting the same essential concerns that guided the development of the National Secular Society in the nineteenth century. The major difference is that in the secular movement today social justice is a concept used mostly in relation to questions of identity rather than class divisions.

Current tensions within the movement with respect to gender can be traced back to an incident known as "Elevatorgate." At the 2011 World Atheist Convention in Dublin, an atheist activist named Rebecca Watson participated in a panel discussion. By her account, several members of the panel and audience had drinks at the hotel bar following the day's events, until finally at about 4 a.m. Watson told her companions she was tired and would go to bed. A man among this group, whom she had never met before, went with her, ostensibly to return to his room. While riding the elevator the man told Watson that he was interested in talking to her more and invited her to his room for coffee. She declined and several days later discussed the incident in a video[63] posted to her website, where she said that she interpreted the man's invitation as a sexual proposition, and that in the context of the closed space of an elevator the advance made her "incredibly uncomfortable." She concluded by making a simple request: "Guys, don't do that."

Watson's description of the elevator encounter was a brief aside in an eight-minute video that focused on other topics, but the response to it in the online atheist community was explosive. Dozens of misogynistic comments appeared on Watson's blog, many of them explicitly violent and suggesting that she should be raped and murdered. She discussed this experience at a Center for Inquiry conference as evidence for her claim that there was a problem with sexism and sexual harassment in the atheist community. PZ Myers covered the incident in a post[64] on his blog *Pharyngula* that also attracted a large number of misogynistic comments, and the incident soon became the topic of a viral blog-based debate. Virtually every significant figure in the secular movement weighed in to offer their opinion on the issue, usually centering on the question of whether the elevator incident was in fact sexual harassment.[65] Gradually the discussion

expanded to the status of women in the secular movement, with a continuing vitriolic backlash from commenters on blogs and discussion forums
referring to atheist women who were speaking out about the issue as
"feminazis," among many other cruder misogynist slurs.

The incident received mainstream media attention when Dawkins
became involved. He appeared in the comments section of *Pharyngula*
to give his take on the issue via a mock letter to an imaginary Muslim
woman that, given his stature, ignited a further frenzy of debate. The
comment reads:

> Dear Muslima
>
> Stop whining, will you. Yes, yes, I know you had your genitals
> mutilated with a razor blade, and . . . yawn . . . don't tell me yet
> again, I know you aren't allowed to drive a car, and you can't leave
> the house without a male relative, and your husband is allowed to
> beat you, and you'll be stoned to death if you commit adultery. But
> stop whining, will you. Think of the suffering your poor American
> sisters have to put up with.
>
> Only this week I heard of one, she calls herself Skep "chick,"
> and do you know what happened to her? A man in a hotel eleva-
> tor invited her back to his room for coffee. I am not exaggerat-
> ing. He really did. He invited her back to his room for coffee. Of
> course she said no, and of course he didn't lay a finger on her,
> but even so . . .
>
> And you, Muslima, think you have misogyny to complain about!
> For goodness sake grow up, or at least grow a thicker skin.
>
> Richard[66]

After a flurry of critical comments on the message board, Dawkins wrote
again to explain his view that the man did not actually attack Watson—
these were "just words"—and insisted that she had not suffered any real
injury:

> Rebecca's feeling that the man's proposition was "creepy" was her
> own interpretation of his behavior, presumably not his. She was
> probably offended to about the same extent as I am offended if a
> man gets into an elevator with me chewing gum. But he does me
> no physical damage and I simply grin and bear it until either I or
> he gets out of the elevator. It would be different if he physically

attacked me. Muslim women suffer physically from misogyny, their lives are substantially damaged by religiously inspired misogyny.[67]

For final emphasis, Dawkins posted one more comment stating clearly that what happened to Watson "was not even slightly bad, it was zero bad. A man asked her back to his room for coffee. She said no. End of story."[68] In response to the many comments noting that the situation was a threatening one because it took place in a confined space from which there was no escape, Dawkins said,

> No escape? I am now really puzzled. Here's how you escape from an elevator. You press any one of the buttons conveniently provided. The elevator will obligingly stop at a floor, the door will open and you will no longer be in a confined space but in a well-lit corridor in a crowded hotel in the center of Dublin.[69]

Dawkins' comments were reported in *Salon*, *New Statesman*, *USA Today*, and *The Guardian*,[70] among many other news organizations. For the first time since the New Atheism had risen to prominence and given new life to the secular movement, he found himself under attack by many of those who had viewed him as a respected leader. Commentators and bloggers, both within the secular movement and outside of it, explained why women find such experiences threatening and accused Dawkins of insensitivity to the threat of sexual violence that women must deal with, particularly in describing Watson's experience as a mere annoyance comparable to being stuck on an elevator with someone chewing gum.[71] Atheist blogger Ophelia Benson suggested that Dawkins' "Dear Muslima" letter indicates that he feels that Western women have nothing to complain about and implies that their experiences have no place in the movement's agenda.[72] Watson herself said, "to have my concerns—and more so the concerns of other women who have survived rape and sexual assault—dismissed thanks to a rich white man comparing them to the plight of women who are mutilated, is insulting to all of us."[73]

Some viewed it as ironic and hypocritical that Dawkins would treat an issue like women's experiences of sexual assault and discrimination so dismissively, given his proclivity to denounce the treatment of women in Muslim societies at every opportunity, as when he told the *Daily Mail*, "I do feel visceral revulsion at the burka because for me it is a symbol of the oppression of women."[74] But his comments make sense if one considers the overall thrust of his thought and his goals for the movement. Dawkins' "Dear Muslima" letter intends to make the point that Muslim women are subject to more direct, extreme, and systematic forms of violence and oppression, and therefore Western women should not complain about their situation, which is relatively much better. This refusal to acknowledge that gender inequality, misogyny, and sexual violence are significant problems in the Western world is an ideological necessity considering that Dawkins' position on religion is predicated on the assumption that religion causes social problems, and that reason resolves them. Equating the West with reason and civilization, and Muslim societies with primitive superstition and barbarism, the ideology of new atheism thus requires a categorical distinction between these contexts in the nature and extent of social problems.

With respect to gender, for the ideology to retain authority, Western problems and inequalities must be relativized—and thus trivialized—through comparisons with the extreme end of the spectrum of gender-based oppression and violence. Hence Dawkins' logic that because there are places where women experience genital mutilation and are subjugated to men by legal authority, feminism is a concept that should direct our concern to those experiences. The Western world is still under threat from religion but is more highly advanced because it has largely embraced scientific rationality, and thus problems with respect to gender are assumed to be solved. While Dawkins' views on race have received much less attention, the same logic and assumptions are at work when he says, "Fifty years ago just about everybody in Britain was somewhat racist. Now only a few people are . . . Some of us lag behind the advancing wave of moral standards, and some of us are ahead."[75] This claim by an upper-class, Oxford-educated white man that in Britain the problem of racism has largely been solved is demonstrative of an unwavering faith that scientific progress brings moral progress. The evidence for this is purely an ideological construction: a binary representation of Western civilization and the barbarism of the Muslim world.

Not all of the Elevatorgate backlash came from men. An atheist writer and activist named Paula Kirby launched an attack on the "feminazis" in the secular movement in an open letter entitled "Sisterhood of the Oppressed."[76] Kirby considers herself a feminist but objects to the radical feminism of what she calls the "Sisters," who go unnamed in the letter but presumably include Rebecca Watson and others who took a similar position on the elevator incident and Dawkins' comments.

Kirby's letter compares atheist feminists to Orwellian thought police, referring to their surveillance of what they perceive as antifeminist remarks made in the online atheist community. She also compares the strategy of the "Sisters" to the Nazis gaining power by fostering a sense of victimhood among the German people, and urging people to rise up and fight back against the Jew-led conspiracy that oppressed them; in the case of the Sisterhood the oppressors are men and women-haters. She also clearly states that the "Sisterhood's sense of victimhood" is not justified.

These comments are in line with the radical individualism promoted by the Center for Inquiry and libertarian rationalists in the movement. Kirby says that rather than trying to change others, women should focus on changing their own behavior and "take responsibility for ourselves and our own successes." The notion of responsibility is a common feature of libertarian atheist discourse, with the idea being that individuals must take it upon themselves to change their conditions through their own actions rather than "blaming" someone else for them. Kirby calls on women to "stop seizing on excuses for staying quiet and submissive, stop blaming it on men or hierarchies or misogyny or, silliest of all, 'privilege,' and start simply practicing being more assertive."[77] This is a sort of victim-blaming: women have an inferior position because that's the position they have taken, and it is up to them to change their behavior. Rather than addressing systematic discrimination and cultural norms, Kirby's view is that nothing needs to change except the individuals themselves, who must find a way to work within this system. Kirby describes herself as a feminist, but her feminism is secondary to her individualism.

Perhaps most revealing of her position is the moment in the letter when Kirby says that she did "a sociology module" as part of her undergraduate degree and therefore knows the arguments about "socialization and normative values, structural discrimination and all that malarkey."[78] The contempt for sociology among New Atheists is on display here. Concepts and theories that have been researched and refined for decades to enrich our understanding of human behavior and the social world are derided as "malarkey" by someone who did one undergraduate module on the subject. Kirby's comments are in line with the scientism that guides the ideological thinking of New Atheists. In this particular instance the comments imply that social and structural limitations are illusions fabricated by social science to excuse individual failings. Such illusions are used by weaker individuals as grounds to artificially adjust an already just social order. Scientism and the critique of social science are here wedded to the libertarian defense of individualism and denial of structural barriers to social mobility. The reaction to feminism within the secular movement, then, brings scientism and libertarian politics together, underscoring the right-wing dimensions of New Atheist ideology.

Elevatorgate, and in particular the reactionary comments by some leading figures (most importantly Dawkins), fomented discontent among feminists and other atheists for whom opposition to religion was related to its role in social oppression. Many activists and self-described feminist atheist bloggers took these events and revelations as an opportunity to reinforce their claim that discrimination and oppression based on gender and sexuality were simmering issues that the movement could no longer ignore, notably Greta Christina's plea in a blog post entitled "Why We Have to Talk About This."[79] A blogger named Jen McCreight joined in the criticism of Dawkins' instantly infamous "Dear Muslima" letter; it resulted in a torrent of reactionary sexism in her comments section, which was becoming a normal occurrence in posts on the topic.[80] Exasperated, McCreight discussed her disillusionment with the movement and her call for a "new wave of atheism" in a post that would prove to be a seminal point in the movement's history:

> I started speaking up about dirty issues like *feminism* and *diversity* and *social justice* because I thought messages like "please stop sexually harassing me" would be simple for skeptics and rationalists. But I was naive. Like clockwork, every post on feminism devolved into hundreds of comments accusing me being a man-hating, castrating, humorless, ugly, overreacting harpy . . . We throw up billboards claiming we're Good Without God, but how are we proving that as a movement? Litter clean-ups and blood drives can only say so much when you're simultaneously threatening your fellow activists with rape and death.[81]

McCreight's call was heard and discussed by a group of bloggers and activists who were sympathetic to the cause. Finally a new group emerged, calling itself "Atheism +," which means atheism *plus* social justice. According to the group's website, "Atheism Plus is a term used to designate spaces, persons, and groups dedicated to promoting social justice and countering misogyny, racism, homo/bi/transphobia, ableism and other such bigotry inside and outside of the atheist community."[82] Examining the group's FAQ page[83] and blogs written by some of its founders indicates that they embrace the scientism that the movement is grounded in and generally endorse a confrontational approach to religion. And yet, they claim that "there is a sizable contingent of atheists who agree that a desire for social justice connects to their atheism in a meaningful way."[84]

The emergence of Atheism + and the growing feminist critiques of inequality and harassment not only within the West but within the atheist movement itself are seen by some in the movement as potentially divisive. They are also a distraction from the New Atheist goals of legitimating scientific authority—a universalizing goal that cannot tolerate differences—and demonstrating the moral superiority of atheism over religion. Dawkins' reaction to the Elevatorgate debates was therefore not only ideological but also strategic, born of a pragmatic desire to maintain movement cohesion and ideological focus. The same concerns presumably motivated a speech given by Center for Inquiry president Ronald Lindsay at an event that became perhaps the most important incident related to Elevatorgate. Lindsay gave the opening remarks at the 2013 Women in Secularism conference, the second in what has become an annual event organized by the Center for Inquiry that features women speaking on such topics as religion's role in violence against women, the overlooked role played by women in the history of secularism, and the status of women in the secular movement today. In seeking to guard the movement against divisiveness, he expressed some views that had consequences for the movement that are still playing out.

Lindsay began in familiar territory, discussing the connection between religion and the subordination of women. But soon his talk turned to what many attendees interpreted as a direct critique of feminism, as Lindsay stated his objections to being silenced because of his gender:

> I'm talking about the situation where the concept of privilege is used to try to silence others, as a justification for saying, "shut up and listen." Shut up, because you're a man and you cannot possibly know what it's like to experience x, y, and z, and anything you say is bound to be mistaken in some way, but, of course, you're too blinded by your privilege even to realize that.[85]

These and other comments were the subject of a Twitter and blog exchange between Lindsay and Rebecca Watson over the course of the conference weekend. On May 17, 2013, the opening day of the event, Watson tweeted, "Very strange to open #wiscfi w a white male CEO lecturing women about using the concept of privilege to silence men." Lindsay responded on the same day that Watson's tweet "indicated as white male I shouldn't have spoken; I should have shut up." Watson blogged[86] about Lindsay's opening remarks the next day, with Lindsay again responding the same day. Lindsay's post was by any measure much harsher than Watson's, opening with the sentence, "Rebecca Watson inhabits an alternate universe."[87] Responding to criticism with insult was an ironic strategy given that he had just disparaged others for silencing tactics. The tone of his reaction was particularly striking given that Watson was one of the invited speakers to the event, sponsored by the Center for Inquiry. Watson was publicly attacked and personally insulted by the host of the event she had been invited to speak at, the very weekend that she was speaking.

Lindsay's speech and subsequent blog post were seen by many as a direct insult to the women gathered and the spirit of the event, which included a panel discussion on the topic of "Gender Equality in the Secular Movement."[88] Amanda Marcotte, a journalist and one of the speakers at the conference, wrote:

> I believe that there's little value in a secularist movement that, for fear of ugliness from sexists and reactionary atheists, avoids tackling religious *patriarchy* and settling for smaller, less important fights against theocratic forces over issues like school prayer . . . Lindsay hijacked a conference that was supposed to be about highlighting women's voices in secularism, and made the conversations mostly about a man's anger that men are sometimes asked to follow the ordinary rule of human discourse to listen to the evidence before you render a judgment on it.[89]

An organization called Secular Woman issued the following statement:

> Given our support and the aims of WiS [Women in Secularism], we find it stunningly unacceptable that Dr. Lindsay chose to greet our members, our Board, and other attendees with his personal, ill-formed criticisms of feminism rather than welcoming us all to the conference we had promoted and paid to attend.[90]

A number of individuals and organizations publicly announced a formal end to their relationship with the Center for Inquiry. Skepticon, an annual conference, said it would no longer accept CFI's sponsorship.[91] Popular blogger Greta Christina, another one of the speakers at the conference, announced that she was boycotting CFI and would no longer participate in their events.[92] This was in response to Lindsay's

> insulting, contemptuous, patronizing, wildly inaccurate, grossly un-professional opening remarks at the recent Women in Secularism 2 conference, in which he used his position of authority with the organization to scold the attendees and speakers, give them an ill-informed lecture on the history of feminism, and request that they talk about sexism and misogyny with more moderation and respect.[93]

The Center for Inquiry board released a statement indicating their "unhappiness with the controversy surrounding the recent Women in Secularism Conference 2" without naming Lindsay or taking a position on his comments, but only suggesting that CFI "believes in respectful debate and dialogue."[94] Christina interpreted this vague statement and refusal to condemn Lindsay's comments as tacit support for his views.[95] She ended her boycott a month after the incident when Lindsay, facing significant pressure from the growing revolt, apologized for his remarks in a very brief blog entry on the CFI website. While he said that he was sorry his talk "caused offense," he said nothing about the content of the speech or whether he still stood by it, but only that after discussing the matter with the organization's board, "I have a better understanding of the objections to the talk."[96]

Perhaps most significantly, Chris Mooney, host of CFI's official pod-cast *Point of Inquiry*, resigned his position and moved his production team (including co-host Indre Viskontas) to a new show hosted by the online news organization *Mother Jones*. In a public letter announcing the move, the group cited the Women in Secularism incident as the trigger for the decision:

> In response to public criticism of Lindsay's speech and blog post, CFI [the Center for Inquiry]'s Board of Directors issued an ambig-uous statement regretting the controversy, but going no further than that . . . The actions of Lindsay and the Board have made it overwhelmingly difficult for us to continue in our goal to provide thoughtful and compelling content, including coverage of feminist issues, as in past interviews with guests like Amanda Marcotte, Katha Pollitt, MG Lord, and Carol Tavris . . . We believe that this

controversy has impaired our ability to produce the highest quality podcast under the auspices of CFI and that our talents will be put to better use elsewhere.[97]

Some in the secular movement saw the aftermath of the elevator incident, including Dawkins' "Dear Muslima" letter, Lindsay's Women in Secularism comments, and the vitriolic blog-based debates as evidence that sexism was not only a problem, but that it was much worse than they thought. There is currently no way of quantifying antifeminism in the movement, either in terms of numbers or the nature of the views held. Blogs and discussion forum comments feature frequent claims that the atheist movement is populated by a significant number of people involved with, or sympathetic to the aims of, men's rights activism (MRA). MRA groups seek to provide a voice for men, whom they claim are increasingly at a disadvantage relative to women, suffer discrimination in some key areas, and are generally unfairly excluded from policy decisions.[98] Two major areas of focus of MRA groups are father's rights with respect to custody and freedom from excessive child support obligations, and domestic violence, which they argue affects men much more than is commonly thought. These groups vary in the nature and tone of their discourse and activism, ranging from a focus on relatively benign issues like equal custody rights to explicit and vehement antifeminism.[99]

There is little we can say without systematic research, but the relationship between the atheist movement and MRA, or at least reactionary antifeminism, demands to be explored further. Many of Lindsay's comments at the Women in Secularism conference and in the ensuing online debate were in the mold of MRA victimhood discourse. There is one clear example of a high-profile atheist activist who is also involved in MRA: Justin Trottier, the founder of the Centre for Inquiry Canada and the most prominent atheist in that country. Trottier was the leader of Toronto's Men's Issues Awareness Campaign in 2011.[100] A report by the Toronto newspaper *Now* suggested that he is also the leader of the Canadian Association for Equality (CAFE), and though Trottier says he does not hold an official leadership position and is not authorized to speak for the organization, he is named as the chair in its application to the Canadian Revenue Agency for charitable status.[101] The following passage is from CAFE's mandate:

While we support all efforts at achieving gender equality, we will work for balance and fairness within this societal project by focusing our limited resources on those areas of gender which are understudied in contemporary culture.

This has led us to a current focus on the status, health and well-being of boys and men, where attention, investment and support for educational and social programs stands at a level that is far from equal to the seriousness of the problem, while also being significantly underdeveloped compared to the resources in other important areas of social improvement.[102]

CAFE has been described in various reports as an MRA organization. Though it publicly claims to be about equality rather than men's rights per se, its website has linked to other MRA organizations, notably promoting a conference for the notoriously misogynist American group A Voice for Men.[103] In 2012 CAFE hosted a public lecture at the University of Toronto by Warren Farrell, author of *The Myth of Male Power*, which was protested by over one hundred students on the grounds that it constituted hate speech.[104] Trottier's involvement with MRA, both substantiated and speculated, is rumored to be the subject of significant turmoil within the Centre for Inquiry Canada that saw Trottier leave—or in some accounts be fired from—his position as national director.[105] He since returned in the role of national outreach coordinator, or as he stated on August 1, 2014, on Twitter, as "Ambassador" for the Centre for Inquiry Canada. The fact that Trottier has been so secretive about his involvement with CAFE compounds the mystery and speculation.

Gender is still a major issue in the movement, and the repercussions of Elevatorgate and the Women in Secularism incident are still playing out. This is true with respect to Dawkins, who has not changed his opinion on the place of feminism and social justice activism in atheism. He has made frequent comparisons to the situation of Western women and that of women in the Middle East on Twitter that are in the same vein as the "Dear Muslima" letter. He has also taken pains to promote Jaclyn Glenn, an atheist with a YouTube channel featuring her homemade skits and comedic commentaries about science and religion. Glenn has a page in the "Secular Stars" section of the Richard Dawkins Foundation website.[106] The page features a number of Glenn's videos that mock the feminist movement within atheism, including one titled "Atheism + Drama," which ridiculed Atheism + and accused it of being divisive.[107] The video featured Glenn as herself in conversation with a mocking caricature of a "radical feminist" (also played by Glenn, outfitted with square-framed glasses to remind us of a stereotypical bookish lesbian) whose every comment involved taking offense at the previous comment. On July 18, 2014, Dawkins tweeted a link to the video, which he called "brilliant." The Richard Dawkins Foundation website also featured Glenn's follow-up video called "Atheists—Beware of the Extreme Feminist!"[108] Dawkins himself also tweets regularly about what he perceives as the excesses of feminism and the social justice movement within atheism; for instance, on June 28, 2014, he wrote: "Learned a useful new phrase this week: Social Justice Warrior. SJWs can't forgive Shakespeare for having the temerity to be white and male." While Dawkins may have written "Dear Muslima" with an eye to the pragmatic concerns of movement cohesion and maintaining a clear focus on particular goals, the tone of the letter and his comments on feminism and social justice since that time are themselves divisively patriarchal, degrading and ridiculing any attempts to address gender issues in the Western context unless it involves the intrusion of Islamic values.

Antifeminism is indicative of a conservative and reactionary dimension within the secular movement motivated by the desire to dismantle religious authority while maintaining traditional but modern structures of power. The question here is who holds these views, and what groups and ideologies they identify with. Are the antifeminists New Atheists, libertarians, or both? Are the libertarians in positions of leadership and public recognition not only economically right-wing, but also conservative on issues of gender and foreign relations? Is their only desire to rid the world of religion, while not fundamentally changing anything else about the existing social arrangement, so that natural inequalities can play out to their natural and logical conclusion? What is the relationship between these political views and the ideology of evolutionism? Are the antifeminists a small but vocal conservative minority, or do they represent the movement mainstream?

These are questions that cannot be answered at the moment, but a relationship between right-wing views on gender and economics is clear in another part of Lindsay's *Women in Secularism* speech that went unnoticed and is much more significant than the "silencing men" comments that instigated the tumult. Lindsay referenced a random blog post he read that "stated that although patriarchy may predate capitalism, we cannot destroy patriarchy without destroying capitalism. Is the destruction of capitalism considered part of a social justice program?"[109] The implication here of a link between feminism and anticapitalist radicalism

is developed further when Lindsay expands on his criticism of the practice of "silencing" opposition:

> It's the approach that the dogmatist who wants to silence critics
> has always taken because it beats having to engage someone in a
> reasoned argument. It's the approach that's been taken by many
> religions. It's the approach taken by ideologies such as Marxism.
> You pull your dogma off the shelf, take out the relevant category or
> classification, fit it snugly over the person you want to categorize,
> dismiss, and silence and . . . poof, you're done. End of discussion.
> You're a heretic spreading the lies of Satan, and anything you say is
> wrong. You're a member of the bourgeoisie, defending your owner-
> ship of the means of production, and everything you say is just a lie
> to justify your power. You're a man; you have nothing to contribute
> to a discussion of how to achieve equality for women.[110]

Here Lindsay's right-wing position becomes clear in a reactionary criticism of tactics used by advocates of social justice to "silence" anyone
who objects to their criticisms of economic and gender inequality. In
this formulation, Marxists and feminists conspire to turn the middle-
class white man into a secular Satan. The subtext of Lindsay's talk is
a message to the middle-class white man, who, Lindsay suggests, is
under attack, vilified by a Marxist–feminist conspiracy to challenge his
dominant position. This speech is an excellent representation of the
beliefs and goals of the atheist Right, bringing its support for capitalism and patriarchy together in a defense of the established socioeconomic structure and its relations of power and authority. The Center
for Inquiry is a charitable educational organization that has tax-exempt
status and by law cannot support any particular political party, and in
any event it is unclear whether people like Lindsay and Flynn would
support the Republican Party given its close association with the Christian Right. But based on the views of its leaders and the content of its
publications, the organization is clearly closer to the right wing of the
political spectrum.

What is most revealing about Lindsay's comments about capitalism
and feminism is that the criticism he received focused exclusively on
the latter. No one mentioned Lindsay's comments about capitalism, and,
in general, the secular movement has not made an issue of capitalism,
class divisions, poverty, concentration of wealth, and so on—unless it is

libertarians defending it. The movement's self-proclaimed advocates of social justice have been vocal about discrimination based on gender, race, and sexuality but are virtually silent on economic oppression (the blog post Lindsay cited that questioned the connection between patriarchy and capitalism is an anomaly in secular movement discourse). This is perhaps a result of the fact that the secular movement is heavily populated by university-educated members of the middle class who do not acutely feel the effects of a vast economic imbalance. Lindsay may have made a strategic choice to link feminists to Marxists, since it is likely that he recognizes that his organization and movement are opposed to the latter—quite a departure from the days of the birth of the secular movement in England, when it was tied to socialism and was composed largely of the working class.

Atheism + and people associated with the social justice movement within atheism have received a good deal of legitimate criticism, and not just from right-wing ideologues in positions of leadership and authority. This has centered around the charge that the group engages in some of the Left's more totalitarian tendencies, using labels like "racist," "misogynist," "ableist" and so on against opponents to discredit them, a strategy of stigmatizing any who challenge their ideological tenets (precisely the subject of Lindsay's talk). The use of these tactics is a subject for further study, but my purpose here is to highlight the conservative dimension of the atheist movement. I have therefore focused on the reaction to the emergence of feminist atheism and Atheism + more so than on those groups themselves, though they clearly demand to be researched and analyzed more rigorously. The most problematic question is how the division between different groups within the movement can be understood after Atheism +, which combines scientific atheism, confrontational strategies, minority discourse involving the notion of individual rights, and a notion of social justice. It therefore does not fit neatly within any of the major ideological categories of New Atheism, secular humanism, or libertarian rationalism and may represent a truly novel development in the secular movement's history.

While gender is the issue of the moment in the movement's internal conversation, the unspoken but most important issue for those researching this phenomenon may be class. Social justice is discussed within the movement almost exclusively within the sphere of identity politics, while class and economic oppression are not on the agenda.

While Atheism + supporters focus on issues of identity and make their views on these matters clear, we know nothing about how they feel about economic inequality, globalization, labor rights, taxation, and social welfare. It is fascinating that today even atheists who advocate for social justice have little to say about capitalism.

Conclusion

A RADIATING BUSH

CHARLES DARWIN VIEWED evolution as a process with no fixed direction and invoked the metaphor of a "radiating bush" to describe adaptation and differentiation. The metaphor is apt for the secular movement, which historically has developed in relation to its socio-political context. We are now seeing a process of differentiation within the movement, with distinct groups seeking to advance their own agendas. There have always been tensions within the secular movement rooted in ideological and political differences that give rise to disagreements about goals and strategies. These unresolved tensions, ongoing since the movement first emerged in the mid-nineteenth century, are indicative of a movement in a state of perpetual latency, punctuated by moments when one group achieves dominance, as was the case for the New Atheism. The future of the movement is unclear, but the increasing diversity of ideological positions is currently producing fragmentation, with a traditional division between atheism and humanism becoming more complex as changing sociocultural circumstances are reflected in groups that combine these belief systems with political ideologies in novel ways. The clearest expressions of these developments are the atheist Right and Atheism +, which represent a break in the historical connection between scientific atheism and classical liberalism. These groups connect atheism to neoconservatism, libertarianism, progressive liberalism, multiculturalism, and identity politics. None of these represents the traditional domain of the secular movement, but they reflect the historical circumstances that shape its ongoing differentiation.

We are now in the midst of a revolutionary moment in atheism's history. New forms of atheism peculiar to the twenty-first century are emerging, most importantly a relationship between atheism and right-wing politics—a radical break from its traditional association with socialism and social justice movements. The two major historical forms of atheism are evolving within the contemporary secular movement, which is giving rise to novel forms that break down the boundaries between perspectives that the New Atheism sought to erect and stabilize. The New Atheism came to prominence in the mid-2000s, when the events of September 11, 2001 were not as distant, and the United States, Canada, and Britain were deeply involved in military conflicts in Iraq and Afghanistan. In the post-9/11 context, where religious fundamentalism on both sides of the "clash of civilizations" was reaching new heights of influence, the New Atheism presented a critique and a promise of social transformation that clearly spoke to many people. However, the cultural project of ideological universalism, which seemed tantalizingly realizable at the height of the New Atheism's popularity and public presence, has given way to more moderate and specific instrumental goals of constructing and defending a minority identity, and the functional differentiation of religious and political spheres. This strategy is a tacit recognition that the narrative of secularization has not been realized as expected and likely will not be in the foreseeable future. The evangelical approach of the New Atheism, which was predicated upon the belief that scientism was the inevitable and proximate trend of history, has thus given way to a defense of strict ideological boundaries through an identity strategy that emphasizes a distinction from, rather than assimilation with, mainstream society. But tensions regarding goals and strategies remain strong.

Atheism + and the feminist revolt in the secular movement illustrate the difficulty in maintaining cohesion within a movement comprising individuals united only by a shared identity rather than by a shared structural location. The debates concerning minority politics, strategies of accommodation and confrontation, and the connection (or lack thereof) between atheism and social justice are all tensions that must be reconciled to some extent for the movement to work in a united fashion to achieve its goals (which themselves are also up for debate). Atheism + explicitly distinguishes itself from secular humanism, making it clear that atheism is a crucial element. While concerned about issues of social justice, changing minds about the existence of God is still central to its mission. It introduces a further complication to movement dynamics by combining scientific atheism and a category-supportive identity strategy with a desire to engage in social justice, thus crossing some traditional ideological and strategic boundaries. It remains to be seen if sufficient "identity work"[1] can be done to overcome these differences and keep the movement from splintering into a number of distinct factions, which in fact seems to already be happening.

Libertarians, the most important part of the atheist Right, are interesting in that they share the scientific atheism of the New Atheism and Atheism +, but their primary goal is protecting individual freedoms rather than ideological legitimation or social justice. Libertarians explicitly claim that there is no unifying set of beliefs that characterizes "secular humanists," since for them humanism is nothing more than the right of self-determination; in this version of humanism there is no responsibility to others. Such atheistic humanism is the polar opposite of Christian humanism and its ethic of responsibility for the suffering of others. Ironically, the Christian Right is closer to the atheistic humanism (as opposed to humanistic atheism) of the libertarian rationalists than it is to Christian humanism. The bottom line is a political one—wherever these groups are positioned on metaphysics is less important than where they are positioned in terms of the practical manifestations of their beliefs. The atheist Right and the Christian Right might disagree about whether the universe came from God or from "nothing"[2], but in terms of how to organize a society, they have much in common. Conversely, progressive humanists and humanistic atheists have much more in common with liberal Christians than with either the atheist Right or Christian Right on matters of practical significance. On the issues of economics, gender, and foreign relations there is significant congruency between the Christian Right and the atheist Right. If these groups were political parties, their platforms would likely be very similar, with the major difference being the issue of whether children should be taught that human beings were created by God or by the invisible hand of natural selection. For all the vitriol launched toward religion, and for all the differences on metaphysical questions of the nature and origin of material reality, when it comes to politics and the ordering of the socioeconomic world—the things that really matter in terms of the conditions and possibilities of life—the New Atheism offers nothing radically different from that offered by conservative Christianity. Atheists are therefore confronted with a decision about what they consider a greater priority: social justice and welfare, or scientific hegemony. The answer to this question should determine whether they side with the secular humanists and "accommodationists," who assign priority to political and moral values, or with the scientific atheists and libertarians, who are "confrontationists" because their greatest priority is maintaining current structures of power and authority.

While there is a great deal of discussion about social justice in the secular movement, it is restricted almost exclusively to equality with respect to gender, race, and sexuality, while economic justice and class are rarely mentioned. Atheists who understand themselves as socially conscious have little to say about capitalism, which is perhaps not surprising given the typically middle-class composition of the membership. The old interests in socialism and the conditions of the working class that featured prominently in the early years of the secular movement are virtually invisible today, as a group of highly educated people with a degree of economic security have turned their attention to identity politics. The only group within the movement that engages with the issue is, of course, the libertarians—but they do so ideologically in order to celebrate capitalism and defend the legitimacy of the vast and expanding chasm that separates the wealthy from the lower classes. The slogan of the atheist bus campaign is quite telling of the social status of the atheists involved in it and their lack of understanding of religion's strong connection to suffering, oppression, and alienation. The message, "There's probably no God, now stop worrying and enjoy your life" can only rest on the assumption that without anxiety about heaven and hell, final destinations, the afterlife, and so on, we would be free of concerns. It also assumes a certain level of comfort and security that most of the people in the world do not share. It is the world's privileged who are free to idly contemplate metaphysical questions. Only those speaking from a position of relative privilege—including the feminists in the secular movement bringing male privilege into critical focus—could assume that metaphysical uncertainties and existential anxieties are the primary obstacles to happiness. The material concerns of the less fortunate among us do not appear in secular movement discourse, which operates within a middle-class intellectual sphere.

The growth of groups advocating the goals of libertarianism and social justice highlights the changing status of the New Atheism, which does not enjoy the same position of dominance in the movement it once did, its "cultural package"[3] having been weakened by its failed prophecy of sudden and mass secularization. These groups abandon the universalizing tendencies of New Atheism and instead adopt a defensive strategy of finding a place in the pluralistic landscape of late modern culture, which is in line with Taylor's account of the expanding religious and nonreligious forms of belief and practice that characterize the "secular age."[4] Despite these developments, Dawkins continues with his strategy of mocking religion and insulting believers as gullible fools, to the chagrin of those who believe that the goals of secularism would be better achieved by forging alliances. Such a strategic choice is understandable if we bear in mind his devotion to the ideology of evolution. He believes that he is engaged in a war of ideas—or "memes"—that will result in one set of memes ultimately selected for survival. Practical theories of social movement strategy and the realities of politics are insignificant when considered in relation to the power of the historical engine of natural selection. By implanting enough memes in enough minds, Dawkins believes that he can "cure" humanity of religion, which he continues to refer to as a mental illness. While he supports atheist activism, practical politics are actually of little interest to him, since he is interested in addressing the issue at the *ultimate*, Darwinian level. The meme of religion, according to Dawkins, is a product of biologically determined psychological predispositions and is therefore extremely powerful, but with enough work, it can be overcome and replaced with the memes of science, reason, and progress. In other words, the secularization of the mind must come before the secularization of the world.

This is a very different approach from that of the early days of secularism, when it was tied to programs for social transformation. Atheism was born of—and took shape in association with—politically radical intellectual and social justice movements, but the progressive element is absent in the New Atheists' view that there is actually no problem with the socio-political arrangement of modernity as presently constituted. Social inequality is not regarded as a contradiction between the promise of the Enlightenment and the reality of modern society, but as a healthy and natural feature of an evolving civilization. For the New Atheists, the only contradiction within modernity is the persistence of dangerous and irrational religious belief, which has proven more resilient than once thought within the secularization paradigm of the social sciences as well as in evolutionistic narratives of progress. The ideology of New Atheism, however, holds to the traditional secularization narrative, and a general faith in progress, that is tantamount to a passive acceptance of the conditions of modern life. Eagleton notes that in some formulations, "the very concept of ideology is synonymous with the attempt to provide rational, technical, 'scientific' rationales for social domination, rather than mythic, religious or metaphysical ones."[5] The New Atheism might be considered a case in point, instituting rational-scientific rationales for domination that replace less efficient (and more dubious) religious ones. In casting religion as a scapegoat for the inequities that plague modernity, asserting science as an unquestionable source of authority, and insisting that techno-scientific progress is equivalent to social and moral progress, it legitimates the current neoliberal world order, while blame for social ills falls to religion—a view firmly in line with the legitimating myth of modernity.[6]

There is disagreement among social scientists regarding the nature and extent of secularization, but there is no foreseeable human future where religion has vanished. The great scholars of the nineteenth and twentieth centuries who believed that religion was in its death throes and on the verge of disappearing from modern societies appear naïve to us today. In Western nations it may be the case that theism is waning, though there is at the same time an emergence of new religious movements and alternative spiritualities, and rising interest in Eastern religious beliefs and practices. The New Atheism's vision of secularization as a universal progression toward a postreligious scientific civilization is a historically and culturally contingent ideology that is utterly out of sync with contemporary social science, which recognizes that while there are undeniable transformations taking place in religious belief and practice, declining church attendance is not the same thing as atheism. Despite their professed attachment to Darwinism, it is also a distortion of the concept of evolution, which Darwin conceived as a radiating bush of adaptation and differentiation that was not leading toward any particular end point. A teleological narrative of linear progress in history breaks from Darwinian logic; it is, rather, a Spencerian vision of social reality. Following a Darwinian cultural theory, a more appropriate hypothesis would be that the trend of history is to produce increasing religious variety, rather than a homogenous faith in science.

As formulated in the New Atheism, the political doctrine of secularization is also a secular eschatology in which, having finally transcended the boundaries imposed on civilization by superstition, humanity is redeemed by science. This teleological narrative positions scientific hegemony and the triumph of modern Western society as the products of an evolutionary historical engine propelling us toward a climactic utopia— much like the utopian promise of evangelical preachers who herald the imminent return of Christ. To this extent it is a religious myth of origins and ultimate destiny, and its ideology of evolutionism provides a conceptual framework for finding meaning and purpose in the chaos of human existence. Groups associated with this doctrine, meanwhile, perform some of the functions traditionally associated with religion, such as providing a sense of community and solidarity. More precisely, these groups are for many a means to address alienation, as people look to atheist communities to provide something essential that religion provided, but with a system of belief they can support. The greatest irony of the New Atheism may be that its very existence undermines the old secularization paradigm, instead pointing to the myriad ways of being religious in the modern world. Just as the radiating bush of life grows unpredictably in relation to changing environments, the evolution of atheism is leading somewhere unexpected.

Notes

INTRODUCTION

1. C. Smith, *The Secular Revolution*
2. See Beattie, *The New Atheists*; Eagleton, *Reason, Faith, and Revolution*; Plantinga, *Where the Conflict Really Lies*; Stahl, "One-Dimensional Rage"; and Wilde, "Antinomies of Aggressive Atheism."
3. Eisenstadt, *Fundamentalism, Sectarianism and Revolutions.*
4. Davie, *The Sociology of Religion.*
5. Williams, *God's Own Party.*
6. Davie, *The Sociology of Religion*, 200–201.
7. Dawkins, *The God Delusion*; Dennett, *Breaking the Spell*; Harris, *The End of Faith*; Hitchens, *God Is Not Great.*
8. Cimino and Smith, "Secular Humanism and Atheism."
9. C. Smith, *American Evangelicalism.*
10. Gryboski, "Creationist Group Challenges Atheists."
11. Stark and Finke, *Acts of Faith.*
12. Cavanaugh, *Myth of Religious Violence.*
13. Taylor, *A Secular Age.*

CHAPTER I

1. See Bullivant, "Defining 'Atheism,'" for a good overview of the problem and the various approaches.
2. Martin, *Cambridge Companion to Atheism.*
3. Berman, *A History of Atheism.*
4. Asad, *Formations of the Secular.*
5. Buckley, *At the Origins of Modern Atheism* and *Denying and Disclosing God.*
6. Hyman, "Atheism in Modern History."
7. Thrower, *Western Atheism.*

8. Hampson, *The Enlightenment*, 37.

9. *Ibid.*

10. Henry, "Religion and the Scientific Revolution."

11. Hyman, "Atheism in Modern History."

12. Lindberg, "Science in Patristic and Medieval Christendom."

13. Buckley, *Denying and Disclosing God.*

14. Kors, *Atheism in France*, and Turner, *Without God, Without Creed.*

15. Turner, *Without God, Without Creed*, xiii.

16. Topham, "Natural Theology and the Sciences."

17. Hyman, "Atheism in Modern History."

18. Byrne, *Natural Religion and the Nature of Religion.*

19. Turner, *Without God, Without Creed*, 35.

20. Berman, *A History of Atheism.*

21. Thrower, *Western Atheism*, 107.

22. Casanova, *Public Religions.*

23. Olson, *Science and Scientism*, 67.

24. Comte, "The Theological Stage," 646.

25. Boyer, *Religion Explained*; Dawkins, *The God Delusion*; and Dennett, *Breaking the Spell.*

26. Comte, *Positive Philosophy*, 310.

27. Comte, "The Theological Stage," 651.

28. *Ibid.*, 650.

29. Olson, *Science and Scientism*, 67.

30. Dennett, *Darwin's Dangerous Idea*, 80, and Dawkins, *The Extended Phenotype*, 113.

31. Dawkins, *The Blind Watchmaker.*

32. Darwin, "Autobiography," 94.

33. Irvine, *Apes, Angels, and Victorians.*

34. Quoted in Dennett, *Breaking the Spell*, 124.

35. Larson, *Evolution*, 108.

36. Browne, *Darwin's Origin of Species.*

37. Desmond and Moore, *Darwin.*

38. Larson, *Evolution.*

39. Bowler, *Evolution*, and Jones, *Social Darwinism and English Thought.*

40. Radick, "Theory of Natural Selection."

41. Budd, *Varieties of Unbelief.*

42. Wiltshire, *Herbert Spencer.*

43. Spencer, *Man Versus the State*, 81.

44. Gondermann, "Progression and Retrogression."

45. Quoted in Durkheim, *Elementary Forms*, 22.

46. Dunbar, "Evolution and the Social Sciences," 32.

47. Desmond and Moore, *Darwin.*

48. Segal, "The Place of Religion."

49. *Ibid.*

50. Berman, *A History of Atheism*.

51. Buckley, *Denying and Disclosing God*.

52. Berman, *A History of Atheism*, ix.

53. Feuerbach, *The Essence of Christianity*, 33.

54. *Ibid.*

55. *Ibid.*, 12.

56. Hyman, "Atheism in Modern History."

57. Beckford, *Religion and Advanced Industrial Society*.

58. Marx, "Contribution to the Critique," 115.

59. *Ibid.*, 115–116.

60. *Ibid.*, 116.

61. *Ibid.*, 119.

62. Marx, "Concerning Feuerbach," 183.

63. *Ibid.*

64. See Fuller, *The New Sociological Imagination*, for an account of the role played by evolutionary biology in the ascendancy of scientific authority over religious authority at the academy.

65. Freud, *Future of an Illusion*, 20–21.

66. *Ibid.*, 21.

67. Freud, *Civilization and Its Discontents*, 22.

68. *Ibid.*

69. Freud, *Future of an Illusion*, 24.

70. Nietzsche, *The Gay Science*, 167.

71. Caputo, "Atheism, A/theology," 270.

72. Ansell-Pearson, *Nietzsche as Political Thinker*, 138.

73. Nietzsche, *The Antichrist*, 177.

74. *Ibid.*, 137.

75. Kaufmann, *Nietzsche*, 371.

76. Nietzsche, *Thus Spoke Zarathustra*, 118.

77. Salaquarda, "Nietzsche and the Judeo-Christian Tradition."

78. Freud, *Future of an Illusion*, 22.

79. Stenmark, "What Is Scientism?"

80. Peris, *Storming the Heavens*.

81. Peris, *Storming the Heavens*, and Froese, "Forced Secularization in Soviet Russia."

82. Larson, *Evolution*, 212.

83. *Ibid.*, 217.

CHAPTER 2

1. *Ibid.*, 118.

2. Huntington, *Clash of Civilizations*.

3. Bullivant, "New Atheism and Sociology," 120.

4. See Baker and Smith, "The Nones"; Lim et al., "Secular and Liminal"; Putnam and Campbell, *American Grace*; and Vargas, "Retrospective Accounts of Religious Disaffiliation."

5. Larson, *Evolution*.

6. Dawkins, *The God Delusion*.

7. Harris, *The End of Faith*, 129.

8. Dawkins and Kidd, *Root of All Evil?*

9. Katherine T. Phan, "Ted Haggard Shares Shocking Details in New Interview," *Christian Post*, January 27, 2011, http://www.christianpost.com/news/ted-haggard-shares-shocking-details-in-new-interview-48697/. After first denying the sex charges—though admitting purchasing drugs—Haggard eventually revealed that he struggled with homosexual desires and had engaged in sexual activity with other men. It would be several years before he would finally describe himself as "bisexual" while insisting that his faith required him to enforce boundaries on his sexual behavior.

10. Dawkins, *The Blind Watchmaker*.

11. Stenmark, "What is Scientism?," 24.

12. Bowler, *Evolution*, 361.

13. Richard Dawkins, "Dawkins on Militant Atheism," *TED: Ideas Worth Spreading*, Video File, accessed July 24, 2010, from http://www.ted.com/talks/richard_dawkins_on_militant_atheism.html.

14. Dennett, *Breaking the Spell*, 17.

15. Hitchens, *Paine's Rights of Man*, and Hitchens, *The Missionary Position*.

16. Hitchens, *The Portable Atheist*, xxii.

17. Christopher Hitchens, "Message to American Atheists," April 22, 2011, http://old.richarddawkins.net/articles/618232-message-to-american-atheists.

18. Grayling, "Can an Atheist?," 475.

19. Most significant among these are *The God Argument*, *The Good Book*, and *Against All Gods*.

20. Terry Eagleton, for example, described the New College as "odious," "elitist," and "the thin edge of an ugly wedge" opening the door to a two-tiered education system in Britain. See Terry Eagleton, "AC Grayling's Private University is Odious," *The Guardian*, June 6, 2011, http://www.theguardian.com/commentisfree/2011/jun/06/ac-graylings-new-private-univerity-is-odious.

21. Holwerda, *The Unbelievers*.

22. Ali, *Infidel*.

23. Ali, *Nomad*.

24. Coyne, "The Best Arguments."

25. Cimino and Smith, *Atheist Awakening*.

26. See McGrath, *The Twilight of Atheism*, and McGrath and Collicutt McGrath, *The Dawkins Delusion?*

27. Martin, *Religion and Power*, 43.

CHAPTER 3

1. See Asad, *Formations of the Secular*; Berger, "Desecularization of the World"; and Casanova, *Public Religions.*

2. Here I refer to Asad, *Formations of the Secular,* who describes secularization as a doctrine that constructs an outside "dark jungle" against which an enlightened space must be defended. I return to this idea in more detail later in the chapter (see note 19).

3. van Dijk, *Ideology: A Multidisciplinary Approach,* 256, 258.

4. Eagleton, *Ideology: An Introduction.*

5. Thompson, *Theory of Ideology.*

6. *Ibid.,* 4.

7. Eagleton, *Ideology: An Introduction,* 5–6.

8. Horkheimer and Adorno, *Dialectic of Enlightenment.*

9. Habermas, *Knowledge and Human Interests,* 4.

10. Stenmark, "What is Scientism?," 19.

11. Gorski, "Scientism, Interpretation, and Criticism," 279.

12. Olson, *Science and Scientism,* 3.

13. *Ibid.,* 60.

14. Flamm, "Strong Believers Beware," 23.

15. Dawkins, *The God Delusion,* 270.

16. *Ibid.,* 271.

17. Hitchens, *God Is Not Great,* 283.

18. *Ibid.*

19. Asad, *Formations of the Secular,* 191.

20. Brooke, "Science and Secularization," 105.

21. Berger, "Desecularization of the World."

22. See Asad, *Formations of the Secular*; Bruce, *God Is Dead*; Casanova, *Public Religions*; and Taylor, *A Secular Age.*

23. Taylor, *A Secular Age.*

24. See Calhoun et al., *Rethinking Secularism*; Gorski et al., *The Post-Secular in Question*; and Mendieta and Antwerpen, *The Power of Religion.* While the postsecular approach is dominating current debate, there are important exceptions and defenders of some version of the secularization paradigm, including Bruce, *Secularization,* and Norris and Inglehart, *Sacred and Secular.*

25. This fact suggests that a unified secularization thesis might be unworkable and that each subthesis should be considered a separate theory in its own right, as argued by Casanova, *Public Religions,* 211.

26. Casanova, *Public Religions.*

27. Asad, *Formations of the Secular,* 1.

28. See Asad, *Formations of the Secular,* and Casanova, *Public Religions.*

29. Asad, *Formations of the Secular.*
30. Bowler, *Evolution.*
31. Szonyi, "Secularization Theories."
32. Casanova, *Public Religions*, 41.
33. *Ibid.*, 17.
34. Hadden, "Toward Desacralizing Secularization Theory."
35. Bellah, "Between Religion and Social Science."
36. Asad, *Formations of the Secular.*
37. Ecklund, *Science vs. Religion.*
38. Hitchens, *God Is Not Great*, 64–65.
39. Martin, *Religion and Power*, 70.
40. Dawkins, *The God Delusion*, 2. The same notion appears in the book *God: The Failed Hypothesis* by American physicist Victor Stenger, a contemporary of the Four Horsemen.
41. Dawkins, *The God Delusion*, 31.
42. *Ibid.*, 48.
43. Buckley, *Denying and Disclosing God.*
44. Dawkins, *The God Delusion*, 125.
45. It should be noted that Dawkins' claim that Darwinian evolutionary theory satisfactorily closes the "gap" on the question of the origin of life is blatantly disingenuous. While Darwinism explains the evolution of organisms in terms of increasing complexity, it has no explanation for how the most primitive organisms came to exist in the first place.
46. Dawkins, *The God Delusion*, 158.
47. *Ibid.*, esp. 67.
48. Dawkins participated in another documentary for Channel 4 called *The Enemies of Reason* where he deals with this conflict between superstition and rationalism. The film follows him in conversations with psychics, astrologers, and so forth, as well as their followers, in an examination of how the continuing popularity of premodern superstitions and pseudosciences demonstrates that we have a long way to go to achieve a rational society and that the "premodern" enchanted world is very much still with us.
49. Dawkins, *The God Delusion*, 284.
50. *Ibid.*, 286.
51. Harris, *The End of Faith*, 232, 66.
52. *Ibid.*, 51.
53. Dawkins, *The God Delusion*, 3.
54. Harris, *The End of Faith*, 72.
55. Dawkins, *The God Delusion*, 163.
56. *Ibid.*, 166.
57. *Ibid.*, 164.
58. Dawkins, *The Selfish Gene*, 190.

59. Dawkins, *The God Delusion*, 174.

60. *Ibid.*, 176.

61. *Ibid.*, 194.

62. Dawkins, "Viruses of the Mind."

63. Dawkins, *The Selfish Gene*, 193.

64. Dennett, *Breaking the Spell*.

65. Dawkins, *The Selfish Gene*.

66. Evangelical pastor and television host Pat Robertson made this claim regarding a tornado in Oklahoma in 2013, just one example of his view that natural disasters are punishment for such sins as toleration of homosexuality and political secularism. He also claimed that the massive earthquake that devastated Haiti in 2010 was the result of a pact that nation had made with the devil to gain his assistance in liberation from French colonial rule. Likewise, Jerry Falwell revealed to his followers shortly after Hurricane Katrina hit New Orleans that the disaster was evidence of God's wrath, a punishment and warning of greater retribution to come for America's tolerance of homosexuality.

67. Dawkins, *The God Delusion*, 200–201.

68. *Ibid.*, 201.

69. Dennett, *Breaking the Spell*, 206–207.

70. *Ibid.*, 207.

71. Dawkins, *The Selfish Gene*, 198.

72. Hitchens, *God Is Not Great*, esp. 165.

73. *Ibid.*, 11.

74. Stahl, "One-Dimensional Rage," 102.

75. *Ibid.*

76. Harris, *The End of Faith*, 26.

77. Stocking, *Race, Culture, and Evolution*, 75.

78. *Ibid.*, 26.

79. *Ibid.*, 27.

80. Harris, *The End of Faith*, 107.

81. Stocking, *Race, Culture, and Evolution*, 122.

82. Harris, *The End of Faith*, 143.

83. *Ibid.*, 145.

84. *Ibid.*, 109.

85. *Ibid.*, 123.

86. *Ibid.*, 132.

87. Dawkins and Kidd, *Root of All Evil?*

88. Glenn Greenwald, "Sam Harris, the New Atheists, and Anti-Muslim Animus," *The Guardian*, April 3, 2013, http://www.guardian.co.uk/commentisfree/2013/apr/03/sam-harris-muslim-animus; Nathan Lean, "Dawkins, Harris, Hitchens: New Atheists Flirt with Islamophobia," *Salon*, March 30, 2013, http://www.salon.com/2013/03/30/dawkins_harris_hitchens_new_atheists_flirt_with_islamophobia; Murtaza Hussain,

Murtaza, "Scientific Racism, Militarism, and the New Atheism," *Al Jazeera*, April 2, 2013, http://www.aljazeera.com/indepth/opinion/2013/04/20134210413618256.html.

89. Sam Harris, "In Defense of Profiling," *Sam Harris* (blog), April 28, 2012, http://www.samharris.org/blog/item/in-defense-of-profiling.

90. Hitchens, *God Is Not Great*, 125.

91. Hitchens, *The Portable Atheist*, xxv.

92. Hitchens, *God Is Not Great*, 281.

93. Davie, *The Sociology of Religion*, 78.

94. Taylor, *A Secular Age*.

95. Davie, *The Sociology of Religion*, 78.

96. Stahl, "One-Dimensional Rage," 97.

97. *Ibid.*, 101.

98. Dawkins, *The Selfish Gene*, 1.

99. *Ibid.*, 191.

100. *Ibid.*

101. Dawkins, *The God Delusion*.

102. *Ibid.*, 347.

103. Dennett, *Breaking the Spell*, 259.

104. *Ibid.*, 103.

105. *Ibid.*, 102.

106. *Ibid.*, 341.

107. Bowler, *Evolution*, 360.

108. Midgley, *Evolution as a Religion*, 151.

109. Ross, *Science Wars*.

110. Ecklund, *Science vs. Religion*.

111. Ross Anderson, "Has Physics Made Philosophy and Religion Obsolete?" *The Atlantic*, April 23, 2012, http://www.theatlantic.com/technology/archive/2012/04/has-physics-made-philosophy-and-religion-obsolete/256203/.

112. David Albert, "On the Origin of Everything," *The New York Times*, March 23, 2012, http://www.nytimes.com/2012/03/25/books/review/a-universe-from-nothing-by-lawrence-m-krauss.html?pagewanted=all&_r=0.

113. Anderson, "Has Physics Made Philosophy and Religion Obsolete?"

114. Lawrence M. Krauss, "The Consolation of Philosophy," *Scientific American*, April 27, 2012, http://www.scientificamerican.com/article/the-consolation-of-philos/.

115. The blog-based debate between Jerry Coyne and philosopher Massimo Pigliucci that came in the wake of this was particularly hostile.

116. Steven Pinker, "Science Is Not Your Enemy," *New Republic*, August 6, 2013, http://www.newrepublic.com/article/114127/science-not-enemy-humanities.

117. Steve Neumann, "The One Thing Neil deGrasse Tyson Got Wrong," *Salon*, June 7, 2014, http://www.salon.com/2014/06/07/the_one_thing_neil_degrasse_tyson_got_wrong/.

118. Dennett, *Darwin's Dangerous Idea*, 82.

119. Dawkins, *The God Delusion*, 328.

120. The version of the article cited here is the one reprinted on Harris's personal website at http://www.samharris.org/site/full_text/the-end-of-liberalism.

121. The remark appears in the comments section of the website: http://old. richarddawkins.net/articles/4563-human-rights-ruling-against-classroom-crucifixes-angers-italy/comments?page=1#comment_411188. Accessed September 17, 2012.

122. Harris, *The End of Faith*, 45.

123. *Ibid.*, 48.

124. *Ibid.*, 52–53.

125. Asad, *Formulations of the Secular*, 59.

126. *Ibid.*

127. *Ibid.*, 60.

128. *Ibid.*

129. Eagleton, *Reason, Faith, and Revolution*, 44.

130. *Ibid.*, 42–43.

131. It goes without saying, of course, that Christian fundamentalism in the United States is a political phenomenon as much as a religious one, and that political and ethical precepts are often actually imposed on the Bible rather than derived from it. The most blatant example of this is the Christian Right's reading of the New Testament that portrays Jesus as a champion of individualism and, more absurdly, free-market capitalism.

132. Lewontin, "Biological Determinism as a Social Weapon," 16.

133. Asad, *Formations of the Secular*.

134. Martin, *Religion and Power*, 34.

135. Fuller, *Dissent Over Descent*, 87.

136. Lindberg, "Science in Patristic and Medieval Christendom."

137. Segal, "The Place of Religion in Modernity," 135.

138. Pinker, *Better Angels of Our Nature*.

139. Eisenstadt, *Fundamentalism, Sectarianism, and Revolution*.

140. Held, *Introduction to Critical Theory*.

CHAPTER 4

1. Campbell, *Sociology of Irreligion*.

2. *Ibid.*, 48.

3. Quoted in *ibid.*, 48.

4. The events discussed in this paragraph are described in Rectenwald, "Secularism and Scientific Naturalism."

5. Rectenwald, "Secularism and Scientific Naturalism."

6. Campbell, *Sociology of Irreligion*.

7. *Ibid.*, 53.
8. *Ibid.*
9. *Ibid.*, see p. 54.
10. Quoted in *ibid.*, 110.
11. *Ibid.*, 110.
12. *Ibid.*, 112.
13. *Ibid.*, 113.
14. C. Smith, *The Secular Revolution.*
15. *Ibid.*, 27.
16. *Ibid.*, 28.
17. *Ibid.*, 2.
18. *Ibid.*, 1.
19. *Ibid.*, 2.
20. *Ibid.*
21. See, for example, Lindberg, "Science in Medieval Christendom"; Shapin, *The Scientific Revolution*; and Smith, *The Secular Revolution.*
22. Bourdieu, "Intellectual Field and Creative Project," 121.
23. *Ibid.*, 118.
24. Smith, *The Secular Revolution*, 60.
25. Lebeau, *The Atheist.*
26. "About American Atheists," *American Atheists*, accessed on February 8, 2015, http://atheists.org/about-us.
27. "About the Secular Coalition for America," *Secular Coalition for America*, accessed February 8, 2015, https://www.secular.org/about/main.
28. "About the Foundation FAQ," *Freedom From Religion Foundation*, accessed February 8, 2015, http://ffrf.org/faq/item/14999-what-is-the-foundations-purpose.
29. Cimino and Smith, "Secular Humanism and Atheism."
30. C. Smith, *American Evangelicalism.* This theory was also employed in Smith's *The Emergence of Liberation Theology.*
31. C. Smith, *American Evangelicalism*, 91.
32. Taylor and Whittier, "Collective Identity," 111.
33. C. Smith, *American Evangelicalism*, 89.
34. Borer, "The New Atheism."
35. Cimino and Smith, "Secular Humanism and Atheism."
36. Cimino and Smith, "Atheisms Unbound."
37. Cimino and Smith, "Secular Humanism and Atheism," 411.
38. *Ibid.*, 418.
39. Campbell, *Sociology of Irreligion.*
40. Buckley, *At the Origins of Modern Atheism* and *Denying and Disclosing God.*
41. Gray, *Straw Dogs*, 126–127.
42. McAdam, "Culture and Social Movements."

43. See Asad, *Formations of the Secular*; Bruce, *God Is Dead*; Casanova, *Public Religions*; and Taylor, *A Secular Age*.

44. Cimino and Smith, "Secular Humanism and Atheism."

45. Melucci, *Nomads of the Present* and *Challenging Codes*.

46. Johnston et al., "New Social Movements."

47. Melucci, "Process of Collective Identity," 41.

48. Polletta and Jasper, "Collective Identity and Social Movements."

49. Armstrong and Bernstein, "Culture, Power, and Institutions."

50. Melucci, "The Process of Collective Identity," 43–44.

51. Snow, "Social Movements as Challenges to Authority," 11.

52. Armstrong and Bernstein, "Culture, Power, and Institutions."

53. *Ibid.*, 79.

54. Melucci, *Challenging Codes*.

55. Melucci, *Nomads of the Present*.

56. C. Smith, *Emergence of Liberation Theology*, 55.

57. *Ibid.*, 56.

58. Kurtz, "The 'True Unbeliever.'"

59. Cimino and Smith, *Atheist Awakening*.

60. Polletta and Jasper, "Collective Identity and Social Movements."

61. Bernstein, "Celebration and Suppression."

62. Bernstein, "Analytic Dimensions of Identity," 281.

63. Castells, *The Power of Identity*.

64. *Ibid.*, 8.

65. *Ibid.*

66. Castells, *The Power of Identity*, 10.

67. Taira, "New Atheism as Identity Politics," 102.

68. Melucci, "The Process of Collective Identity," 50.

69. J. Gamson, "Must Identity Movements Self-Destruct?"

70. Ghaziani, "Post-Gay Collective Identity Construction."

71. Armstrong and Bernstein, "Culture, Power, and Institutions."

72. Johnston and Klandermans, "Cultural Analysis"; Melucci, *Challenging Codes*; and Polletta and Jasper, "Collective Identity and Social Movements."

73. Snow and McAdam, "Identity Work Processes."

CHAPTER 5

1. Bernstein, "Analytic Dimensions of Identity."

2. Melucci, "Process of Collective Identity," 45.

3. Berezin, "Emotions and Political Identity."

4. Einwohner et al., "Identity Work in Social Movements."

5. Murphy, "March of the Godless."

6. Major sponsoring organizations include American Atheists, the American Humanist Association, the Richard Dawkins Foundation for Reason and Science, the United Coalition of Reason, the Center for Inquiry, the Stiefel Freethought Foundation, the Secular Coalition for America, the Secular Student Alliance, and the Freedom From Religion Foundation (Reason Rally, accessed August 13, 2013, reasonrally.org/sponsors-2).

7. Staggenborg, *Social Movements*, 100.

8. Richard Dawkins, "The Out Campaign," Richard Dawkins Foundation for Reason and Science, July 7, 2007, http://old.richarddawkins.net/articles/1471.

9. *Ibid.*

10. *Ibid.*

11. Out Campaign, accessed October 3, 2012, http://outcampaign.org.

12. Ariane Sherine, "Atheists-Gimme Five," June 20, 2008, *The Guardian*, http://www.guardian.co.uk/commentisfree/2008/jun/20/transport.religion. The word "probably" was initially used for legal reasons, since claiming that "there is no God" could lead to the advertisers having to prove it. When the campaign came to North America, the use of the word "probably" was explained by organizers as a reflection of the proper scientific position on the existence of God, which is not certainty, but skepticism based on lack of evidence.

13. Riazat Butt, "Atheist Bus Campaign Spreads the Word of No God Nationwide," January 6, 2009, *The Guardian*, http://www.guardian.co.uk/world/2009/jan/06/atheist-bus-campaign-nationwide.

14. *Ibid.*

15. Interview with Ariane Sherine, *Q: with Jian Ghomeshi*, Podcast Audio, January 12, 2009, http://www.cbc.ca/q/podcasts/q/index.html.

16. Atheist Bus Campaign, "A Quick International Round-up," accessed April 12, 2009, http://www.atheistbus.org.uk/a-quick-international-round-up/?cp=4.

17. Atheist Convention, "The Atheist Foundation of Australia is back on the Buses!," March 15, 2012, http://www.atheistconvention.org.au/2012/03/15/atheist-foundation-of-australia-back-on-buses/.

18. Johnston and Klandermans, "The Cultural Analysis of Social Movements."

19. Atheist Nexus, accessed October 1, 2013, from http://www.atheistnexus.org/.

20. Cimino and Smith, "Atheisms Unbound."

21. Darwin Day, accessed August 13, 2013, http://darwinday.org.

22. Center for Inquiry, "Carl Sagan Day," accessed December 12, 2012, http://www.centerforinquiry.net/carlsaganday.

23. Center for Inquiry, "Campaign for Freedom of Expression," accessed October 1, 2013, http://www.centerforinquiry.net/campaign_for_free_expression.

24. Center for Inquiry, "International Blasphemy Right Day, 2011," accessed October 30, 2011, http://www.centerforinquiry.net/oncampus/events/ibrd_2011_event/.

25. Melucci, "Identity and Mobilization" and *Nomads of the Present*.

26. D'Emilio, *Sexual Politics, Sexual Communities.*

27. Pinel and Swann, "Finding the Self."

28. Snow and McAdam, "Identity Work Processes."

29. Smith, "Becoming an Atheist."

30. See McGrath, *Twilight of Atheism.*

31. J. Smith, "Becoming an Atheist," 224.

32. Non-Believers Giving Aid, accessed May 3, 2013, http://givingaid. richarddawkins.net/campaign.

33. Freedom From Religion Foundation, "Ten 'Out of Closet' Freethought Billboards Go up in Tulsa," May 24, 2011, http://ffrf.org/news/news-releases/ item/2755-update-ten-out-of-the-closet-freethought-billboards-go-up-in-tulsa.

34. Freedom From Religion Foundation, "Join FFRF's Out of Closet Virtual Billboard Campaign," accessed July 11, 2011, http://ffrf.org/out/.

35. Dawkins, *The God Delusion,* 4.

36. *Ibid.,* 44.

37. Reason Rally, accessed October 3, 2013, http://reasonrally.org/about/.

38. This is the estimated attendance reported by Fearnow, Benjamin and Mickey Woods, "Richard Dawkins Preaches to Nonbelievers at Reason Rally," *The Atlantic,* March 25, 2012, http://www.theatlantic.com/national/archive/2012/03/ richard-dawkins-preaches-to-nonbelievers-at-reason-rally/255012/. However, estimates vary considerably depending on the source.

39. Reason Rally, accessed October 3, 2013, http://reasonrally.org/about/.

40. Kimberley Winston, "Atheists Rally on National Mall; the Reason Rally Largest Gathering of Non-Believers," *The Huffington Post,* May 24, 2012, http:// www.huffingtonpost.com/2012/03/24/atheist-rally_n_1377443.html.

41. Lori Aratani, "Atheists, Others Gather at Reason Rally," *The Washington Post,* March 24, 2012, http://www.washingtonpost.com/local/atheists-others-to-gather-at-reason-rally/2012/03/23/gIQAvqY2WS_story.html?tid=pm_local_pop.

42. *The Four Horsemen,* 2007, accessed March 2, 2013, https://www.youtube.com/ watch?v=vZ-xK_PEDgc.

43. Atheist Alliance International, 2007, "Atheist Alliance International Convention, 2007," Richard Dawkins Foundation, DVD.

44. Cimino and Smith, "Secular Humanism and Atheism."

45. To provide evidence for his belief that Christianity is much less pervasive in Britain than commonly thought, Dawkins commissioned a study through his foundation that concluded that most British are only nominal Christians because, among other reasons, most who identified as Christians could not name the first book of the New Testament (Paula Kirby, "How Religious are UK Christians?" The Richard Dawkins Foundation, February 14, 2012, http://old.richarddawkins.net/ articles/644941-rdfrs-uk-ipsos-mori-poll-1-how-religious-are-uk-christians).

Soon after the study was reported Dawkins was challenged on this point by an interviewer who asked him for the full title of Darwin's *Origin of Species*. Dawkins' inability to provide the answer (the full title is "On the Origin of Species by Means of Natural Selection, or the Preservation of Favoured Races in the Struggle for Life")—and his muttering "Oh, God" as he became flummoxed—were a major embarrassment (Peter McGrath, "Richard Dawkins Can't Recall the Full Title of Origin of Species: So What?" *The Guardian*, February 15, 2012, http://www.guardian.co.uk/science/blog/2012/feb/15/richard-dawkins-title-origin-species).

46. Grothe and Dacey, "Atheism Is Not a Civil Rights Issue."

47. TV Ontario, "PZ Myers on Science and Atheism: Natural Allies," Video File, accessed August 4, 2011, http://www.youtube.com/watch?v=3UoMnBmSlhE.

48. PZ Myers, "Why Are You an Atheist?," *Pharyngula*, February 1, 2012, http://scienceblogs.com/pharyngula/2011/02/why_are_you_an_atheist.php.

49. Cragun et al., "Discrimination toward the Non-Religious."

50. See Bainbridge, "New Age Religion"; Cragun et al., "Discrimination Toward the Non-Religious"; Edgell et al., "Atheists as 'Other'"; Gervais et al., "Do You Believe in Atheists?"; and Swan and Heesacker, "Anti-Atheist Bias in the United States."

51. Edgell et al., "Atheists as 'Other.'"

52. Neela Banerjee, "Soldier Sues Army, Saying His Atheism Led to Threats," *The New York Times*, April 26, 2008, http://www.nytimes.com/2008/04/26/us/26atheist.html?pagewanted=all.

53. Abby Goodnough, "Student Faces Town's Wrath in Protest Against a Prayer," *The New York Times*, January 26, 2012, http://www.nytimes.com/2012/01/27/us/rhode-island-city-enraged-over-school-prayer-lawsuit.html?_r=1.

54. *Ibid.*

55. *Ibid.*

56. Paul Fidalgo, "Atheist Group Settles Landmark Discrimination Case with Michigan Country Club," Center for Inquiry, February 27, 2013, http://www.centerforinquiry.net/newsroom/atheist_group_settles_landmark_discrimination_case_with_michigan_country_cl/.

57. *CBC News*, "Atheist Ads Vanish from Kelowna Buses," May 5, 2011, http://www.cbc.ca/news/canada/british-columbia/story/2011/05/05/bc-kelowna-atheist-bus-ads-missing.html.

58. Johnston and Klandermans, "Cultural Analysis of Social Movements."

59. Cimino and Smith, "Secular Humanism and Atheism."

60. Flynn, "'A' Word Won't Go Away."

61. Flynn, "Secularism's Breakthrough Moment," 17.

62. Flynn, "'A' Word Won't Go Away," 16.

63. Aratani, "Atheists, Others Gather at Reason Rally."

64. PZ Myers, "Nisbet and Mooney in the WaPo: Snake Oil for the Snake Oil Salesmen," Richard Dawkins Foundation, April 14, 2007, http://old.

richarddawkins.net/articles/881-nisbet-and-mooney-in-the-wapo-snake-oil-for-the-snake-oil-salesmen.

65. Military Association of Atheists and Freethinkers, accessed October 5, 2013, http://www.militaryatheists.org.

66. American Atheists, accessed October 1, 2013, http://www.atheists.org.

67. American Atheists, "Atheists Have Achy-Breaky Hearts, Want Apology from Billy Ray Cyrus for Bigoted Slur," February 25, 2011, http://www.atheists.org/press_releases/atheists_have_achy_breaky_hearts_for_bigoted_slur.

68. Epstein, *Good Without God*, xii.

69. ThinkAgainCFI, "Canada's Office of Religious Freedom: Protect Persecuted Atheists," Centre for Inquiry Canada. Video retrieved March 28, 2013, http://www.youtube.com/user/ThinkAgainCFI.

70. Cimino and Smith, "Secular Humanism and Atheism," 408.

71. *Ibid.*

72. *Ibid.*

73. Ghaziani, "Post-Gay Collective Identity Construction."

74. Gamson, "Must Identity Movements Self-Destruct?"

75. Ghaziani, "Post-Gay Collective Identity Construction."

76. Bernstein, "Celebration and Suppression"; Gamson, "Must Identity Movements Self-Destruct?"; and Ghaziani, "Post-Gay Collective Identity Construction."

77. Gamson, "Must Identity Movements Self-Destruct?," 391.

78. Polletta and Jasper, "Collective Identity and Social Movements."

79. See C. Smith, "American Evangelicalism," and Cimino and Smith, "Secular Humanism and Atheism."

80. Taylor and Whittier, "Collective Identity in Social Movement Communities."

81. Ghaziani, "Post-Gay Collective Identity Construction."

82. Cimino and Smith, "Secular Humanism and Atheism."

83. Borer, "New Atheism and the Secularization Thesis."

84. Flamm, "Strong Believers Beware," 24.

85. Bernstein, "Identities and Politics."

86. Council for Secular Humanism, Video File, accessed November 12, 2011, http://www.secularhumanism.org/laconference/live.html. This video serves as the reference for the following discussion of this debate and the source of all the quotations. Edited versions of the four presentations were published in the June/July 2011 issue of *Free Inquiry* (vol. 31, no. 4).

87. Cimino and Smith, "Atheisms Unbound," 21.

88. Mooney and Kirshenbaum, *Unscientific America*.

89. Mooney, "Do the New Atheists Make America More Unscientific?," 7.

90. Elissa Gootman, "Atheists Sue to Block Display of Cross-Shaped Beam in 9/11 Museum," *The New York Times*, July 28, 2011, http://www.nytimes.com/2011/07/29/nyregion/atheists-sue-to-ban-display-of-cross-shaped-beam-in-911-museum.html?_r=1.

91. American Atheists, "Now Is Not the Time for Atheists to Back Down," accessed December 20, 2011, http://atheists.org/blog/2011/08/05/now-is-not-the-time-for-atheists-to-back-down.

92. Adam Isaak (Producer), "The Future of Atheism: Beyond the Question of God," *Point of Inquiry*, Podcast Audio, December 3, 2010, http://www.pointofinquiry.org/archive.

93. Cimino and Smith, "New Atheism and the Empowerment of American Freethinkers."

94. Baggini, "Toward a More Mannerly Secularism."

95. Hoffman, "Why Hard Science Won't Cure Easy Religion," 47.

96. Barbara Bradley Hagerty, "A Bitter Rift Divides Atheists," *NPR*, October 19, 2009, http://www.npr.org/templates/story/story.php?storyId=113889251.

97. Kurtz, "Multi-Secularism: The New Agenda," 6.

98. Kurtz, "The 'True Unbeliever.'"

99. Kurtz, "Multi-Secularism: The New Agenda," 8.

100. Adam Isaak (Producer), "Secular Humanism versus . . . Atheism?," *Point of Inquiry*, Podcast Audio, June 26, 2009, http://www.pointofinquiry.org/archive.

101. Adam Isaak (Producer), "A Kinder, Gentler Secularism," *Point of Inquiry*, Podcast Audio, August 14, 2009, http://www.pointofinquiry.org/archive.

102. PZ Myers, "What Ever Happened to Paul Kurtz?," *Pharyngula*, May 25, 2010, http://scienceblogs.com/pharyngula/2010/05/what_ever_-happened-_to_paul_kur.php.

103. Epstein, *Good Without God*, xiv.

104. *Ibid.*, 9.

105. *Ibid.*, 11.

106. Stedman, *Faitheist*.

107. Isaak, "A Kinder, Gentler Secularism."

108. Lindsay, "Secular Humanism," 4–5.

109. Campbell, *Sociology of Irreligion*.

110. Rectenwald, "Secularism and Scientific Naturalism," 247.

111. Campbell, *Sociology of Irreligion*, 53.

112. Susan Jacoby, "A Woman's Place? The Dearth of Women in the Secular Movement," *The Humanist*, 2012, September/October, http://thehumanist.org.

CHAPTER 6

1. Touraine, *Can We Live Together?*, 94.

2. See Hunsberger and Altemeyer, *Atheists*, and LeDrew, "Discovering Atheism."

3. See Smith, "Becoming an Atheist" and "Creating a Godless Community"; Pasquale, "Portrait of Secular Group Affiliates"; Guenther, "Bounded by Disbelief"; and Guenther et al., "From the Outside In."

4. Morris and Staggenborg, "Leadership in Social Movements," 172.

5. Melucci, *Challenging Codes.*

6. Dawkins, *The God Delusion*, 2.

7. See Bernstein, "Celebration and Suppression," "Identities and Politics," and "Analytic Dimensions of Identity."

8. Bernstein, "Analytic Dimensions of Identity."

9. Snow and McAdam, "Identity Work," 48.

10. Pinel and Swan, "Finding the Self."

CHAPTER 7

1. Stahl, "One-Dimensional Rage."

2. See Eagleton, *Reason, Faith and Revolution*, and Schulzke, "The Politics of New Atheism."

3. Kettell, "Faithless."

4. Kurtz, "Multi-Secularism," 6.

5. Flamm, "Strong Believers Beware," 26.

6. Pinker, *Better Angels*, 121.

7. *Ibid.*, 123.

8. *Ibid.*, 122.

9. Dawkins, *The God Delusion*, 316.

10. *Ibid.*, 316.

11. Hitchens, *The Portable Atheist.*

12. Sam Harris, "Islam and the Future of Liberalism," *Sam Harris* (blog), March 13, 2012, http://www.samharris.org/blog/item/islam-and-the-future-of-liberalism/.

13. Sam Harris, "Why Don't I Criticize Israel?," *Sam Harris* (blog), July 27, 2014, http://www.samharris.org/blog/item/why-dont-i-criticize-israel/.

14. *Ibid.*

15. David Samuels, "How Atheist Author Sam Harris Unites the Christian Right, Radical Islamists and Secular Leftists," *Tablet Magazine*, May 29, 2012, http://tabletmag.com/jewish-life-and-religion/100757/qa-sam-harris.

16. *Ibid.*

17. *Ibid.*

18. Interview with Sam Harris, *The Joe Rogan Experience*, Podcast Audio, August 3, 2012, http://podcasts.joerogan.net/podcasts/jre-192-sam-harris-brian-redban.

19. Sam Harris, "In Defense of Profiling," April 28, 2012, http://www.samharris.org/blog/item/in-defense-of-profiling/.

20. Sam Harris, "In Defense of Torture," *The Huffington Post*, May 25, 2011, http://www.huffingtonpost.com/sam-harris/in-defense-of-torture_b_8993.html.

21. Harris, *End of Faith*, 198.

22. Sam Harris, "The Riddle of the Gun," *Sam Harris* (blog), January 2, 2013, http://www.samharris.org/blog/item/the-riddle-of-the-gun/.

23. Hitchens, *Hitch-22*, 308.

24. Hitchens, *The Portable Atheist*, xxiv.

25. Hitchens, "Believe It or Not."

26. Ayaan Hirsi Ali, "A Weak America Roars but Retreats When the Going Gets Tough," American Enterprise Institute, June 24, 2011, http://www.aei.org/publication/a-weak-america-roars-but-retreats-when-the-going-gets-tough/.

27. Jerome Taylor, "Atheists Richard Dawkins, Christopher Hitchens and Sam Harris Face Islamophobia Backlash," *The Independent*, April 12, 2013, http://www.independent.co.uk/news/uk/home-news/atheists-richard-dawkins-christopher-hitchens-and-sam-harris-face-islamophobia-backlash-8570580.html.

28. Ronald A. Lindsay, "A Closer Look at the Republican Brain," Center for Inquiry, April 15, 2012, http://www.centerforinquiry.net/blogs/ronaldlindsay.

29. Mooney, *The Republican Brain*.

30. His point centred on Trofim Lysenko, who devastated Soviet agriculture by applying Lamarckian evolutionary principles to food production.

31. Ronald A. Lindsay, "A Closer Look at the Republican Brain," Center for Inquiry, April 15, 2012, http://www.centerforinquiry.net/blogs/ronaldlindsay.

32. Ronald A. Lindsay, "Humanism and Wealth," Center for Inquiry, July 12, 2012, http://www.centerforinquiry.net/blogs/entry/humanism_and_wealth/.

33. Kaminer, "Epistemic Closure."

34. *Ibid.*, 14.

35. Machan, "Myth of Surplus Wealth," 13.

36. *Ibid.*

37. Tibor Machan, "The Fountainhead: An American Novel by Douglas J. Den Uyl," Foundation for Economic Education, March 1, 2000, http://fee.org/freeman/detail/the-fountainhead-an-american-novel-by-douglas-j-den-uyl.

38. See Shermer, *Science of Good and Evil* and *The Believing Brain*.

39. Shermer, *Mind of the Market*.

40. Michael Shermer, "Science, Skepticism and Libertarianism," *Point of Inquiry*, Podcast Audio, 47 minutes, May 22, 2009, http://www.pointofinquiry.org/michael_shermer_science_skepticism_and_libertarianism/.

41. Flynn, "Letters."

42. Becker, "Secular Humanism," 20.

43. Flynn, "Note from the Editor."

44. Jackie Calmes and Robert Pear, "Benefits Programs Face Bipartisan Effort to Cut Them," *New York Times*, September 8, 2011, http://www.nytimes.com/2011/09/09/us/politics/09social.html.

45. PZ Myers, "About," *Pharyngula* (blog), accessed February 1, 2014, http://scienceblogs.com/pharyngula/2006/07/22/about-about/.

46. Sam Harris, "How Rich Is Too Rich?," *Sam Harris* (blog), August 17, 2011, http://www.samharris.org/blog/item/how-rich-is-too-rich/.

47. Sam Harris, "How to Lose Readers (Without Even Trying)," *Sam Harris* (blog), August 24, 2011, http://www.samharris.org/blog/item/how-to-lose-readers-without-even-trying/.

48. Dawkins, *The God Delusion*, 125, 218.

49. Cowen, "Income Inequality Is Not Rising Globally. It's Falling".

50. For his endorsement of libertarianism, see Tyler Cowen, "The Paradox of Libertarianism," Cato Unbound, July 8, 2007, http://www.cato-unbound.org/2007/03/11/tyler-cowen/paradox-libertarianism.

51. Tyler Cowen, "Income Inequality Is Not Rising Globally. It's Falling," *New York Times*, July 19, 2014, http://www.nytimes.com/2014/07/20/upshot/income-inequality-is-not-rising-globally-its-falling-.html.

52. Eric A. Posner and Glen Weyl, "Thomas Piketty Is Wrong: America Will Never Look Like a Jane Austen Novel," *The New Republic*, July 31, 2014, http://www.newrepublic.com/article/118925/pikettys-capital-theory-misunderstands-inherited-wealth-today.

53. Shermer, *Mind of the Market*.

54. Kurtz, "America a Post-Democratic Society?," 21.

55. *Ibid.*

56. Kurtz, "Principles of Fairness."

57. Kurtz, "Multi-Secularism."

58. Lindsay, "Expressing One's Views," 4–5.

59. Lindsay, "Secular Humanism," 4.

60. *Ibid.*, 5.

61. *Ibid.*, 6.

62. See Mahlamäki, "Religion and Atheism," and Furseth, "Atheism, Secularity and Gender."

63. Rebecca Watson, "About Mythbusters, Robot Eyes, Feminism, and Jokes," *Skepchick* (blog), June 20, 2011, http://skepchick.org/2011/06/about-mythbusters-robot-eyes-feminism-and-jokes/.

64. PZ Myers, "Always Name Names!," *Pharyngula* (blog), July 2, 2011, http://scienceblogs.com/pharyngula/2011/07/02/always-name-names/.

65. For an overview of the incident and links to many of the blogs in question, see "Elevatorgate," *Freethought Kampala*, accessed May 18, 2014, https://freethoughtkampala.wordpress.com/2011/09/11/elevatorgate/.

66. See Phil Plait, "Richard Dawkins and Male Privilege," *Discover*, July 5, 2011, http://blogs.discovermagazine.com/badastronomy/2011/07/05/richard-dawkins-and-male-privilege/#.VM3tfSlX_ww.

67. *Ibid.*

68. *Ibid.*

69. *Ibid.*

70. See Tracy Clark-Flory, 2011, "Richard Dawkins: Skeptic of Women?," *Salon*, July 8, 2011, http://www.salon.com/2011/07/08/atheist_flirting/; David Allen Green, "Sharing a Lift with Richard Dawkins," July 6, 2011, *New Statesman*, http://www.newstatesman.com/blogs/david-allen-green/2011/07/richard-dawkins-chewing-gum; Kimberly Winston, "Atheists Address Sexism Issues," USATODAY.COM, September 15, 2011, http://www.usatoday.com/news/religion/story/2011-2009-15/atheist-sexism-women/50416454/1; and Emily Band, "Richard Dawkins, Check the Evidence on the 'Chilly Climate' for Women," *The Guardian*, July 24, 2011, http://www.theguardian.com/commentisfree/2011/jul/24/richard-dawkins-women-chilly-climate.

71. Emily Band, "Richard Dawkins, Check the Evidence on the 'Chilly Climate' for Women," *The Guardian*, July 24, 2011, http://www.theguardian.com/commentisfree/2011/jul/24/richard-dawkins-women-chilly-climate.

72. Ophelia Benson, "Guest Post: Saying Antifeminist Things Seems to Be the Path to YouTube Stardom," *Butterflies and Wheels* (blog), July 24, 2014, http://freethoughtblogs.com/butterfliesandwheels/2014/07/guest-post-saying-antifeminist-things-seems-to-be-the-path-to-youtube-stardom/.

73. Rebecca Watson, "The Privilege Delusion," *Skepchick* (blog), July 5, 2011, http://skepchick.org/2011/07/the-privilege-delusion/.

74. Liz Thomas "Fury over Richard Dawkins's 'Bin-Liner' Burka Jibe as Atheist Tells of His 'Visceral Revulsion' at Muslim Dress," *Mail Online*, August 10, 2010, http://www.dailymail.co.uk/news/article-1301750/Fury-Richard-Dawkinss-burka-jibe-atheist-tells-revulsion-Muslim-dress.html.

75. Dawkins and Kidd, *Root of All Evil?*

76. Paula Kirby. 2012, "Sisterhood of the Oppressed," July 1, 2012, https://docs.google.com/file/d/0B02RDDb71N8Xc2EwYmw5T2Z4eDg/edit?pli=1.

77. *Ibid.*

78. *Ibid.*

79. Greta Christina, "Why We Have to Talk About This: Atheism, Sexism, and Blowing up the Internet," *Greta Christina's Blog*, July 12, 2011, http://gretachristina.typepad.com/greta_christinas_weblog/2011/07/why-we-have-to-talk-about-this.html.

80. Jen McCreight, "Richard Dawkins, Your Privilege Is Showing," *Blag Hag* (blog), July 2, 2011, http://freethoughtblogs.com/blaghag/2011/07/richard-dawkins-your-privilege-is-showing/.

81. Jen McCreight, "How I Unwittingly Infiltrated the Boy's Club & Why It's Time for a New Wave of Atheism," *Blag Hag* (blog), August 18, 2012, http://freethoughtblogs.com/blaghag/2012/08/how-i-unwittingly-infiltrated-the-boys-club-why-its-time-for-a-new-wave-of-atheism/.

82. "Atheism Plus," Atheism +, accessed May 5, 2014, http://atheismplus.com/?page_id=127.

83. "Atheism Plus FAQ," Atheism +, accessed May 5, 2014, http://atheismplus.com/faq.php.

84. "Atheism Plus," Atheism +, accessed May 5, 2014, http://atheismplus.com/?page_id=127.

85. Ronald A. Lindsay, "My Talk at WIS2," Center for Inquiry, May 17, 2013, http://www.centerforinquiry.net/blogs/entry/my_talk_at_wis2/.

86. Rebecca Watson, "The Silencing of Men," *Skepchick* (blog), May 18, 2013, http://skepchick.org/2013/05/the-silencing-of-men/.

87. Ronald A. Lindsay, "Watson's World and Two Models of Communication," Center for Inquiry, May 18, 2013, http://www.centerforinquiry.net/blogs/entry/watsons_world_and_two_models_of_communication/.

88. "Schedule: Women in Secularism 2: 2013 Conference in Washington, DC," Women in Secularism, accessed June 21, 2014, http://previous.womeninsecularism.org/2013/schedule.html#_=_.

89. Amanda Marcotte, "An Open Letter to the Center for Inquiry," Raw Story, May 20, 2013, http://www.rawstory.com/rs/2013/05/an-open-letter-to-the-center-for-inquiry/.

90. Elsa Roberts, "Statement of Objection to Center for Inquiry CEO Ron Lindsay's Actions Regarding Feminism," Secular Woman, May 22, 2013, http://www.secularwoman.org/Statement_of_Objection.

91. Lauren Lane, "Skepticon Says Goodbye To a Sponsor," Skepticon, June 19, 2013, http://skepticon.org/skepticon-says-goodbye-to-a-sponsor/.

92. Greta Christina, "An Open Letter to the Center for Inquiry, Withdrawing my Participation and Support," *Greta Christina's Blog*, June 17, 2013, http://freethoughtblogs.com/greta/2013/06/17/open-letter-to-cfi-withdrawing-support/.

93. Greta Christina, "Parsing the Center For Inquiry's Non-Statement about Ron Lindsay and the Women in Secularism 2 Conference," *Greta Christina's Blog*, June 17, 2013, http://freethoughtblogs.com/greta/2013/06/17/parsing-cfis-non-statement/.

94. "Center for Inquiry Board of Directors Statement on the CEO and the Women in Secularism 2 Conference," Center for Inquiry, June 17, 2013, http://www.centerforinquiry.net/news/board_statement_wis/.

95. Christina, "Parsing the Center For Inquiry's Non-Statement about Ron Lindsay and the Women in Secularism 2 Conference".

96. Ronald A. Lindsay, "Some Remarks on My Talk at WIS2," Center for Inquiry, June 22, 2013, http://www.centerforinquiry.net/blogs/entry/some_remarks_on_my_talk_at_wis2/.

97. Chris Mooney, Adam Isaak, and Indre Viskontas, "Point of Inquiry Team Resigns, Launches New Show with Mother Jones," accessed June 9, 2014,

https://docs.google.com/document/d/1SEaa9gaIpeqpf1SA7GoUfoYwyL-B82oTppr7lbj6rx4/edit?pli=1.

98. Girard, "Backlash or Equality?"

99. Dragiewicz, *Equality with a Vengeance.*

100. Robert Cribb, "A Widely Observed Transformation in Male Social Status is Upon Us, Causing a Man-Power Backlash," *Toronto Star,* October 19, 2011, http://www.thestar.com/life/2011/10/19/cribb_men_are_the_new_underclass.html#.

101. Ben Spurr, "Men's Rights Whitewash," *NOW Magazine,* May 31, 2014, https://nowtoronto.com/news/story.cfm%3Fcontent%3D198263.

102. "Mandate/Mandat," Canadian Association for Equality, accessed July 15, 2014, http://equalitycanada.com/about/mandate/.

103. Ben Spurr, "Men's Rights Group Used Feminists' Names on Charity Application," *NOW Magazine,* June 24, 2014, https://nowtoronto.com/news/story.cfm%3Fcontent%3D198600.

104. Dan Smeenk, "Arrest, Assaults Overshadow 'Men's Issues' Lecture," *The Varsity,* November 17, 2012, http://thevarsity.ca/2012/11/17/arrest-assaults-overshadow-mens-issues-lecture/.

105. There are, for example, a number of blog posts that discuss the issue, although there is much rumor and hearsay within them: Teen Skepchick, "Emotions Overrule Rationality at CFI: Canada," *Skepchick* (blog), November 29, 2011, http://skepchick.org/2011/11/emotions-overrule-rationality-at-cfi-canada/; Jacob Fortin, "CFI Canada Members Have a Lot to Be Worried About," *The Good Atheist* (blog), November 22, 2011, http://www.thegoodatheist.net/2011/11/22/cfi-canada-members-have-a-lot-to-be-worried-about/; Laurence A. Moran, "The Implosion of CFI Canada," *Sandwalk: Strolling with a Skeptical Biochemist* (blog), November 26, 2011, http://sandwalk.blogspot.se/2011/11/implosion-of-cfi-canada.html; and Hemant Mehta, "What's Happening with CFI Canada?," *Friendly Atheist* (blog), November 26, 2011, http://www.patheos.com/blogs/friendlyatheist/2011/11/26/whats-happening-with-cfi-canada/.

106. "Secular Stars," Richard Dawkins Foundation, accessed August 24, 2014. https://richarddawkins.net/community/secularstars/.

107. "Atheism + Drama," Richard Dawkins Foundation, July 18, 2014, https://richarddawkins.net/2014/07/atheism-drama/.

108. Jaclyn Glenn, "Atheists—Beware of the Extreme Feminist!," YouTube (video), accessed July August 4, 2014, https://www.youtube.com/watch?v=hbRwe9srFfA&feature=youtube_gdata_player.

109. Ronald A. Lindsay, "My Talk at WIS2," Center for Inquiry, May 17, 2013, http://www.centerforinquiry.net/blogs/entry/my_talk_at_wis2/.

110. *Ibid.*

CONCLUSION

1. Snow and McAdam, "Identity Work Processes."
2. Krauss, *A Universe From Nothing*.
3. McAdam, "Culture and Social Movements."
4. Taylor, *A Secular Age*.
5. Eagleton, *Ideology*, 37.
6. Cavanaugh, *Myth of Religious Violence*.

Bibliography

Ali, Ayaan Hirsi. 2008. *Infidel*. New York: Free Press.

Ali, Ayaan Hirsi. 2010. *Nomad: From Islam to America—A Personal Journey Through the Clash of Civilizations*. New York: Free Press.

Ansell-Pearson, Keith. 1994. *An Introduction to Nietzsche as Political Thinker*. Cambridge: Cambridge University Press.

Armstrong, Elizabeth A. and Mary Bernstein. 2008. "Culture, Power, and Institutions: A Multi-Institutional Politics Approach to Social Movements." *Sociological Theory* 26(1): 74–99.

Asad, Talal. 2003. *Formations of the Secular: Christianity, Islam, Modernity*. Stanford, CA: Stanford University Press.

Baggini, Julian. 2007. "Toward a More Mannerly Secularism." *Free Inquiry* 27(2): 41–44.

Bainbridge, William Sims. 2007. "New Age Religion and Irreligion." In *The SAGE Handbook of the Sociology of Religion*, ed. J. A. Beckford and N. J. Demerath, pp. 248–266. Los Angeles: SAGE Publications.

Baker, Joseph O'Brian and Buster Smith. 2009. "The Nones: Social Characteristics of the Religiously Unaffiliated." *Social Forces* 87(3): 1252–1263.

Beattie, Tina. 2007. *The New Atheists: The Twilight of Reason and the War on Religion*. London: Darton, Longman and Todd.

Becker, Lauren. 2012. "Secular Humanism with a Pulse: The New Activists." *Free Inquiry* 32(5): 20–21.

Beckford, James A. 1989. *Religion and Advanced Industrial Society*. London: Unwin Hyman.

Bellah, Robert. 1971. "Between Religion and Social Science." In *The Culture of Unbelief*, ed. Rocco Caporale and Antonio Grummelli, pp. 271–296. Berkeley: University of California Press.

Berezin, Mabel. 2001. "Emotions and Political Identity: Mobilizing Affection for the Polity." In *Passionate Politics: Emotions in Social Movements*, ed. J. Goodwin, J. M. Jasper, and F. Polletta, pp. 83–98. Chicago: University of Chicago Press.

Berger, Peter L. 1999. "The Desecularization of the World: A Global Overview." In *The Desecularization of the World: Resurgent Religion and World Politics*, ed. Peter L. Berger, pp. 1–18. Grand Rapids, MI: William B. Eerdmans Publishing Company.

Berman, David. 1988. *A History of Atheism in Britain: From Hobbes to Russell*. London: Croom Helm.

Bernstein, Mary. 1997. "Celebration and Suppression: The Strategic Uses of Identity by the Lesbian and Gay Movement." *American Journal of Sociology* 103(3): 531–565.

Bernstein, Mary. 2002. "Identities and Politics: Toward a Historical Understanding of the Lesbian and Gay Movement." *Social Science History* 26(3): 531–581.

Bernstein, Mary. 2008. "The Analytic Dimensions of Identity: A Political Identity Framework." In *Identity Work in Social Movements*, ed. Jo Reger, Daniel J. Myers, and Rachel L. Einwohner, pp. 277–301. Minneapolis: University of Minnesota Press.

Borer, Michael Ian. 2010. "The New Atheism and the Secularization Thesis." In *Religion and the New Atheism: A Critical Appraisal*, ed. Amarnath Amarasingam, pp. 125–137. Leiden: Brill.

Bourdieu, Pierre. 1971. "Intellectual Field and Creative Project." In *Knowledge and Control*, ed. M. F. D. Young. London: Cullier-Macmillan.

Bowler, Peter J. 2003 [1983]. *Evolution: The History of an Idea*. Berkeley: University of California Press.

Boyer, Pascal. 2001. *Religion Explained: The Evolutionary Origins of Religious Thought*. New York: Basic Books.

Brooke, John Hedley. 2010. "Science and Secularization." In *The Cambridge Companion to Science and Religion*, ed. Peter Harrison, pp. 103–123. Cambridge: Cambridge University Press.

Browne, Janet. 2006. *Darwin's Origin of Species: A Biography*. New York: Grove Press.

Bruce, Steve. 2002. *God is Dead: Secularization in the West*. Malden, MA: Blackwell Publishers.

Bruce, Steve. 2011. *Secularization: In Defence of an Unfashionable Theory*. Oxford: Oxford University Press.

Buckley, Michael J. 1987. *At the Origins of Modern Atheism*. New Haven, CT: Yale University Press.

Buckley, Michael J. 2004. *Denying and Disclosing God: The Ambiguous Progress of Modern Atheism*. New Haven, CT: Yale University Press.

Budd, Susan. 1977. *Varieties of Unbelief: Atheists and Agnostics in English Society 1850–1960*. London: Heinemann.

Bullivant, Stephen. 2010. "The New Atheism and Sociology: Why Here? Why Now? What Next?" In *Religion and the New Atheism: A Critical Appraisal*, ed. Amarnath Amarasingam, pp. 109–124. Leiden: Brill.

Bullivant, Stephen. 2013. "Defining 'Atheism.'" In *The Oxford Handbook of Atheism*, ed. S. Bullivant and M. Ruse, pp. 11–21. Oxford: Oxford University Press.

Byrne, Peter. 1989. *Natural Religion and the Nature of Religion: The Legacy of Deism*. London: Routledge.

Calhoun, Craig. 1993. "'New Social Movements' of the Early Nineteenth Century." *Social Science History* 17(3): 385–427.

Calhoun, Craig, Mark Juergensmeyer, and Jonathan VanAntwerpen, eds. 2011. *Rethinking Secularism*. New York: Oxford University Press.

Campbell, Colin. 1971. *Toward a Sociology of Irreligion*. London: Macmillan.

Caputo, John D. 2007. "Atheism, A/theology, and the Postmodern Condition." In *The Cambridge Companion to Atheism*, ed. M. Martin, pp. 267–282. Cambridge: Cambridge University Press.

Casanova, Jose. 1994. *Public Religions in the Modern World*. Chicago: University of Chicago Press.

Castells, Manuel. 2004. *The Power of Identity* (2nd ed.). Malden, MA: Blackwell Publishing.

Cavanaugh, William T. 2009. *The Myth of Religious Violence: Secular Ideology and the Roots of Modern Conflict*. Oxford: Oxford University Press.

Cimino, Richard and Christopher Smith. 2007. "Secular Humanism and Atheism Beyond Progressive Secularism." *Sociology of Religion* 68(4): 407–424.

Cimino, Richard and Christopher Smith. 2010. "The New Atheism and the Empowerment of American Freethinkers." In *Religion and the New Atheism: A Critical Appraisal*, ed. Amarnath Amarasingam, pp. 139–156. Leiden: Brill.

Cimino, Richard and Christopher Smith. 2012. "Atheisms Unbound: The Role of the New Media in the Formation of a Secularist Identity." *Secularism and Nonreligion* 1: 17–31.

Cimino, Richard and Christopher Smith. 2014. *Atheist Awakening: Secular Activism and Community in America*. New York: Oxford University Press.

Comte, Auguste. 1896. *The Positive Philosophy of Auguste Comte*, vol. 2 (trans. Harriet Martineau). London: George Bell & Sons.

Comte, Auguste. 1961. "The Theological Stage." In *Theories of Society: Foundations of Modern Sociological Theory*, Vol. 1, ed. Talcott Parsons, Edward Shils, Kaspar D. Naegele, and Jesse R. Pitts, pp. 646–655. New York: The Free Press of Glencoe, Inc.

Coyne, Jerry A. 2014. "The 'Best Arguments for God's Existence' Are Actually Terrible." *The New Republic*, January 16. http://www.newrepublic.com/article/116251/best-arguments-gods-existence-dont-challenge-atheists.

Cragun, Ryan T., Barry Kosmin, Ariela Keysar, Joseph H. Hammer, and Michael Neilson. 2012. "On the Receiving End: Discrimination toward the Non-Religious in the United States." *Journal of Contemporary Religion* 27(1): 105–127.

Darwin, Charles. 2003 [1859]. *The Origin of Species*. New York: Penguin Books.

Darwin, Charles. 2007 [1876]. "Autobiography." In *The Portable Atheist: Essential Readings for the Nonbeliever*, ed. C. Hitchens, pp. 93–96. Philadelphia: Da Capo Press.

Davie, Grace. 2004. "New Approaches in the Sociology of Religion: A Western Perspective." *Social Compass* 51(1): 73–84.

Davie, Grace. 2013. *The Sociology of Religion: A Critical Agenda*. London: Sage.

Dawkins, Richard. 1982. *The Extended Phenotype: The Gene as the Unit of Selection*. Oxford: W. H. Freeman & Company.

Dawkins, Richard. 1986. *The Blind Watchmaker*. New York: Penguin Books.

Dawkins, Richard. 1989 [1976]. *The Selfish Gene*. Oxford: Oxford University Press.

Dawkins, Richard. 1995. "Viruses of the Mind." In *Dennett and His Critics: Demystifying Mind*, ed. Bo Dahlbom, pp. 13–27. Malden, MA: Blackwell Publishers.

Dawkins, Richard. 2006. *The God Delusion*. Boston: Houghton Mifflin Company.

Dawkins, Richard (Presenter/Writer) and Kidd, Deborah (Producer). 2006. *Root of All Evil?* [Documentary]. United Kingdom: Channel 4.

D'Emilio, John. 1983. *Sexual Politics, Sexual Communities: The Making of a Homosexual Minority in the United States 1940–1970*. Chicago: University of Chicago Press.

Dennett, Daniel. 1992. *Consciousness Explained*. New York: Back Bay Books.

Dennett, Daniel. 1995. *Darwin's Dangerous Idea: Evolution and the Meanings of Life*. New York: Simon and Schuster.

Dennett, Daniel. 2006. *Breaking the Spell: Religion as a Natural Phenomenon*. New York: Penguin Books.

Desmond, Adrian and James Moore. 1991. *Darwin*. New York: W. W. Norton & Company.

Dragiewicz, Molly. 2011. *Equality with a Vengeance: Men's Rights Groups, Battered Women, and Antifeminist Backlash*. Lebanon, NH: Northeastern University Press.

Dunbar, Robin I. M. 2007. "Evolution and the Social Sciences." *History of the Human Sciences* 20(2): 29–50.

Durkheim, Émile. 1995 [1912]. *The Elementary Forms of Religious Life* (trans. Karen E. Fields). New York: The Free Press.

Eagleton, Terry. 1991. *Ideology: An Introduction*. New York: Verso.

Eagleton, Terry. 2009. *Reason, Faith and Revolution: Reflections on the God Debate*. New Haven, CT: Yale University Press.

Ecklund, Elaine Howard. 2010. *Science vs. Religion: What Scientists Really Think*. New York: Oxford University Press.

Edgell, Penny, Joseph Gerteis, and Douglas Hartmann. 2006. "Atheists as 'Other': Moral Boundaries and Cultural Membership in American Society." *American Sociological Review* 71(2): 211–234.

Einwohner, Rachel L., Jo Reger, and Daniel J. Myers. 2008. "Identity Work, Sameness, and Difference in Social Movements." In *Identity Work in Social Movements*, ed. J. Reger, D. J. Myers, and R. L. Einwohner, pp. 1–17. Minneapolis: University of Minnesota Press.

Eisenstadt, Shmuel. 1999. *Fundamentalism, Sectarianism and Revolutions: The Jacobin Dimension of Modernity*. Cambridge: Cambridge University Press.

Epstein, Greg M. 2010. *Good Without God: What a Billion Nonreligious People Do Believe*. New York: Harper.

Feuerbach, Ludwig. 1957 [1841]. *The Essence of Christianity*. New York: Harper and Row.

Flamm, Matthew Caleb. 2011. "Strong Believers Beware." *Free Inquiry* 31(1): 23–26.

Flynn, Tom. 2006. "Secularism's Breakthrough Moment." *Free Inquiry* 26(3): 16–17.

Flynn, Tom. 2008. "Why the 'A' Word Won't Go Away." *Free Inquiry* 28(2): 15–16.

Flynn, Tom. 2011. "Letters." *Free Inquiry* 31(2): 11–12.

Flynn, Tom. 2012. "A Note from the Editor." *Free Inquiry* 32(5): 21.

Freud, Sigmund. 1989 [1927]. *The Future of an Illusion*. New York: W. W. Norton and Company.

Freud, Sigmund. 1989 [1929]. *Civilization and its Discontents*. New York: W. W. Norton and Company.

Froese, Paul. 2004. "Forced Secularization in Soviet Russia: Why an Atheistic Monopoly Failed." *Journal for the Scientific Study of Religion* 43(1): 35–50.

Fuller, Steve. 2006. *The New Sociological Imagination*. London: SAGE Publications.

Fuller, Steve. 2008. *Dissent Over Descent: Intelligent Design's Challenge to Darwinism*. Cambridge: Icon Books.

Furseth, Inger. 2009. "Atheism, Secularity, and Gender." In *Atheism and Secularity, Volume 1: Issues, Concepts, and Definitions*, ed. Phil Zuckerman, pp. 209–227. Santa Barbara, CA: Praeger.

Gamson, Joshua. 1995. "Must Identity Movements Self-Destruct? A Queer Dilemma." *Social Problems* 42(3): 390–407.

Gamson, William A. 1992. "The Social Psychology of Collective Action." In *Frontiers in Social Movement Theory*, ed. Aldon D. Morris and Carol McClurg, pp. 53–76. New Haven, CT: Yale University Press.

Gamson, William A. 1998. "Social Movements and Cultural Change." In *From Contention to Democracy*, ed. Marco G. Giugni, Doug McAdam, and Charles Tilly, pp. 57–77. Lanham, MD: Rowman and Littlefield.

Gervais, Will M., Azim F. Shariff, and Ara Norenzayan. 2011. "Do You Believe in Atheists? Distrust Is Central to Anti-atheist Prejudice." *Journal of Personality and Social Psychology* 101(6): 1189–1206.

Ghaziani, Amin. 2011. "Post-Gay Collective Identity Construction." *Social Problems* 58(1): 99–125.

Girard, April L. 2009. "Backlash or Equality? The Influence of Men's and Women's Rights Discourses on Domestic Violence Legislation in Ontario." *Violence Against Women* 15(1): 5–23.

Gondermann, Thomas. 2007. "Progression and Retrogression: Herbert Spencer's Explanations of Social Inequality." *History of the Human Sciences* 20(3): 21–40.

Gorski, Philip S. 1990. "Scientism, Interpretation, and Criticism." *Zygon* 25(3): 279–307.

Gorski, Philip, David Kyuman Kim, John Torpey, and Jonathan VanAntwerpen, eds. 2012. *The Post-Secular in Question: Religion in Contemporary Society.* New York: NYU Press.

Gray, John. 2002. *Straw Dogs: Thoughts on Humans and Other Animals.* London: Granta Books.

Grayling, A. C. 2007. *Against All Gods: Six Polemics on Religion and an Essay on Kindness.* London: Oberon Books.

Grayling, A. C. 2007. "Can an Atheist Be a Fundamentalist?" In *The Portable Atheist: Essential Readings for the Nonbeliever,* ed. Christopher Hitchens, pp. 473–476. Philadelphia: Da Capo Press.

Grayling, A. C. 2013. *The God Argument: The Case Against Religion and for Humanism.* New York: Bloomsbury.

Grayling, A. C. 2013. *The Good Book: A Humanist Bible.* New York: Walker Publishing Company.

Grothe, D. J. and Austin Dacey. 2004. "Atheism Is Not a Civil Rights Issue." *Free Inquiry.*

Guenther, Katja M. 2014. "Bounded by Disbelief: How Atheists in the United States Differentiate themselves from Religious Believers." *Journal of Contemporary Religion* 29(1): 1–16.

Guenther, Katja M., Kerry Mulligan, and Cameron Papp. 2013. "From the Outside In: Crossing Boundaries to Build Collective Identity in the New Atheist Movement." *Social Problems* 60(4): 457–475.

Habermas, Jurgen. 1970. *Toward a Rational Society: Student Protest, Science, and Politics.* Boston: Beacon Press.

Habermas, Jurgen. 1971. *Knowledge and Human Interests.* London: Heinemann.

Hadden, Jeffrey. 1987. "Toward Desacralizing Secularization Theory." *Social Forces* 65(3): 587–611.

Hampson, Norman. 1968. *The Enlightenment: An Evaluation of its Assumptions, Attitudes and Values.* London: Penguin Books.

Harris, Sam. 2004. *The End of Faith: Religion, Terror, and the Future of Reason.* New York: W. W. Norton & Company.

Harris, Sam. 2006. *Letter to a Christian Nation.* New York: Vintage Books.

Harris, Sam. 2010. *The Moral Landscape: How Science Can Determine Human Values.* New York: Free Press.

Hart, David Bentley. 2010. *Atheist Delusions: The Christian Revolution and Its Fashionable Enemies.* New Haven, CT: Yale University Press.

Held, David. 1980. *Introduction to Critical Theory: Horkheimer to Habermas.* Berkeley: University of California Press.

Henry, John. 2010. "Religion and the Scientific Revolution." In *The Cambridge Companion to Science and Religion,* ed. P. Harrison, pp. 39–58. Cambridge: Cambridge University Press.

Hitchens, Christopher. 1995. *The Missionary Position: Mother Theresa in Theory and Practice.* New York: Verso.

Hitchens, Christopher. 2004. "Believe It or Not; Making a Patriotic Case for Those of Little Faith." *Washington Post*, April 25.

Hitchens, Christopher. 2007. *God Is Not Great: How Religion Poisons Everything.* Toronto: Emblem.

Hitchens, Christopher, ed. 2007. *The Portable Atheist: Essential Readings for the Nonbeliever.* Philadelphia: Da Capo Press.

Hitchens, Christopher. 2008. *Thomas Paine's Rights of Man.* New York: Atlantic Monthly Press.

Hitchens, Christopher. 2010. *Hitch-22: A Memoir.* Allen & Unwin.

Hoffman, R. Joseph. 2006. "Why Hard Science Won't Cure Easy Religion." *Free Inquiry* 26(3): 47–49.

Holwerda, Gus. 2013. *The Unbelievers.* Documentary Film.

Horkheimer, Max and Theodor W. Adorno. 1995 [1944]. *Dialectic of Enlightenment.* Stanford, CA: Stanford University Press.

Hunsberger, Bruce E. and Bob Altemeyer. 2006. *Atheists: A Groundbreaking Study of America's Nonbelievers.* Amherst, NY: Prometheus Books.

Hunt, Scott A., Robert D. Benford, and David A. Snow. 1994. "Identity Fields: Framing Processes and the Social Construction of Movement Identities." In *New Social Movements: From Ideology to Identity*, ed. Hank Johnston, Enrique Larana, and Joseph R. Gusfield, pp. 185–208. Philadelphia: Temple University Press.

Huntington, Samuel J. 1996. *The Clash of Civilizations and the Remaking of World Order.* New York: Touchstone.

Hyman, Gavin. 2007. "Atheism in Modern History." In *The Cambridge Companion to Atheism*, ed. M. Martin, pp. 27–46. Cambridge: Cambridge University Press.

Irvine, William. 1955. *Apes, Angels, and Victorians: The Story of Darwin, Huxley, and Evolution.* New York: Time Inc.

Jervis, Robert. 2003. "Understanding the Bush Doctrine." *Political Science Quarterly* 118(3): 365–388.

Johnston, Hank and Bert Klandermans. 1995. "The Cultural Analysis of Social Movements." In *Social Movements and Culture*, ed. Hank Johnston and Bert Klandermans, pp. 3–24. Minneapolis: University of Minnesota Press.

Johnston, Hank, Enrique Larana, and Joseph R. Gusfield. 1994. "Identities, Grievances, and New Social Movements." In *New Social Movements: From Ideology to Identity*, ed. Hank Johnston, Enrique Larana, and Joseph R. Gusfield, pp. 3–35. Philadelphia: Temple University Press.

Jones, Greta. 1980. *Social Darwinism and English Thought: The Interaction between Biological and Social Theory.* Sussex, UK: The Harvester Press.

Kaminer, Wendy. 2010. "Epistemic Closure–Left and Right." *Free Inquiry* 30(2): 14, 44.

Kaufmann, Walter. 1974 [1950]. *Nietzsche: Philosopher, Psychologist, Antichrist.* Princeton, NJ: Princeton University Press.

Kettell, Steven. 2013. "Faithless: The Politics of New Atheism." *Secularism and Nonreligion* 2: 61–78.

Kors, Alan Charles. 1990. *Atheism in France, 1650–1729, Volume 1: The Orthodox Sources of Disbelief.* Princeton, NJ: Princeton University Press.

Krauss, Lawrence. 2012. *A Universe from Nothing: Why There Is Something Rather than Nothing.* New York: Free Press.

Kurtz, Paul. 2005. "Is America a Post-Democratic Society?" *Free Inquiry* 25(1): 19–25.

Kurtz, Paul. 2006. "The Principles of Fairness: Progressive Taxation." *Free Inquiry* 26(6): 4–7.

Kurtz, Paul. 2008. "Multi-Secularism: The New Agenda." *Free Inquiry* 28(2): 4–8.

Kurtz, Paul. 2010. "The 'True Unbeliever.'" *Free Inquiry* 30(1): 4–5.

Larson, Edward J. 2006. *Evolution: The Remarkable History of a Scientific Theory.* New York: Modern Library.

LeBeau, Bryan F. 2003. *The Atheist: Madalyn Murray O'Hair.* New York: New York University Press.

LeDrew, Stephen. 2013. "Discovering Atheism: Heterogeneity in Trajectories to Atheist Identity and Activism." *Sociology of Religion* 74(4): 431–453.

Lewontin, Richard. 1977. "Biological Determinism as a Social Weapon." In *Biology as a Social Weapon*, ed. The Ann Arbor Science for the People Editorial Collective. Minneapolis, MN: Burgess Publishing Company.

Lim, Chaeyoon, Carol Ann MacGregor, and Robert D. Putnam. 2010. "Secular and Liminal: Discovering Heterogeneity Among Religious Nones." *Journal for the Scientific Study of Religion* 49(4): 596–618.

Lindberg, David C. 2010. "Science in Patristic and Medieval Christendom." In *The Cambridge Companion to Science and Religion*, ed. P. Harrison, pp. 21–38. Cambridge: Cambridge University Press.

Lindsay, Ronald A. 2010. "Expressing One's Views on Religion." *Free Inquiry* 30(5): 4–6.

Lindsay, Ronald A. 2011. "Secular Humanism: Its Scope and Its Limits." *Free Inquiry* 31(1): 4–6.

Machan, Tibor. 2011. "The Myth of Surplus Wealth." *Free Inquiry* 31(2): 13.

Mahlamäki, Tiina. 2012. "Religion and Atheism from a Gender Perspective." *Approaching Religion* 2(1): 58–65.

Martin, David. 2014. *Religion and Power: No Logos Without Mythos.* Surrey, UK: Ashgate.

Martin, Michael, ed. 2007. *The Cambridge Companion to Atheism.* Cambridge: Cambridge University Press.

Marx, Karl. 1983 [1844]. "From 'Contribution to the Critique of Hegel's Philosophy of Right: Introduction.'" In *The Portable Karl Marx*, ed. E. Kamenka, pp. 115–124. New York: Penguin Books.

Marx, Karl. 2002 [1845]. "Concerning Feuerbach." In *Marx on Religion*, ed. J. Raines, pp. 182–184. Philadelphia: Temple University Press.

McAdam, Doug. 1982. *Political Process and the Development of Black Insurgency, 1930–1970*. Chicago: University of Chicago Press.

McAdam, Doug. 1994. "Culture and Social Movements." In *New Social Movements: From Ideology to Identity*, ed. Hank Johnston, Enrique Larana, and Joseph R. Gusfield, pp. 36–57. Philadelphia: Temple University Press.

McGrath, Alister. 2006. *The Twilight of Atheism: The Rise and Fall of Disbelief in the Modern World*. New York: Galilee.

McGrath, Alister and Joanna Collicutt McGrath. 2007. *The Dawkins Delusion? Atheist Fundamentalism and the Denial of the Divine*. London: SPCK.

Melucci, Alberto. 1988. "Getting Involved: Identity and Mobilization in Social Movements." *Research in Social Movements, Conflicts and Change* 1: 329–348.

Melucci, Alberto. 1989. *Nomads of the Present: Social Movements and Individual Needs in Contemporary Society*. Philadelphia: Temple University Press.

Melucci, Alberto. 1995. "The Process of Collective Identity." In *Social Movements and Culture*, ed. Hank Johnston and Bert Klandermans, pp. 41–63. Minneapolis: University of Minnesota Press.

Melucci, Alberto. 1996. *Challenging Codes: Collective Action in the Information Age*. New York: Cambridge University Press.

Mendieta, Eduardo and Jonathan VanAntwerpen, eds. 2011. *The Power of Religion in the Public Sphere*. New York: Columbia University Press.

Midgley, Mary 2002 [1985]. *Evolution as a Religion: Strange Hopes and Stranger Fears*. London: Routledge.

Mooney, Chris. 2010. "Do the New Atheists Make America More Unscientific?" *Free Inquiry* 30(2): 7, 43.

Mooney, Chris. 2012. *The Republican Brain: The Science of Why They Deny Science—and Reality*. Hoboken, NJ: John Wiley and Sons, Inc.

Mooney, Chris and Sheril Kirshenbaum. 2009. *Unscientific America: How Scientific Illiteracy Threatens Our Future*. New York: Basic Books.

Morris, Aldon D. and Suzanne Staggenborg. 2007. "Leadership in Social Movements." In *The Blackwell Companion to Social Movements*, ed. David A. Snow, Sarah A. Soule, and Hanspeter Kriesi, pp. 171–196. Malden, MA: Blackwell.

Murphy, Caryle. 2002, November 3. "March of the Godless Takes to the Mall; Nonbelievers Fight Religion in Government." *Washington Post*, p. C03.

Nietzsche, Friedrich. 1966 [1885]. *Thus Spoke Zarathustra: A Book for All and None*. New York: Penguin Books.

Nietzsche, Friedrich. 1974 [1887]. *The Gay Science*. New York: Vintage Books.

Nietzsche, Friedrich. 2003 [1895]. *The Antichrist*. London: Penguin Books.

Norris, Pippa and Inglehart, Ronald. 2004. *Sacred and Secular: Religion and Politics Worldwide*. Cambridge: Cambridge University Press.

Olson, Richard G. 2008. *Science and Scientism in Nineteenth-Century Europe.* Urbana: University of Illinois Press.

Onfray, Michel. 2007. *In Defence of Atheism: The Case Against Christianity, Judaism, and Islam* (Jeremy Leggatt, Trans.). Toronto: Penguin Canada.

Pasquale, Frank. 2010. "A Portrait of Secular Group Affiliates." In *Atheism and Secularity,* ed. Phil Zuckerman, pp. 43–88. Santa Barbara, CA: Praeger.

Pasquale, Frank. 2010. "The Quintessential Secular Institution." *Free Inquiry* 30(1): 55–56.

Peris, Daniel. 1998. *Storming the Heavens: The Soviet League of the Militant Godless.* Ithaca, NY: Cornell University Press.

Pinel, Elizabeth C. and William B. Swann Jr. 2000. "Finding the Self through Others: Self-Verification and Social Movement Participation." In *Self, Identity, and Social Movements,* ed. S. Stryker, T. J. Owens, and R. W. White, pp. 132–152. Minneapolis: University of Minnesota Press.

Pinker, Steven. 2002. *The Blank Slate: The Modern Denial of Human Nature.* New York: Viking.

Pinker, Steven. 2011. *The Better Angels of Our Nature: Why Violence Has Declined.* New York: Viking.

Plantinga, Alvin. 2011. *Where the Conflict Really Lies: Science, Religion, and Naturalism.* New York: Oxford University Press.

Polletta, Francesca and James M. Jasper. 2001. "Collective Identity and Social Movements." *Annual Review of Sociology* 27: 283–305.

Putnam, Robert D. and David E. Campbell. 2010. *American Grace: How Religion Divides and Unites Us.* New York: Simon & Schuster.

Radick, Gregory. 2009. "Is the Theory of Natural Selection Independent of its History?" In *The Cambridge Companion to Darwin,* ed. J. Hodge and G. Radick, pp. 147–172. Cambridge: Cambridge University Press.

Rectenwald, Michael. 2013. "Secularism and the Cultures of Nineteenth-Century Scientific Naturalism." *British Journal for the History of Science* 46(2): 231–254.

Rose, Hilary and Steven Rose. 2010. "Darwin and After." *New Left Review* 63: 91–113.

Ross, Andrew. 1996. *Science Wars.* Durham, NC: Duke University Press.

Salaquarda, Jorg. 1996. "Nietzsche and the Judeo-Christian Tradition." In *The Cambridge Companion to Nietzsche,* ed. B. Magnus and K. M. Higgins, pp. 90–118. Cambridge: Cambridge University Press.

Schulzke, Marcus. 2013. "The Politics of New Atheism." *Politics and Religion* 6(4): 778–799.

Segal, Robert A. 2004. "The Place of Religion in Modernity." *History of the Human Sciences* 17(4): 131–149.

Shapin, Steven. 1996. *The Scientific Revolution.* Chicago: University of Chicago Press.

Shermer, Michael. 2004. *The Science of Good and Evil: Why People Cheat, Gossip, Care, Share, and Follow the Golden Rule.* New York: Holt Paperbacks.

Shermer, Michael. 2009. *The Mind of the Market: How Biology and Psychology Shape our Economic Lives.* New York: Times Books.

Shermer, Michael. 2011. *The Believing Brain: From Ghosts and Gods to Politics and Conspiracies—How We Construct Beliefs and Reinforce Them as Truths.* New York: Times Books.

Smith, Christian. 1991. *The Emergence of Liberation Theology: Radical Religion and Social Movement Theory.* Chicago: University of Chicago Press.

Smith, Christian. 1998. *American Evangelicalism: Embattled and Thriving.* Chicago: University of Chicago Press.

Smith, Christian, ed. 2003. *The Secular Revolution: Power, Interests, and Conflict in the Secularization of American Public Life.* Berkeley: University of California Press.

Smith, Jesse M. 2011. "Becoming an Atheist in America: Constructing Identity and Meaning from the Rejection of Theism." *Sociology of Religion* 72(2): 215–237.

Smith, Jesse M. 2013. "Creating a Godless Community: The Collective Identity Work of Contemporary American Atheists." *Journal for the Scientific Study of Religion* 52(1): 80–99.

Snow, David A. 2004. "Social Movements as Challenges to Authority: Resistance to an Emerging Conceptual Hegemony." *Research in Social Movements, Conflicts and Change* 25: 3–25.

Snow, David A. and Doug McAdam. 2000. "Identity Work Processes in the Context of Social Movements: Clarifying the Identity/Movement Nexus." In *Self, Identity, and Social Movements,* ed. S. Stryker, T. J. Owens, and R. W. White, pp. 41–67. Minneapolis: University of Minnesota Press.

Sokal, Alan and Jean Bricmont. 1998. *Fashionable Nonsense: Postmodern Intellectuals' Abuse of Science.* New York: Picador.

Spencer, Herbert. 1965 [1884]. *The Man Versus the State.* Caldwell, OH: Caxton Printers.

Staggenborg, Suzanne. 2008. *Social Movements.* Oxford: Oxford University Press.

Stahl, William A. 2010. "One-Dimensional Rage: The Social Epistemology of the New Atheism and Fundamentalism." In *Religion and the New Atheism: A Critical Appraisal,* ed. Amarnath Amarasingam, pp. 97–108. Leiden: Brill.

Stark, Rodney and Roger Finke. 2000. *Acts of Faith: Explaining the Human Side of Religion.* Berkeley: University of California Press.

Stedman, Chris. 2012. *Faitheist: How an Atheist Found Common Ground with the Religious.* Boston: Beacon Press.

Stenger, Victor. 2008. *God: The Failed Hypothesis: How Science Shows That God Does Not Exist.* Amherst, NY: Prometheus Books.

Stenger, Victor. 2009. *The New Atheism: Taking a Stand for Science and Reason.* Amherst, NY: Prometheus Books.

Stenmark, Mikael. 1997. "What is Scientism?" *Religious Studies* 33(1): 15–32.

Stocking, George. 1968. *Race, Culture, and Evolution: Essays in the History of Anthropology.* Chicago: University of Chicago Press.

Swan, Lawton K. and Martin Heesacker. 2012. "Anti-Atheist Bias in the United States: Testing Two Critical Assumptions." *Secularism and Nonreligion* 1: 32–42.

Szonyi, Michael. 2009. "Secularization Theories and the Study of Chinese Religions." *Social Compass* 56(3): 312–327.

Taira, Teemu. 2012. "New Atheism as Identity Politics." In *Religion and Knowledge: Sociological Perspectives*, ed. Mathew Guest and Elisabeth Arweck, pp. 97–114. Farnham, UK: Ashgate.

Taylor, Charles. 2007. *A Secular Age*. Cambridge, MA: Belknap Press of Harvard University Press.

Taylor, Verta and Nancy E. Whittier. 1992. "Collective Identity in Social Movement Communities: Lesbian Feminist Mobilization." In *Frontiers in Social Movement Theory*, ed. Aldon D. Morris and Carol McClurg Mueller, pp. 104–129. New Haven, CT: Yale University Press.

Thompson, John B. 1984. *Studies in the Theory of Ideology*. Cambridge: Cambridge University Press.

Thrower, James. 2000. *Western Atheism: A Short History*. Amherst, MA: Prometheus Books.

Tilly, Charles. 1978. *From Mobilization to Revolution*. Reading, MA: Addison-Wesley.

Tilly, Charles. 2004. *Social Movements, 1768–2004*. Boulder, CO: Paradigm.

Topham, Jonathan R. 2010. "Natural Theology and the Sciences." In *The Cambridge Companion to Science and Religion*, ed. P. Harrison, pp. 59–79. Cambridge: Cambridge University Press.

Touraine, Alain. 2000. *Can We Live Together?: Equality and Difference*. Stanford, CA: Stanford University Press.

Turner, James. 1985. *Without God, Without Creed: The Origins of Unbelief in America*. Baltimore: John Hopkins University Press.

van Dijk, Tuen. 1998. *Ideology: A Multidisciplinary Approach*. Thousand Oaks, CA: Sage Publications.

Vargas, Nicholas. 2012. "Retrospective Accounts of Religious Disaffiliation in the United States: Stressors, Skepticism, and Political Factors." *Sociology of Religion* 73(2): 200–223.

Wilde, Lawrence. 2010. "The Antinomies of Aggressive Atheism." *Contemporary Political Theory* 9(3): 266–283.

Williams, Daniel K. 2012. *God's Own Party: The Making of the Christian Right*. New York: Oxford University Press.

Wilson, Edward O. 1975. *Sociobiology: The New Synthesis*. Cambridge, MA: Belknap Press of Harvard University Press.

Wiltshire, David. 1978. *The Social and Political Thought of Herbert Spencer*. Oxford: Oxford University Press.

Zuckerman, Phil. 2010. *Society Without God: What the Least Religious Nations Can Tell Us About Contentment*. New York: New York University Press.

Zuckerman, Phil. 2011. *Faith No More: Why People Reject Religion*. New York: Oxford University Press.

Index